The Gendered Newsroom

The Gendered Newsroom

How Journalists Experience the Changing World of Media

Louise North

Monash University

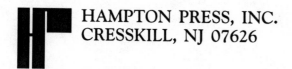

HAMPTON PRESS, INC.
CRESSKILL, NJ 07626

Printed in the United States of America

Library of Congress Cataloging-in-Publication Data

North, Louise.
    The gendered newsroom : how journalists experience the changing world of media / Louise North.
        p. cm. — (The Hampton Press communication series)
    Includes bibliographical references and index.
    ISBN 978-1-57273-872-0 (hardbound) — ISBN 978-1-57273-873-7 (paperbound)
    1. Women journalists—Australia.   2. Women in journalism—Australia.
3. Sex role in the work environment—Australia.   4. Sex discrimination in employment—Australia.   I. Title.
    PN5517.W58N67 2009
    079.940982—dc22   2008047695

Hampton Press, Inc.
23 Broadway
Cresskill, NJ 07626

In memory of my grandmother
Doris Isabella Parr

October 13, 1914–August 15, 2006

Contents

Preface and Acknowledgments

In 1985, I began work as a cadet journalist for a small weekly newspaper on the Central Coast of New South Wales, in Australia—one of many cadets who start in the news media industry every year idealistically dreaming of changing the world. Having a university degree was not a prerequisite to gaining a cadetship[1] in those days; perhaps if I had, I may have been more quickly aware of the gender inequalities and hegemonic masculinity that dominated the majority of newsrooms I was to work in during the next 19 years. At that newspaper a woman was the deputy editor, and the male sports reporters considered me their equal—whether practising cricket in the nets after work or in the newsroom producing all manner of news and sports stories. Journalism was an intense working life, but I was struck by the camaraderie among journalists at that paper. We typed stories on clunking, big typewriters in a tin shed with a cement floor, stared in awe at the massive computers in a hermetically sealed room where our stories were input by typesetters, we cut stories on the 'stone' with the compositors haranguing us for not getting it right the first time. I didn't realise that the industry was on the verge of massive technological advances and that our industry would change so dramatically in such a short period of time.

Journalism, however, is about change on a broader scale and at the personal level. I moved on to other newspapers, upgraded from a typewriter to a computer and moved, too, from reporting to subediting and laying out news pages. My world became restricted to the fast-paced, deadline-driven newsroom, and the larger world of 'contacts' (people) and the community largely disappeared for me.

I moved interstate and intrastate to work on other newspapers and in so doing gained a lot of newsroom and life experience. On the way I began to see

---

[1]A cadetship is a four-year, on-the-job training program, and the people undertaking the training are called 'cadets.' After competing the training, some in less than four years, cadets become graded journalists.

xi

and experience the oppressiveness of working in newsrooms where men were making the majority of the news decisions, and where I couldn't seem to move beyond the middle ranks of editorial seniority. This realisation, not surprisingly, coincided with my starting a Bachelor of Arts degree which included Gender Studies units. Of all the newsrooms I worked in, one in particular stands out as exceedingly oppressive for women. The masculine newsroom culture reflected an almost exclusive male dominance at every level of editorial decision making: TVs blared with male sport, snide sexist jokes were common currency, and insinuations that pornography was on some computer screens were part and parcel of daily life on the subs desk. There were regular angry verbal outbursts between male journalists, often fuelled by alcohol, and an editor who often strode through the newsroom swearing. It became an oppressive place for me and other women to work, but not all saw it like I did, at least not publicly. Women, or certain types of women, were tolerated. Young, career-driven women who were loathe to speak about the sexist environment in which they worked, or who didn't experience it in that way, were acceptable. Older women who loved male sport and accepted crude jokes could be tolerated as 'one of the boys.' Those journalists with a feminist philosophy were generally not acceptable. Like news agendas, newsroom culture is never explicit, but rather implicit; you learn how it works very quickly and develop strategies to survive, or you move on. It was the lack of opportunity for career progression and the shutting-out tactics once you were located as an outsider that cemented your status. Outsiders could be feminists, or nonheterosexual, or non–sports loving.

In the 2000s young women are making giant leaps into the lower ranks of the profession worldwide, and in Australia university journalism and media courses are overwhelmingly female dominated. Yet female journalists remain clustered en masse in the lower-paid, lower-status reporting positions while men still dominate in decision-making (editing) roles. One of the last newspapers I worked for in the early 2000s, the News Limited–owned *The Mercury* in Hobart, Tasmania, had all its influential editorial roles filled by men: editor, deputy editor, day editor, night editor, sports editor, racing editor, chief sub-editor, features editor, chief-of-staff, and all nine photographers.[2] I looked for answers outside of my personal observations and found my politics in feminist theories. It wasn't always welcomed in the newsroom, and so I learned to fit in and develop strategies for surviving the masculine newsroom. Generally that tactic involved not having an opinion about news content (especially if it involved a criticism of the lack of women or the way the newspaper stereotyped women)—even though I was employed as a sub-editor,[3] and part

---

[2]Although by 2004 the company proudly acknowledges that women are making significant inroads into editorial decision making roles. The Chief-of-staff position is now filled by a woman (Davies Bros, 2004: 3).

[3]Sub-editors' tasks range from copy editing, headline writing, and picture captioning, to copy selection and designing news pages.

of my job was making some decisions about news content. It also involved accepting a masculine and often sexist culture and not complaining. Between 1997 and 2006 I completed three degrees. Each degree gave me an insight and a framework with which to understand the industry to which I had so far devoted my working life.

The industry, or more precisely the gendered production of news in the Australian print news media, formed the basis of my doctoral dissertation undertaken when I was a postgraduate student at the University of Tasmania. It forms the basis of this book. Both the research and writing of this book depended on the support and encouragement of many people. The supervisor of my thesis, Associate Professor Barbara Baird, deeply influenced my thinking early in the project and provided generous support throughout that process. American feminist media studies scholar Dr Carolyn Byerly and Australian political scientist Dr Elizabeth van Acker gave valuable feedback on the finished thesis. Dr Byerly has since become an important source of professional support.

Of course, the research would not have been possible without the many journalists who gave so willingly of their time during the interview process and ensuing correspondence over the years. I particularly thank the three journalists at The Mercury Newspaper in Hobart, Tasmania, who gave permission to use parts of their newsroom dialogues, found in Chapter Nine. I'd also like to thank The Mercury's current editor, Garry Bailey, for allowing his paraphrased comments found in Chapter Nine to go without a pseudonym, and also for allowing use of published material in this book.

A number of institutions and people attached to them have also been important sources of professional and personal support. The University of Tasmania offered me financial assistance provided by an Australian Postgraduate Award scholarship for the three-year duration of my PhD research. Staff and postgraduate students at the School of Gender, Work and Social Inquiry at the University of Adelaide also offered critical feedback on one chapter during a seminar series in which I was invited to participate. Particular thanks to Margie Ripper and Kathy Muir.

Also thanks to the University of Tasmania Rosamond McCulloch Studio management committee who offered me a two-month residency at the Cite International des Arts in Paris in 2005, where part of this book was written, and from where I drew much creative inspiration.

I am indebted to Hampton Press for bringing this book to fruition. Many thanks to Lee Becker, Hampton Press's Communication Series editor, who invited me to write the book, and to Barbara Bernstein who put the process in motion.

Personal support is crucial when one is hunkered down for months and even years on projects such as this. My mother, Maureen, has marvelled at my life's path, which has been so very different to her own, and I thank her for letting me grow and learn in my own way without prejudice. Lynne

Smith was instrumental in my decision to take up academic study in 1997 and Carol Altmann sustained me through the rollercoaster ride on the path to book completion. Her enthusiasm for this project has been infectious, and her intellectual and emotional support critical to completing the book, while reminding me that there is a life outside and beyond.

My biggest supporter, my late grandmother Doris Parr, did not get to share in the final celebrations. But I revelled in her weekly phone calls where she listened intently to the machinations of my life and my research. This is for her.

Chapter One

Introduction

The Newsroom (A)gender

In the mainstream print news media in Australia, content is determined predominantly by men. Men constitute the overwhelming proportion of editorial decision makers in mainstream newspapers around the world, and Australia is no exception. In 2006 the nation's 21 major metropolitan newspapers were all edited by men, with one exception (MacLean, 2006, p. 17). There is no doubt that journalism is a far cry from the male bastion it was 50 years ago, when there was just a handful of women who entered the fray. In the past 30 years women have been entering the profession in unprecedented numbers, this being one of the most dramatic changes to occur in the industry since World War II. Female students take up university communication and media studies courses in Australia at more than double the rate of male students (Putnis & Axford, 2002). Yet this influx both within the academic institutions and the industry has not changed the newsroom location of male and female journalists. This location is best illustrated by a pyramid in which men are found in the upper echelons of decision making and women en masse in the lower-graded, lower-paid, less prestigious positions. Even though women represent more than a third of the working journalists around the world, the percentage of women editors, heads of departments, or media owners is just 0.6 percent (Peters, 2001, p. 4).

Whereas a 'body count' has been the centre of feminist media research (and I will explore this further in later chapters), along with the representation of women in the media, we need now to turn to examining the gendered nature of production processes and find out how journalists have experienced industry change.

The shift to a focus on production is crucial not only because the field lacks a substantial body of empirical data and theory, but because feminist media studies scholars need the information to better understand how journalists experience change in today's global media. A focus on production that considers gender will allow for a better consideration of the gendering of

1

journalists as occupational subjects while also contributing to our understanding of news content.

In this book I engage with the question of how gender shapes newsroom
culture, and in so doing am concerned with production practices and cultural
processes. The book considers the dilemmas, constraints, negotiations, and compromises that shape journalists' day-to-day routines. It probes specific questions
about gender in asking: What is journalism and what is a journalist? How is
newsroom culture embodied? How do female journalists experience newsroom
culture? What are women's embodied responses to newsroom culture? How has
global industry change impacted on the workplace and what does this mean
for journalists? How does feminism get played out in the newsroom? What is
the relationship of newsroom culture to the content of the news?

My aim, then, is to explore the gendered production of news—and
in particular the experiences of women—in the Australian print media. It
is located within a theoretical framework underpinned by feminist media
studies about news, while also drawing from media studies, cultural studies,
journalism studies, the sociology of media, organisational and occupational
studies, and feminist theories of work and the body. Feminist media studies
has not focussed on empirical or theoretical research about gender and news
production. This book, therefore, responds to a call by U.S. feminist media
studies scholar Carolyn Byerly, and also British cultural studies theorist Angela
McRobbie, for more research that can draw on the strong but small body of
work completed so far.

In my attempt to understand how Australian print news media journalists
experience newsroom culture, I have conducted 17 in-depth, semistructured
interviews. The interviewees range in age and industry experience, and at the
time of interview occupied positions within both regional and metropolitan
newspapers across four of the country's eight states and territories. I have
deliberately restricted my inquiry to the print news media in Australia. Other
mediums such as television, radio, and the Internet have their own set of
complex cultures that are not always applicable to print journalism.

The research is based on the belief that all organisations—including
news organisations—are gendered, albeit in different ways. The book builds
on the work of a group of feminist media scholars in the United States, the
United Kingdom, the West Indies, India, The Netherlands, and Sweden,
whose central concern is the gendered production of news (Aldridge, 2001a,
2001b; Byerly, 1999, 2004a; Carter, Branston, & Allen, 1998; de Bruin, 1999,
2000a, 2000b; de Bruin & Ross, 2004; Joseph, 2000; Ross, 2001; van Zoonen,
1998a). In particular, the extensive body of feminist research by Byerly during
the past 15 years on gendered production practices and newsroom culture has
influenced my thinking and inspired me to attend to the dearth of research
in Australia on news production and especially gendered news production. It

would be incorrect to assume that the experiences of journalists in Australia are the same as those found by international researchers.

Byerly has been influential in redirecting feminist media studies away from a focus on the text to one of production, and in doing so has raised some important points for feminist media studies scholars to explore. Her research also resonates with me personally and professionally, as we have both worked as print news journalists. I have found many of my own journalistic experiences reflected in Byerly's work. Her newsroom anecdotes about her experience as a journalist, and her blending of feminist activism and scholarship, opened up a new way of thinking about the direction of my own academic research. This is not to imply that gender is the only factor that influences newsroom practices and processes, employment opportunities, and news content, although it is my central concern here. Although gendered, there are specific issues relating to race, class, ethnicity, and age—to name a few—that need more research. Other important variables that this book integrates with discussions of gendering processes are organisational structure, media ownership, concentration, commercialism, technology, and globalisation.

Byerly's research is primarily concerned with women's (and gays,' lesbians' and racial minorities') relationship to news media. It is the emancipatory nature of Byerly's work that sets her apart from most of her contemporaries. She aims to bring feminist activism, journalism, and academia into a constant dialogue. Byerly may well lament "that the struggle is not yet over" (2004a, p. 110), but her work in academia is a rare attempt to further debate between journalists and feminist activists in a bid to ensure that women's needs—as viewers and producers of news—and interests are met by the news media. In a similar way, I too have involved myself in feminist activism, drawing on my professional and academic knowledge to help nongovernment women's organisations to better understand news media practices so they can more easily access the media. By presenting and running workshops, talking to women's community groups, being involved in a state government women's consultative committee and a taskforce on women and work, maintaining links with the industry, and more recently tutoring and teaching within academia, I hope to bring a feminist perspective to all those with whom I am in dialogue. Like Byerly, then, my research is grounded in my lived experience and embodied history as a former news journalist and feminist activist, having spent 19 years as a print journalist in regional and metropolitan newspapers in Australia. My professional history and activism also shapes how I position myself in relation to the literature and the interview material in this book. My gender, race, class, sexuality, and age are other important factors that influence my scholarship, and all are explored at various points in the book. An understanding about how I integrate my professional and academic work will be discussed later in this chapter.

Why Move from Textual Analysis to Production Studies?

Liberal feminist politics in particular, has been concerned with the representation of women in the media. In the academy, this perspective tended to dominate feminist research of the media up until the late 1990s. This focus has been at the expense of research that questions how gender relations in the newsroom actually shape and inform these representations. This is not to say that textual analysis has not been a purposeful area of study for feminist media theorists. Because media messages, or content, are said to influence institutions and the ideas of individuals about the world, textual analysis has been invaluable. As Janet Wolff argues, texts are the space where:

> . . . . ideologies are constructed, and the social relations are forged. The very codes of art and literature, the narrative structures of the text, are part of the ongoing process of the construction of meaning and, hence, of the social world. (Wolff, 1997, p. 171)

It has been argued, however, that the almost exclusive focus on textual analysis tends to underplay the material sources of power. Those material sources of power that need further investigation include production practices, including issues that arise around media ownership and media concentration.

U.S. Suffragist Susan B. Anthony believed that as long as newspapers were controlled by men, women's ideas and deepest convictions would be prevented from reaching the public (cited in Gallagher, 1987, p. 11). Perhaps this is why she established the newspaper *Revolution*, which was printed in New York City from 1868 to 1870 (and edited by Elizabeth Cady Stanton, a leading figure in the women's rights movement in the U.S.) and focussed on injustices suffered by women. This numerical equity theme carried over to early second-wave feminist critiques of women and the media.

Byerly's recently published research goes beyond the concern with numbers of women employed in media industries. She is concerned with feminist interventions in the newsroom and their incremental and uneven success (Byerly, 2004a).[4] In exploring feminist intervention she refocusses a debate that is often weighed down by a singular focus on a 'misogynist media.' She acknowledges

---

[4] In late 2005, Byerly moved her focus. An essay in *Feminist Media Studies* ("After September 11: The Formations of an Oppositional Discourse") is concerned with exploring 'oppositional discourses'—those discourses that opposed the U.S. Government's official accounts of the 9/11 events and its call for attacks on Afghanistan and, later, Iraq. Those oppositional discourses were mainly circulated via the Internet and gave voice to those left out of the mainstream media debate (mainly women, and people of colour). Byerly champions the possibility that the Internet is an antidote to corporate domination in the media. The Internet, then, is an alternative space for marginalised voices.

overt acts of coercion "to manufacture the consent of both women and men in perpetuating particular masculine systems in newsrooms and, by extension, the stories those newsrooms produce" (Byerly, 2004a, p. 112), but also examines the subtle mechanisms that work alongside this enforced hegemony. This extends earlier research, which argues that it is time that feminist media scholars move on from a simplistic misogynist media position and instead employ a feminist analysis that seeks to reveal "how feminism, over time, has deeply embedded itself in the fabric of media messages and the industries that produce them" (Byerly, 1999, pp. 383–384).

McRobbie (2000) addresses this point when she argues for a return to cultural production as a key area for contemporary media studies. To the question of 'why return?,' McRobbie (2000, p. 255) posits that "for too long in feminist media studies there has been a concern with media texts and their various meanings at the expense of any detailed sociological considerations of those who actually make these texts." Cultural studies scholars have also been more concerned with media texts and those who consume them, and McRobbie (2000) argues that this focus has either downplayed or dismissed both journalists' agency and institutional relations inherent in newsmaking. McRobbie (1997) notes that she has taught with the principle in mind that some of her young female students would enter the industry and find opportunities to change the industry 'from within.' Over a period of 13 years teaching feminist cultural/media studies to university students in London, she "cannot think of a single women's or girls' magazine whose (full-time or freelance) staff does not include some of my ex-students" (1997, p. 204). Here McRobbie suggests that although women's and girls' magazines will remain bound by the genre, there is potential for change linked to journalistic agency. This is a debateable point. As the book unfolds we will see that newsroom culture is a powerful, pervasive, and often silently persuasive mechanism for keeping 'idealists' (read 'cadet' journalists) in check and following mainstream views on the news agenda; or, more specifically, the views of newspaper owners and editors.

Byerly (1998), in her analysis of feminist media studies, suggests that researchers should give more attention to the modes of production. Feminist scholars and other critical scholars who approach their work from the left "have largely failed to theorise or examine the motives, ideas and agendas of those whose works we so readily analyse" (Byerly, 1998, p. 16). Byerly suggests that feminist and other critical scholars "move backward from texts and give consideration to the people, circumstances, policies and structures within which texts are produced" (1998, p. 17). The shift to production is necessary because feminist media studies scholars need the information to understand where women "fit into the scheme of today's global media in terms of access to capital and ownership, employment, and decision making" (Byerly, 1998,

p. 3). Having this information will allow feminist media scholars to detail and analyse women's location in media history, a history that, as Byerly notes, stands a chance to surface more clearly as a result of more emphasis on production studies. Focussing on media professionals' agency is not to detract from the importance of political-economic structures, which define the macro context within which the media operates. It is, however, to centre on the exploration of the relationship between the macro structures and the micro relations of everyday working life.

There is a lack of research into production processes and their nature and effect on news; into the gendered nature of production; into news production within feminist media studies; and into production, and more specifically, into gendered production in Australia. A search of the relevant scholarly journals that regularly publish material about Australian media, *Australian Journal of Communication*, *Media International Australia*, and *Continuum: Journal of Media and Cultural Studies* between 2000 and mid-2007 turns up just one article (i.e., Lester, 2006) that attends to production studies (journalist-source relations and outcomes), and certainly none that address gender and production.[5] Internationally, the journal *Feminist Media Studies*, in the seven years since its inception, has virtually ignored production studies, with just one very short essay that attends to a brief discussion about gendered Internet production (Pitt, 2003) and my own article about journalists' discourses of sexually harassing behaviour in the newsroom, published in 2007.

What does this gap mean about the direction of media studies in Australia and internationally? Most likely, an absence of production studies, and production studies that focus on gender, is about 'fashion' in academic study. Much of the research about media leans towards a focus on representation and content analysis. Greg Noble, an Australian cultural studies theorist, highlights this shift, not only in cultural studies (an area that overlaps significantly with media studies), but the academy more broadly. Noble (2005, p. 13) notes that the early themes associated with cultural studies research included "a desire to give voice to the lived experiences of everyday life." Despite this, he says, "the concern with ethnographic work seems to have diminished over the last decade" (Noble, 2005, p. 13).

> It [cultural research] asks us to consider the ways of best capturing the lived experience of the cultural and social complexity of [the] contemporary globalised world, as well as the broader socio-structural conditions of that experience. (Noble, 2005, p. 14)

---

[5]My own article "Naked Women, Feminism and Newsroom Culture" in the *Australian Journal of Communication* (2004) is the exception.

Noble acknowledges that there is a more pressing issue: whether we can afford the 'luxury' of ethnography. The problem he identifies is the duration and intensity of fieldwork, and the financial costs involved. "As the research landscape increasingly demands more and more publications, and quicker postgraduate theses, our capacity to generate long-term ethnographic projects is diminished" (Noble, 2005, p. 14). It seems a problem, then, that will be increasingly difficult to address.

Feminist Literature on News Production

The main concern of feminist research that has focussed on women's access to newsmaking apparatus has been women's employment and advancement in the media industry where news is defined, formulated, and distributed. This has been central to feminist media studies, especially during the late 1990s. The majority of international scholars who have written about the gendered production of news have been published in just two edited collections (Carter, Branston, & Allan, 1998; and de Bruin & Ross, 2004). My point here is that research into the gendered production of news still has many gaps. In Australia it is virtually nonexistent.

Some researchers have focussed on the absence of 'stories' about talented female journalists throughout history and have attempted to 'right' an imbalance in the research by bringing to light individual talented women journalists who have stood out in a male enclave. Australian academic Sharyn Pearce (1998), in her book *Shameless Scribblers*, examines the contributions of eight Australian female journalists from 1880 until 1995. In it she concentrates on the manner in which the journalists presented issues of key importance in women's lives. Pearce suggests that perhaps this neglect of the achievements of women journalists is due to the fact that journalism has rarely been seen as 'high art.' (I would suggest that this would also mitigate against acknowledgment of the achievements of *all* journalists.) Pearce offers as an example typical of this attitude when author Patrick White derogatively described Australian literature as 'dun-coloured journalistic realism.' Another possible reason for this negligence could be related to journalism's popular image, "its reputation as a male enclave, a masculine profession" in an industry predominantly owned by rich and powerful men. As such:

> The conspicuous success of individual women journalists could be dismissed as aberrations infrequently tolerated within a patriarchal framework, or, alternatively, they could be overlooked by the more hyped performances of prominent and influential men. (Pearce, 1998, p. vi)

The idea of a critical mass has been central to research focussing on the 'body count.' The question posed has been 'How many women would it take to effect change in news content?' Twenty-five years ago, Zillah Eisenstein (1997/1981) was very optimistic in her liberal approach, suggesting that male-dominated organisations were more likely to become responsive to women's needs and concerns when there are sufficient numbers of women within them asking for change. This type of feminist research on media production assumes that a 'critical mass' of women integrated into positions at all levels in the media will benefit feminist projects. This perspective posits that if women did dominate the media and constitute a majority, media content, the language, the style, and the nature of news would change, because these have been formed and refined by generations of men. As Yehiel Limor and Aliza Lavie (2002) point out, this approach, however, is grounded in essentialist assumptions about men and woman. Margaret Gallagher (1995, p. 3) also had high hopes that a "critical mass of women will have some success in changing the long established media practices, routines and priorities which individual female professionals have been powerless to shift." U.K. media theorist Linda Christmas (1997, p. 7) agrees with a consensus figure on women's presence in the newsroom, "a critical mass . . . by consensus, thought to be around 30 per cent." This argument, however, fails to take into account that female journalists have constituted about a third of journalists worldwide since Gallagher's ground-breaking 1995 report. It also denies complexities of vertical segregation within the industry in which female journalists are still located en masse in the lower ranks while men dominate the decision-making roles.

Many female journalists themselves indicate that the news would be different if more women held decision-making positions in media organisations. For example, surveys conducted by the International Women's Media Foundation support this notion.[6] By 2002, Gallagher has changed her position and admits that "it is now clear that 'the problem' is both more deeply rooted and more over-arching than can be solved by numerical redistribution" (Gallagher, 2002, p. 4).

The majority of feminist media research posits no essentially different view between male and female journalists about, for example, news selection. As established Netherlands feminist media researcher Liesbet van Zoonen (1994, pp. 54, 58) argues, women do seem to hold more explicit, but not fundamentally different, views on journalism then men. Sue A. Lafky (1991) also finds that among American journalists, there are few significant differences between how men and women journalists define news. Karen Ross (n.d., cited in Byerly, 1998)

---

[6]The foundation, launched in 1990, notes on its website (www.iwmf.org/ accessed June 12, 2005) that its mission is to "strengthen the role of women in the news media around the world, based on the belief that no press is truly free unless women share an equal voice."

similarly reports little difference between the way in which male and female reporters in Britain in the mid-90s covered news about female politicians. In terms of professional values, David Weaver's (1997) study also finds that there are few significant differences between how male and female journalists report news. "This [findings] suggests that newsroom and community environments are stronger influences on journalists' professional values (and probably on the kind of news content they produce) than is gender" (Weaver, 1997, p. 39). This raises the question of whether news coverage is likely to significantly change as increasing numbers of women enter the industry. Furthermore, this approach is based on the notion that the occupation of 'journalist' has no gender, and that journalists' knowledge is not gendered. But as Ross (2001) points out, there are contradictions within Weaver's findings, and although gender differences appear to be diminishing in general terms, there nonetheless seems to be some distinctions when considering subject source and tone.

An analysis of my interview material in later chapters, however, suggests that a newspaper's news agenda is learnt by journalists through a series of rewards and punishments. Male and female journalists are more likely to select and produce stories that fit the status quo, and therefore reward a certain type of gendered subjectivity. There are a number of reasons for this, not the least being the intensification of work practices and the focus on covering the same news as the opposition.

The tide has begun to turn in terms of a shift in recent academic debates from numbers to more systematic research on the interaction of gender and organisational variables (de Bruin, 2000a). "Counting men and women, although necessary and useful, is also seen as only scratching the surface of the realities of media" (de Bruin, 2000a, p. 5). In other words, the early critical mass arguments put forward by Gallagher and Christmas, for example, although important, need to be made in more complex ways than merely number crunching.

Van Zoonen was one of the first to critically address newsroom culture and to see the newsroom as gendered. For van Zoonen (1998a, p. 137) organisational agency is central. She defines agency as being "what journalists do within the structural constraints posed by the organisation of the profession and is thus always embedded in organisational routines and pressures" (1998a, p. 128). The process by which journalists become acquainted with unwritten rules, norms, and values of journalism and learn to perform accordingly is termed by van Zoonen (1989, p. 2) 'professional socialisation.' It is this socialisation that encourages journalists to take up the dominant discourses in the newsroom. It soon becomes apparent to journalists that if they fail in this acceptance of norms, they will be viewed with suspicion and even alienated from other workers and networking opportunities vital to promotion. They also face being excluded from covering important breaking stories where prestige is claimed and used as a basis for promotion and job satisfaction.

Linda Steiner's (1998) account of how power works in the newsroom furthers this debate. She maintains that focussing only on the impact of the power of media representation fails to adequately address how news stories are selected and organised. This focus gives insufficient attention "to how journalists, with what experiences and acting by what processes, produce the news" (1998, p. 145). Steiner poses a series of important questions that offer ways to unravel how gender is critically embedded in news culture. They are significant questions that this book responds to. She asks:

> Do reporters' perceptions enter into their work, for example, in their definitions of newsworthiness, choice of assignments, approaches to sources, or ethical decision-making? What have been the power relations operating in the production of news work? Who has helped whom? Who provided encouragement and mentoring? What are the consequences of working with stubborn colleagues or dictatorial editors? What about sexual harassment in the newsroom? Or being underpaid, or underappreciated, or underutilised? Or being positioned as the token woman on staff? (1998, pp. 145–146)

Recent Areas of Concern for Feminist Studies of News Media

In terms of book-length publications about media production studies there exists a similar gap worldwide, as I have noted with academic journal publications, with a few notable exceptions. While I argue that production studies that include an analysis of gender are paramount to understanding newsroom culture, other writers consider more overarching themes. In Australia, feminist media scholars Elspeth Probyn and Catharine Lumby (2003) have provided a forum for scholars to probe media ethics. Although contributions to their edited collection, *Remote Control: New Media, New Ethics*, are not focussed on gender, the fact that feminist media studies scholars are directing debates about media ethics is noteworthy. In their introduction, Probyn and Lumby explain the often fractured relationship between the industry's code of ethics and journalists, arguing that journalists simply do not, or cannot, abide by the code because it fails to take account of the realities and complexities of popular media. Problematically, they don't attend to the constraints within which individual journalists who make (un)ethical decisions are constituted and regulated as journalists in the first place. Some of those constraining forces could include media concentration, the decline of traditional news media, the influx of women into the media, the differing ethical concerns for male and female journalists, and the gendered occupational culture in which journalists make decisions. Rather, the book's various authors consider important, but limited, ethical debates about pornography and the Internet, indigenous issues, the ethics around 'food' journalism, and debates over talkback radio and a so-called 'cash for comment' affair.

In 2007, former journalist and now academic Libby Lester published a book focussing on the news media coverage and journalists' understanding of the environment in Australia's island-state of Tasmania. It is specifically concerned with the reporting of the Franklin Dam blockade of the early 1980s. The state government's proposed damming of the Franklin River in Tasmania's wild south-west sparked an unprecedented public outcry and unprecedented media coverage of environmental issues. Although Lester's focus is broadly about the rise of the concept of 'wilderness' in media coverage, her interviews with journalists allow an analysis of journalist-source relations. In doing so, Lester examines how journalists come to understand 'news'—in this case, specifically, the Franklin blockade and the influences on journalists in the reporting process. Although this is a valuable contribution to media production studies, it is limited by its Tasmanian media focus and the specificity of one media debate. This is not to say that the debate is undeserving of a book; it is more to highlight the lack of full engagement with organisational and production studies that may have enhanced the analysis. Problematically, for me, it also ignores the gendered dynamics of journalist-source relations, and therefore arguably gives a partial account of those relationships in which Lester focusses.

The first edited collection that focussed primarily on gender and newsroom culture was Cynthia Carter, Gill Branston, and Stuart Allan's important book *News, Gender and Power* (1998). In exploring how gender relations affect the practice of journalism, the contributors have laid the foundation for feminist media scholars interested in production studies. The contributors, who include Jenny Kitzinger, van Zoonen, and Steiner, probe how gender shapes the forms, practice, institutions, and audiences of journalism. In doing so they draw on feminist theory to explore media issues such as ownership and control, employment and occupation status, the production of news, newsroom culture, and the changing gender of journalism.

Carter, Branston, and Allan set the stage for Marjan de Bruin and Ross's edited collection *Gender and Newsroom Culture: Identities at Work* (2004). It is a book that emerges from, and extends on, feminist research from the mid-1990s onwards in media studies and organisational studies that began to focus in the dynamics between gender and the (media) organisation. Since the 1980s, women in organisations had been a study topic in media studies and organisational studies, but "the behaviour of women and men was seen as determined by their positions, reflecting the patriarchal society that structured apparently 'gender-neutral' organisations" (de Bruin & Ross, 2004, p. viii). The essays in this book extend on the 1990s trend of understanding the behaviour of male and female journalists in media organisations "as the result of practices and interaction in a culture in which gender is a major 'given' " (de Bruin & Ross, 2004, p. viii). The authors in their collection analyse gendered symbols, values, meanings, and signification as the key to understanding relationships in organisations, rather than power differences based on organisational rank. The book contains a mix of methods and approaches, and importantly encompasses smaller qualitative projects that offer richly textured accounts that contribute to an understanding of the different contexts and cultures from which the work originates, including Africa, the West Indies, and India. Many of the essays have proven a valuable tool to my own research enabling an international perspective on the gendered production of news and reinforcing my position that research with an Australian context was long overdue, and that a small-focus qualitative approach had merit.

Bringing an international perspective to media research has been at the core of Ross and Byerly's edited collection, *Women and Media: International Perspectives* (2004). In the first section of the book the essays analyse the ways in which mainstream media continue to commodify and sexualise women in news media and film. In the second section the emphasis is on the ways that women have gained some control of news messages and images, provoking a shift in both content and context, and particularly how feminist media activism has helped change the industry. Byerly (2004a), for example, in her essay "Feminist Intervention in Newsrooms" argues that changes in U.S. news are the result of both internal newsroom campaigns by women journalists and external campaigns waged by community-based women's groups making specific demands for change. Ammu Joseph (2004) also looks at the ways in which women in newsrooms in India have had a positive effect on media culture. For the editors, Ross and Byerly, illuminating knowledge of these events is important in order to gain a full appreciation of women's self determination in communicating within and across nations (2004, p. 6)

Ross continues her prolific work in media studies with a book based on empirical research with Byerly. Published in 2006, *Women and Media: A Critical Introduction* examines the ways in which women have worked inside and outside mainstream media organisations since the 1970s. The book, firstly, provides an overview of the key issues and developments in feminist media critiques and interventions over the last 30 years, before concluding with a new study of women's media activism across 20 nations. The study is based around 100 interviews with women media workers and activists, some from Australia, and provides insights into women's newsroom experiences. It focusses on the ways that women have organised their internal and external campaigns to improve media content (or working conditions) for women and established women-owned media to gain a public voice.

Gendered Occupations: How Advantage is Conferred

There is little doubt that feminist intervention and other socio/economic/ political changes have facilitated change in terms of the gender makeup of most occupations and workplaces, with newsrooms no exception. Traditional employment structures have privileged men's working lives across all occupations, whereas women's participation in the workforce has been, and continues to be, largely confined to a limited number of occupations. The jobs on which women dominate, quantitatively, continue to be reflective of their domestic and caring responsibilities; for example, childcare, cleaning, nursing, hospitality, and teaching. In Australia in 1975, 43 percent of women were in the labour market, leaving the majority outside it participating in various forms of unpaid care and home life (Woods, 2000, n.p). By 2005, 56.7 percent of women were in the labour market (AMP NATSEM, 2005, p. 4). At the same time the proportion of men in the Australian labour force has decreased from 80.5 percent in 1975 to 72.1 percent in 2005 (Abhayaratna & Lattimore, 2006, p. 10; Woods, 2000, n.p.). The 'ideal,' or 'imagined' worker, however, remains 'benchmark man.' As Margaret Thornton (2001, p. 78) explains it, the 'benchmark man' is "invariably white, Anglo-Celtic, heterosexual, able-bodied and middle class, and who constitutes the standard against which women and Others are measured."

Women's entry into journalism in Australia has been one of the most significant changes in the industry. This has taken place alongside the emergence of the second wave feminist movement and feminist-inspired government legislation providing mechanisms for equal opportunity. Less than 50 years ago journalism worldwide was an almost exclusively male profession (Peters, 2001), with a sprinkling of pioneering women.[7] But women have since entered the media in unprecedented numbers. The number of female students studying journalism in Australia has risen dramatically (Putnis & Axford, 2002, p. 2) and women are gaining a foothold in the industry, especially in its lower-status ranks (Peters, 2001, p. 4), in line with the labour market in general.

The professionalisation, or credentialing, of the occupation of journalism is a phenomena of the last two decades in Australia, indicating a shift in how the industry accepts journalists into the 'fold.' Formerly, the industry would train its staff in-house with on-the-job experience highly valued. Cadetships were completed in four years, and those with a university education were in the minority. Today the public/student-funded university system trains the

---

[7]Pearce's (1998) book about Australian women's contribution to journalism from 1880–1995 highlights those pioneering women.

majority of prospective journalists in Australia. A university degree of some description is necessary, and a journalism degree preferred, to apply for the few, hotly contested cadetships offered by major metropolitan newspapers in Australia each year.

Gallagher finds that women now account for at least 50 percent of the students in journalism and mass communication fields in the world (Gallagher, 1995, p. 5).[8] This varies from around 20 percent in Iraq to nearly 80 percent in New Zealand, Estonia, Hong Kong, and Iceland (1995, p. 5). More specifically related to journalism, Bettina Peters (2001), citing a 1993 study, notes that the average percentage of female students among those undertaking journalism degrees is about 40 percent worldwide. Women dominate communication and media studies courses in Australian universities. In 1999, there were 8,726 female students enrolled compared to 3,597 males (Putnis & Axford, 2002, p. 2).

But this influx does not mean women are advantaged in promotional opportunities once in the industry. The irony is that although more women are undertaking journalism degrees and gaining lower-status jobs in the newsroom, there has been no flow-on effect to the more senior editorial decision-making positions, which remain dominated by men (Melin-Higgins, 1996). Jobs in the top end of the industry remain elusive for women. Gallagher (1995) reports that just 3 percent of media organisations worldwide are headed by women. If the figures are broadened to take in the highest management level, women's share of the jobs rises to 9 percent (Gallagher, 1995, p. 47). Peters (2001, p. 4) more recently finds, however, that even though women represent more than a third of the working journalists around the world, the percentage of women editors, heads of departments, or media owners is only 0.6 percent. Unfortunately, there is no comprehensive and detailed research about Australia in that report.

In Australia in the early 1990s, according to Gallagher (1995, p. 12) women on average made up 39 percent of the media workforce. The only source that offers a more detailed and overall picture of the Australian journalistic landscape can be drawn from reports lodged by newspaper organisations to the Equal Opportunity for Women in the Workplace Agency (EOWA). Under the Equal Opportunity for Women in the Workplace Act 1999—formerly the Affirmative Action (Equal Employment Opportunity for Women) Act 1986—Australian companies (private sector, community organisations, non-government schools, unions, group training companies, and higher educations institutions) with 100 or more employees must establish a workplace program to remove the barriers to women entering and advancing in their organisation

---

[8]Gallagher's valuable and much cited report draws on statistics from 1990 to 1995 for the United Nations Educational, Scientific and Cultural Organisation (UNESCO). It covered 43 nations and 239 organisations.

and report to the EOWA each year.[9] I have drawn extensively on the reports submitted because they provide the most detailed statistics available about the Australian media workforce. I am, however, wary of making any definitive statements here because of the diverse methods that various organisations use to collate and report their statistics.

Other ways of accessing information lack academic rigour, but do provide additional layers of information about the Australian media. For example, an industry magazine and some newspapers have published articles that address the prejudice that female journalists encounter, and I discuss them more fully later in the chapter. In 2006, an article published in the News Limited–owned national broadsheet newspaper *The Australian*, although not discussing gender, provided evidence of gender bias in the upper ranks. The story "Paper Sales Defy Internet Growth" (MacLean, 2006, p. 17) has an accompanying list that details 21 of Australia's major metropolitan newspapers, their editors, and circulation figures under their leadership. Although this is interesting reading about leadership and circulation trends, it also shows that there is just one female editor of a metropolitan newspaper in Australia—Jeni O'Dowd, who heads the weekly publication *The Sunday Telegraph* (News Limited, Sydney). In 2001, there were two female editors leading Australian metropolitan newspapers—Colleen Ryan at the up-market daily *The Australian Financial Review* (owned by News Limited rival John Fairfax Holdings Ltd, which has substantial interests in metropolitan, suburban, regional, and more recently rural newspapers), replaced after three years by Glenn Burge, who now works for the newspaper as a reporter; and O'Dowd at *The Sunday Telegraph*. Senior Australian journalist and the then federal vice-president of the industry union, the Media, Entertainment and Arts Alliance (MEAA), Claire Miller, notes, however, that:

> Lower down the newspaper and news magazine ranks, women can be found as deputy or assistant editors in news, business and sport, but rarely the section editor in their own right. The exception is the 'softer' sections such as lifestyle, real estate, arts and features. (Miller, 2001, p. 3)

In terms of Australian journalists' wages, there is a disparity on average weekly earnings between male and female journalists in all age groups, and it worsens with age (Jackson, 2003b, p. 3). A specially collated report from the Australian Bureau of Statistics requested by News Limited reporter Sally Jackson

---

[9]The reports are public documents under the *Equal Opportunity for Women in the Workplace Act 1999* and can be found at www.eowa.gov.au (accessed July 9, 2007). The reports, among other things, list total workforce numbers, which include editorial, production, advertising, and other ancillary staff.

addresses the common industry conception that motherhood depresses incomes for female journalists. I more fully discuss this issue in later chapters in which interviewees raise the point that female journalists who have children are less suited to 'being a journalist.' Jackson reports that the breakdown is as follows for childless women working full-time in the media: those aged 55-plus earn 20 percent less than their male counterparts; those 45–54 earn 21 percent less; 35–44 earn 15 percent less; those aged 25–34 earn 8 percent less; and those 15–24 earn 2.5 percent less (Jackson, 2003b, p. 3). The point here is that even female journalists without children who work full-time (seemingly able to be compared to male journalists whether they have children or not) lag behind their male counterparts in remuneration. The MEAA federal secretary, quoted by Jackson in the article, says that women in journalism are affected by a lack of objective criteria for upgradings, the promotion of 'like by like,' and bias in the allocation of rounds.[10]

Statistics from EOWA reports are available that demonstrate a prevalence of women journalists in part-time, casual,[11] and temporary positions. However, because of the way that various organisations collate and report their statistics, it is difficult to make comparisons. Some figures are skewed in relation to the gender breakdown of part-time staff because some organisations have included freelance contributors and columnists—roles that are often dominated by men. Also, a thorough critique is problematic because some organisations have conflated part-time, temporary, and casual staff figures, and others do not separate between editorial staff and overall company staff. For example, the 2003 report to the EOWA by Tasmanian metropolitan newspaper The Mercury and its subsidiary papers shows an unusually high number of male casuals—33 compared to 11 females. However, it makes clear that the majority of the casual males are freelance contributors. In the 2006 report there is a massive jump in casual staff (77 casual males and 74 casual females) (Davies Bros Pty Ltd, 2003 and 2006, p. 4). This is not due to a rise in overall staff figures, but rather a conflation of editorial casuals with the rest of the company's staff including, administration, sales, and service staff. At West Australian Newspapers, which publishes the metropolitan broadsheet The West Australian, there were 21 male and 38 female casuals, part-time, or temporary journalists on staff in 2002. By 2006 there has been a substantial rise in female causal, part-time, or temporary

---

[10]The statistics are also interesting for the fact that The Australian reporter asked for them to be collated in that way. According to the ABS, this information is not freely available, and a cost applies for an ABS researcher to collate specific information—i.e., the information is not publicly available.

[11]Casual staff have irregular, nonpermanent working shifts. There is no guarantee of regular work. Casuals usually fill in for staff on sick or holiday leave. They are usually paid at a lower rate than permanent or temporary staff.

staff, with 50 women filling these roles, compared to 18 men in those positions (West Australian Newspapers Pty Ltd, 2002 and 2006, p. 2).

At the Adelaide metropolitan daily *The Advertiser* there were 22 casual or part-time women and 15 casual or part-time men in the editorial department in 2003, and in 2006 27 women and 15 men (Advertiser Newspapers Pty Ltd, 2003 and 2006, p. 2). At Queensland Newspapers, which publishes the Brisbane metro *The Courier-Mail* and weekly *Sunday Mail*, there were 105 casual male journalists and 58 female journalists (Queensland Newspapers Pty Ltd, 2003, p. 2). In its 2006 report, however, there are 21 casual women and 50 casual men in the editorial department (Queensland Newspapers Pty Ltd, 2006, p. 1). It is evident that some newspapers have used the categories to include contributors and others have not. It is also clear, and frustrating, that constant category variations each year by the same organisation makes it impossible to accurately assess gender segregation.

As Gallagher (1995) and Byerly (1998) have lamented, accessing reliable and accurate comparable statistics on employment in media industries is a major hurdle to media research worldwide. Relatively little systematic study has been made of women's employment status in media organisations around the world (Gallagher 1995, p. 10). The situation is the same in Australia, making it difficult to draw conclusions or compare statistics over time and between national newspapers, and also between countries—especially in regard to gendered staff numbers—due to the inconsistent use of report categories by various newspaper organisations.

The reports to EOWA do, however, offer an overall picture of the gendered newsroom. In 2003, *The Mercury* signed off its report to the Federal Government detailing that the number of full-time professional females (primarily journalists) had dropped to 17.8 percent of the journalistic workforce, well below the level of five years earlier at 25.6 percent (Davis Bros Ltd, 2003, p. 4; and 1998, p. 7). This equates to 20 full-time female 'professionals' (comprising primarily journalists) and 58 full-time male professionals employed by the company in 1998. In 2003, it employed 13 full-time female professionals compared to 60 full-time male professionals (Davis Bros Ltd, 2003, p. 4; and 1998, p. 3). The 1998 figure is the highest participation of female journalists compared to male journalists at *The Mercury*, according to the EOWA statistics, which, from 2004 no longer allow for comparisons because of a change in the company's reporting categories. Both statistics (17.8 and 25.6 percent) demonstrate that the company is well below worldwide industry levels of around 35 percent (Gallagher, 1995, p. 12). The 2004 report, while not making a clear breakdown in the number of male and female journalists, happily reported in detail that:

> For the first time in its 150 year history, the newspaper appointed women to three key roles in the news section during the reporting year. These

included the first women to be appointed Chief of Staff, the newspaper's
Chief Reporter, and the Chief Political Journalist. It is apparent that
women are moving progressively into some other areas, both within the
management and supervisory levels. This includes responsible operational
jobs that may have been seen previously as male dominated. This trend
has been demonstrated in the past few years by the appointment of women
to senior positions in Marketing and Editorial Departments. (Davies Bros
Ltd, 2004, p. 3)

It should be noted the careful wording of the sentence "the newspaper
appointed women to *three key roles* in the news section during the reporting
year." There were indeed *three roles* that senior women variously filled; however,
judging from the bylines in the newspaper at that time and information in the
newspaper, *just two* women filled those three roles that year. There is no 'trend'
here except for the one that turns a blind eye to a declining number of female
journalists in the editorial department. In the company's 2006 report there is
no longer a 'professional' category, and it is impossible to decipher which category includes editorial staff (Davis Bros Pty Ltd, 2006, p. 4). It now has the
categories 'senior managers' and 'managers.' In the 'senior manager' category
there are 7 women and 18 men and in the 'manager' category there is 1 woman
and 11 men. One is left wondering why the categories are constantly shifting,
if not to make it impossible to compare and contrast a deeply and consistently
gender-segregated workforce.

Internationally, Gallagher (1995) has found that most nations still have
less than 50 percent of women working across all media (television, radio, and
newspapers). In central and eastern Europe (along with the Nordic states) female
journalists comprise 45 percent of the journalistic workforce but in western
Europe, the numbers fall to 35 percent. In Canada and the United States the
figure is 39 percent, Latin America is around 25 percent and in Japan only 8
percent. Peters (2001), whose study took in 39 countries, representing almost
70 percent of members of the industry body the International Federation of
Journalists (IFJ), shows the number of women journalists in the industry at 38
percent, up from a reported 27 percent in the early 1990s.

Gallagher also notes that there are a higher proportion of women working
in radio and television than in print media (Gallagher, 1995, p. 17). By 2001,
Peters' survey contradicts Gallagher's, suggesting that in most countries more
women work in newspapers than in any other media.[12] Yet in a broad-reaching
2005 worldwide report it was found that female reporters have gained more

---

[12]The IFJ survey on the status of women journalists (Peters, 2001) shows that there are exceptions
to this rule. For instance in the United States, more women work in magazines (37 percent) than
any other media, and only 10 percent work in newspapers. In Morocco almost 45 percent of female
journalists work in broadcasting, closely followed by newspapers (38 percent).

ground in radio and TV than in newspapers. The Global Media Monitoring Project (2005, p. 18)[13] found that just 29 percent of news stories were written by female newspaper reporters in 2005. In 2000, television gave most space to female reporters (36 percent). In 2005 it was overtaken by radio, where 45 percent of stories were reported by women (2005, p. 61–62). The third GMMP also found that the percentage of news items reported by female journalists had risen from 28 percent in 1995 to 31 percent in 2000, and to 37 percent in 2005.

Gallagher's (1995, p. 15) worldwide study found that women were 26 percent of the permanent full-time media workforce; 79 percent of the permanent part-time workforce and 44 percent of the temporary or casual media workforce. "In all regions women are more likely to be found in part-time and temporary work than in full-time employment" (Gallagher, 1995, p. 15).

The majority of global media workforce literature doesn't, however, address occupational segregation. Gallagher's (1995, p. 39–45) report is an exception, although there are no comparable statistics specifically for Australia. It briefly engages with statistics that demonstrate a gendered numerical difference between journalists' tasks (horizontal segregation) such as reporting, sub-editing, and editing. The statistics show a predominance of men in sub-editing and editing positions.

Some feminist media scholars (for example Byerly, 1999; and Mills, 1988) have argued that feminism as a political movement has impacted on the industry at a macro level by opening up jobs, providing the structures to monitor inequality (such as, in Australia, reporting to the Federal Government agency EOWA and having those reports accessible to the public via the organisation's website), and fostering an awareness within the industry of need for change in the way it represents women.

The shifts that Mills and Byerly refer to may be driven more by economics than feminism. Newspaper owners and editors have increasingly recognised the need to capture new markets, as traditional readership niches decline and technological advances change the way audiences access news. This is evident in Australia. In 2004, for example, *The Age*'s (Melbourne broadsheet) incoming editor-in-chief, British journalist Andrew Jaspan, the former editor of the Scottish independently-owned broadsheet *Sunday Herald*, was reported as saying that the youth and women's market were central to increasing the newspaper's readership (Catalano, 2004, p. 5). Jaspan acknowledges that newspapers are mostly 'run by men with very much a male-orientated agenda,' admitting that at a micro level, personal bias and antifeminist sentiment continue to shape

---

[13]The 2005 international Global Media Monitoring Project surveyed the representation of women and men in news content. It also offered statistics on who reported the news. Groups in 76 countries submitted data for analysis on February 16, 2005, with just under 13,000 stories monitored on TV, radio, and in newspapers.

news content and newsroom culture (see Chapter Eight). Despite increased participation by women in media industries and 20 years of equal employment opportunity laws in Australia, women still struggle to attain the status of their male colleagues. The increasing quantitative success of women in journalism is linked to broader social and cultural changes that have allowed women an increased presence in the workforce. Gallagher (2001, p. 63) suggests that the most common obstacle to career development reported by women journalists is the problem of male attitudes.

The above statistics about the gendered nature of newsroom staffing describe a form of news media with declining readership worldwide. The number of newspaper readers in Australia is clearly in decline.[14] There has also been a decline in the number of metropolitan daily newspapers. In 2005, there were only 11, but as recently as the 1980s, there were 17 (Beecher, 2005, p. 15). All afternoon newspapers have been axed, taking with them a combined circulation of 1.5 million at their peak. Moreover, the proportion of the population that is buying or reading newspapers has collapsed (Beecher, 2005, p. 15). This is hardly surprising given the volume of information and entertainment that is now available electronically in the home and office and the various technologies with which to access it. Beecher (2005, p. 15), a former journalist, notes that times have changed considerably from 1947, when, in Australia's largest capital city, Sydney, 1.2 million newspapers were sold daily to a population of 1.5 million. Today, with Sydney's population at 4.5 million, there are less than 700,000 newspapers sold daily. Roy Morgan research published in March 2005 reveals that Saturday newspapers in metropolitan and major regional markets were also showing consistent readership losses (www.bandt. com.au/news/38/0c02d238.asp). Perhaps newspapers are old fashioned, on the dying end of the media business, where journalists get paid less for a less sexy job. Perhaps the femininisation of the newspaper workforce can be seen as a response to the declining readership of newspapers.

Feminisation Debates

Although women have been increasingly rewarded with more positions in the newsroom, their structural position has not changed since the 1960s. Swedish academic Margareta Melin-Higgins (1996) argues that women are confined to 'softer' specialised news-topics which among journalists are rated as having lower status. Melin-Higgins notes, however, that it is increasingly argued by feminist media theorists that the 'feminisation' of the news, whereby 'softer'

---

[14]As it is in the United States, where in 1964, 81 percent of Americans read a daily newspaper; today that figure hovers around 54 percent (Beecher, 2005, p. 15).

stories take up increasing space in newspapers and are considered important to the public, could actually give female journalists increasing status. 'Soft' news includes social issues, consumer issues, healthcare, education, childcare, housing and, according to Monika Djerf-Pierre and Monica Lofgren-Nilsson (2001), the environment. I see their final point considering the environment as 'soft' news more complex in an Australian context. Since in the early 2000s, the environment has carried much political weight in Australia and could therefore be considered 'hard' news—although, I would add that those stories that offer a 'green' political position could be seen as 'soft' news. From mid 2006 climate change also became a major debate in Australia, gaining momentum after the government acknowledged climate change as a significant, if debatable, problem. Therefore, to a degree, 'soft' and 'hard' are culturally specific concepts. Hard news includes politics, business, union issues, military, technology, science, and crime.

Of more importance is their position that changes in the news genre are difficult to describe as a whole when different gender orders and journalistic cultures "produce and support different femininities and masculinities in different newsrooms at different times" (2001, p. 20). Djerf-Pierre and Lofgren-Nilsson (2001) are adamant that to fully understand the changing gender of journalism, three existing and interacting forces and structures need to be considered. That is, firstly, the social, economic, political, and cultural forces of the existing gender system in a given society in a given historical period. Secondly, it is necessary to analyse journalistic culture; and thirdly to explore the strategies of individuals or groups of women and men trying to change or reproduce the existing structure of power in journalism. For Djerf-Pierre and Lofgren-Nilsson (2001, p. 20) feminist media research should develop closer links with theoretical perspectives on organisation and gender "in order to fully grasp the gendered nature of news." These are valuable insights and important points that I take up in the following chapters.

From the masculine bastion of days gone by, when 'cowboys' and 'corrupt marionettes' (Melin-Higgins, 1996) were terms used to describe what a journalist is, the argument in the 2000s is that news has become more feminine in form and content. In other words, a feminisation is taking place. So is this change due to the increased number of women in the industry? The increased presence of women in newsrooms hasn't encouraged the substantive changes in newswork practices that many had expected, but it has brought about other changes that hadn't been envisaged and about which feminists feel ambivalent. I'd argue this along with Jane Arthurs. In her discussion of the televisual industry in Britain, she contends that: "More women in the industry is not enough. There need to be more women with a politicised understanding of the ways in which women's subordination is currently reproduced, and with the will to change it" (Arthurs, 1994, p. 100).

Theoretical Framework

Feminist research on male-dominated occupations has provided a theoretical framework for my analysis of the male-dominated occupation of journalism. Feminist theorists have variously researched how women have negotiated male-dominated industries such as medicine (Pringle, 1998), engineering (Lewis, McLean, Copeland, & Lintern, 1998; McLean et al., 1997), and the legal profession (Pierce, 1995; Thornton, 1996). I discuss their work and their exploration of embodied subjectivity in more depth in the following chapter, but provide a brief outline here to make the point that this book also moves beyond just numbers to consider issues of culture, the impact of feminism, and the fragmented nature of patriarchy—all questions that have been dealt with in feminist studies of other occupations.

For example, Australian researcher Rosemary Pringle's study of male and female doctors in Australia and Britain (1998) explores the changes that have occurred through the increased number of women in the profession. She considers the implications of this transformation for the practice of medicine and, in turn, for conventional assumptions about gender, power, inequality, and patriarchy. Rather than dwelling on the realities of male medical power, Pringle points to its "vulnerabilities and cracks" (1998, p. 3). This shift away from a focus on male power in a male-dominated profession has been helpful to my analysis of the occupation of journalism.

Sue Lewis, Christopher McLean, Jane Copeland, and Sue Lintern (1998) and McLean, Lewis, Copeland, Lintern, and Brian O'Neill (1997) in interviews with Anglo male engineering students and staff at two Australian universities are similarly concerned with masculine power. They are looking at a profession that hasn't yet been infiltrated by women and make a different point from Pringle—that patriarchy impedes the progress of women. Both papers demonstrate that engineering, both in its educational and professional contexts, is dominated by a particular type of masculine culture that excludes women, and some men, from full participation. McLean et al. argue (1997, p. 143) that it is the specific masculine nature of engineering culture that acts as a major impediment to change.

Thornton's (1996, p. 1) Australian study of women in the legal profession is concerned with the issues pertaining to the conditions under which women have been 'let in' to the profession. Thornton (1996, p. 2) argues that women are constituted as 'non men' as 'others' to the benchmark man, "the paradigmatic incarnation of legality who represents the standard against whom others are measured and who is invariably White, heterosexual, able-bodied, politically conservative, and middle-class." Thornton (1996, p. 8) also demonstrates how body politics are deployed to "affirm and reconstitute the feminine so as to diminish the authority of women as legal knowers." Corporeality, then, is highlighted by Thornton as one of the ongoing sites of contestation.

Jennifer Pierce (1995) demonstrates how sex segregation is maintained and reproduced through case studies of two U.S. law offices and explains how the gendered division of labour is maintained. For Pierce, the embodied worker is central to understanding law firm culture.

Conclusion

It is from these five feminist tracts on organisational and occupational cultures that I draw ideas about the newsroom culture of the Australian print media. I call on similar methodological frameworks to those used in the studies mentioned above, of semistructured in-depth interviews, to flesh out how newsroom culture is embodied. It will be argued, as I have already alluded, that journalism has similar characteristics to the legal and engineering professions that Pierce (1995), Thornton (1996), and Mclean et al. (1997) describe. Journalism, however, is specific—it has its own mythologies, ideologies, and gendered ways of being that individuals call on to negotiate the newsroom.

The study of the newsroom experiences of men and women journalists in the Australian print media is as important an area of research as those described above and may even raise the stakes. The news media represents the world to us, shapes our knowledges and histories, and influences our thinking about everything from seemingly simple and nonpolitical issues such as fashion and health, to international politics. This news is not produced by disembodied workers. The overriding questions then are 'Do men and women experience newsroom culture differently and, if so, does this effect news decisions? Does gender effect who is allocated what stories, what gets published and what doesn't, and how are stories displayed or given more or less prominence than others?' By extension, issues such as how cadets learn what is news, how career progress is made in an industry that has no formal methods of merit-based advancement, how sexual harassment affects female journalists, and why women are, in most cases, en masse in lower-paid, less-senior ranks than their male colleagues are important questions on the path to understanding gendered subjectivities in the newsroom. This is critical to an understanding of the news we read everyday.

Chapter Two

The Research

Bringing the Personal into Politics of Objectivity

This chapter details the framework that underpinned the research for the book and engages with a debate about the processes that effect research outcomes. In taking up an interdisciplinary feminist theoretical approach, I am aware that other research styles would pose challenges to such an approach, and it is this point that is worthy of consideration.

A total of 17 print news media journalists, male and female, senior and junior, who work, or had recently worked, in metropolitan and regional newspapers in Australia were sought for the purpose of conducting semistructured, in-depth interviews. The eight men and nine women interviewed ranged in age, education, journalistic experience, and seniority. There were two regional daily newspaper editors and three regional daily cadets, a metropolitan news editor, feature writers, political round reporters, and sub-editors. Two former metropolitan reporters were included in the research. Five of the nine female interviewees had completed a Bachelor degree, not necessarily in journalism; and one had also been awarded a Masters degree in journalism while working in the industry. Two of the eight male interviewees had completed a Bachelor degree. The majority of interviewees had been in the industry on average 15 years, but a few had less than two years' experience, while some had 38 or 39 years' experience. The participants' ages varied from 19 to 56. The participants worked variously for four metropolitan and two regional dailies owned at the time of interview by a broad cross-section of media companies—News Limited, John Fairfax Holdings, Australian Provincial Newspapers (APN), and Rural Press.

News Limited dominates the print media landscape in Australia, owning 70 percent of the mainstream press including the majority of metropolitan dailies and community newspapers in most of the states and territories. Its closet rival in terms of newspaper ownership is John Fairfax Holdings Ltd, which merged with Rural Press in late 2006. The group dominates the Victorian and NSW landscape, publishing major metropolitan dailies *The Financial Review* and *The Sydney Morning Herald* (Sydney) and *The Age* (Melbourne) along with a host of regional newspapers. Rural Press was a specialist agricultural and regional publisher that was led by its flagship weekly newspaper, *The Land*, before the merger and the nation's capital newspaper, *The Canberra Times* (more details of the companies are provided in Chapter Five). APN publishes 23 daily and about 100 non-daily regional newspapers in Australian and New Zealand.

The interviews took place in four states of Australia between December 2003 and April 2004, primarily at participants' workplaces. In two instances, editors whom I interviewed had arranged for other staff I had contacted to be interviewed in a private office in the newsroom. A few interviews took place in coffee shops close to the participants' workplace. In one city, all three interviewees came to a private room in a motel to be interviewed. I didn't question these decisions, as I had given all 17 interviewees the option of an interview location that they felt most appropriate. In two instances interviews took place in participants' homes. Interviews lasted from 40 minutes to more than two hours.

A purposive rather than a random strategy was applied for securing participants. I closely monitored the diversity of the group, in terms of age, gender, editorial position, and geographic location. As well, as far as I am aware, all of the interviewees are white. Although this could be argued to limit the research, it is also reflective, in my observation, of the Anglocentric dominance of journalists in the Australian print news media. Finally, even though it was important for me to scan as widely as possible for research participants, inevitably the research was restricted by the economic constraints of being a postgraduate student at the time, which meant not being able to travel as widely or for as long as I would have wished to conduct a larger number of interviews.

I do not claim this research to be neutral or unbiased, as I devised the theme areas, asked the questions, shaped conversations, interpreted transcripts, developed a thesis, and selected pertinent excerpts. As I have indicated, my work has been informed by my own experience as a print media journalist and influenced by my own pre-existing ideas about feminism, particularly the ideas of feminist media studies scholars. In making this contribution about gender and media, I therefore acknowledge that I am playing an active role in constituting knowledge about the media; I cannot pretend that I am merely interpreting it. As Mary Hawkesworth posits:

> Discussions of the 'situatedness' of knowers suggest that the claims of every knower reflect a particular perspective shaped by social, cultural, political and personal factors and that the perspective of each knower contains blind spots, tacit presuppositions, and prejudgements of which the individual is unaware. (1989, p. 554)

A 'snowballing' method was used to recruit participants. It is generally accepted by qualitative researchers that this is the most efficient and productive way of recruiting a heterogeneous group of participants. This method has been successfully used in other small-scale media research projects. For example, Meryl Aldridge's (2001b) study of 27 newspaper journalists in the United Kingdom; de Bruin's (2004) study of 10 male and 10 female journalists (the majority in the print media) working in the Caribbean media; Melin-Higgins' (2004) follow-up study of nine (three men and six women) of her earlier 33 interviewees (radio, TV, and newspapers) from a 1992 study; and Minelle Mahtani's (2005) transnational study between 2000 and 2004 of 20 female journalists (TV, radio, and newspapers) from Mumbai, Toronto, Sydney, and Melbourne.

Initial contact was made with two journalists who I knew from my experience in the industry and two contacts given to me via academic sources. They participated in the interviews and also provided contact details for other journalists who they believed may have been interested in contributing to the project. To avoid unwanted intrusion into people's privacy, it was requested that the journalist contact the person recommended to me before I made initial contact. Each of the contacts provided were emailed or phoned and the project briefly outlined. If agreeable, added information was provided about general topics to be covered in the interview. These included, but were not confined to, discussions about career trajectory, career aspirations, frustrations, compromises, negotiations in day-to-day work routines, if or how gender impacts on the treatment and opportunities offered to journalists, and a discussion about how feminism may have impacted on newsroom culture and workplace practices. After the journalists had received this information they were contacted again, and we discussed possible dates, times, and suitable locations for interviews to take place. I suggested interview locations (ones that had a power point that allowed me to run a tape recorder) only if a participant seemed unsure of a suitable location. I then sought their support in suggesting other journalists who may be interested in the project and who may agree to be interviewed.

Of those journalists recommended by colleagues, none rejected participation in the project. The initial contact point was important to the success of gaining participants. All interviewees went out of their way to participate and were available for interview when they said they would be. Many came into their workplaces on days off. In one city the participants all came to a motel where I had established an interview area on their scheduled days off work, and many scheduled our interview during a break in their busy working days. All of the interviewees whom I needed to contact after the initial interview to clarify details in their transcript responded. The majority also replied to emails in early 2006 asking if they would update me about their current position in the industry.

After the interviews were completed and professionally transcribed, a copy was sent to all participants. Interviewees were invited to read the transcript and make any corrections in transcription, verify their account, and edit material. Participants were able to withdraw the entire interview from the project during this time, but none did. All participants were then allocated a pseudonym so as to provide anonymity and, as such, any perceived risks associated with identification in published materials were avoided.

Bringing the Personal into Politics of Objectivity

One of the central understandings of feminist epistemology is that impartial or detached observation is not possible (Fonow & Cook, 1991). Positivists have argued that rationality, viewed as a trademark of masculinity, is preferable in all scholarship. However, building on one's own personal and professional experience has been a hallmark of feminist scholarship, and feminist media researchers have effectively used this method to strengthen their research. Many feminist media scholars are former journalists who bring to their research years of personal experience.

How these women locate their personal experiences in journalism within their academic work, however, varies considerably. Byerly, as mentioned, uses her professional experience as a way of enhancing dialogue between feminist activism and professionalism and therefore has an emancipatory focus. British scholar and former journalist Christmas (1997, p. 1) has a more liberal take on women's slow progress in the industry, suggesting that women journalists themselves effect change and "set their own agenda." Lafky, too, has a liberal feminist frame to her work and, as with Christmas, keeps her past experience as a journalist from her work, although it is acknowledged in small biographies accompanying some of her essays, suggesting that this adds some credibility to the work. Indian media scholar and journalist Joseph (2000), unlike Christmas, specifically states that she does not wish to advise women journalists what they should or should not do in order to address gender inequality. She also eschews anecdotal experience to inform her work. Rather, she places the emphasis on an analysis of material from interviews with female journalists and excludes her experience from this analysis. Australian feminist Lumby's is a complex subject position. In *Bad Girls: The Media Sex and Feminism* (1997), she makes the point that feminism challenges established ways of speaking, from journalism to scholarship. Lumby not only produces a theory of the postmodern breakdown between zones of discourse, she performs and embodies it in the way that she moves between those ways of speaking (Wark, 1999, p. 70).

It seems that one's personal history (or 'objective' current location) shapes, but doesn't necessarily determine, one's methodological or epistemological position. These positions are also shaped by the theoretical assumptions and tools one takes up.

As with Byerly, I consider my personal and professional experience and feminist commitment in the newsroom as informing my theorising. Professional anecdotes, therefore, form a small but important part of this book. Moreover, my professional background, understood through a particular feminist theoretical lens, underpins the research as a whole and is central to why I focus, in particular, on women's experiences in the newsroom. My working experience in the print news media also underpins the book's focus on the print news media in Australia. Experience in journalism and in the newsroom offers a significant insight that can be utilised to support theories and interview material. I am keenly aware that this method challenges many research assumptions, especially those that argue that the researcher should be objective and 'above' involvement. Yet, if one acknowledges that, firstly, all research has a political dimension, and as Pamela Creedon (1993) notes, that when the political dimension of research challenges the orthodoxy (dominant values), it creates controversy, this makes my approach valid.

Shifting Terrain: The Insider-Outsider Positions in Interviews

Some feminist literature on methodology suggests that an articulation of the self in the research process should be fully explored in the research and writing of such work. In this section I explore the dual positions in which I find myself during the research/interviewing process: white, middle-class feminist academic, and a female journalist. I raise this because in this research, my position as journalist, academic, and feminist created a shifting position. As Lila Abu-Lughod (1991, p. 141) astutely notes: "Standing on shifting ground makes it clear that every view is a view from somewhere and every act of speaking, a speaking from somewhere." I'm not suggesting that acknowledging the researcher's subject position mitigates the validity of one's knowledge, although those with positivist epistemologies often assume it does. As Laurel Richardson (1994, pp. 517–518) so poignantly argues, "a postmodernist position does allow us to know 'something' without claiming to know everything. Having a partial, local, historical (situated) knowledge is still knowing." Donna Haraway's (1988) concept of 'situated knowledges' is similarly useful here. Haraway suggests that the only way to create a larger, more critical vision is 'to be somewhere in particular.'

The insider/outsider distinction emanates from the notion that a researcher can (and should, according to the positivist approach, which emphasises the erasure of self) detach oneself from the research subject. The positivist position, which advocates a passive detached approach to research, suggests that the less involvement from the researcher the 'truer' the 'data.' Feminist methodology questions that proposition. The positions for researchers of either 'insider' or 'outsider' have been debated by social scientists from the late 1960s and early 1970s (Pierce, 1995, p. 191). The debate has mainly centred around ethnographic research and who should be allowed to do such research, particularly on minority communities (Bridges, 1973, p. 392). In the methodological literature, "a researcher who shares the same gender and racial, ethnic and social class background as the subject is considered to be an 'insider,' whereas a sociologist whose status differs from those of the subjects is an 'outsider' " (Pierce, 1995, p. 190). This, I suggest, could be extended to include 'profession,' not only because academics are increasingly drawn from industry to teach and research in universities, but because we are in an era of postgraduate study in which increasingly students are of mature age and have a profession in which they still work while completing higher degrees. This is, of course, the case in which I found myself. This dichotomous position of neither one nor the other, however, leaves little room for the shifting and sometimes intertwined positions that I have experienced—sometimes insider, then outsider, depending, among other variables, on the topic being covered in the interview.

In theorising whether the terms 'insider' and 'outsider' are still relevant and useful concepts to enact in the field, Pierce (1995, p. 191) concludes that "ethnographers move back and forth in continuous tack between the statuses of insider, outsider." Patricia Hill Collins (1986) terms this position the 'outsider within.'

The insider position often secured me the interviews I may not have garnered had I been 'just' another postgraduate student asking for an interview. I was keenly aware that my experience in the industry was a fact that I raised very early on in either my phone calls to prospective interviewees or in the formulaic letter I emailed to contacts whom other journalists suggested might become participants in my research. As a journalist still situated in the industry, my interviewees often drew me into the insider position via comments such as 'you know what I mean' or 'you must have experienced that' or 'I don't know if you have found that.' Male interviewees were more likely to bring me into the insider position when were discussing journalism and not gender, whereas female interviewees, especially those about the same age as myself, were more likely to make a point about similarly gendered experiences.

The insider position bears me fruit as a researcher. Because I know the journalistic discourse and am aware of certain similarities in news production and newsroom culture across Australian newspapers, there is more opportunity to explore the nuances. But there are also problems. As a feminist academic, I was clearly an outsider to many of the journalists I interviewed. My academic training, and pre-existing feminist position had taught me to question and challenge dominant paradigms and the patriarchal institution within which I worked for most of my working life. Yet, I constantly found myself in relation to the journalists I interviewed as another journalist, finding that when I stepped out of that mode it created stiffness in my dialogue and in their response. A part of this had to do with wanting to maintain equality in the interview. I had hoped to elicit their stories in a way that empowered the interviewees while also benefiting my research. I often took up a 'dialogical' (Frankenberg, 1993, p. 30) approach to the interviews, positioning myself as explicitly involved in the questions and at times sharing information with interviewees about my own working life, and sometimes about my personal circumstances or experiences. In order to gain the interviewees' trust and acceptance and allay any initial nervousness about the interview, I always began the interviews with questions about the participant's career trajectory. This method provided easy and instant engagement, but sometimes created frustrations. One of the oldest male interviewees talked over the top of most of my initial questions to the point where I just sat there and nodded and waited for an hour for him to detail every move in his 38-year career. This was also the case with the oldest female interviewee with whom I had worked at an early stage of my journalistic career. I let her talk for a considerable time before I brought her back to a more directed focus on my questions. But even so, there were fascinating points made that may not have arisen if I had been too directed (to my theme areas) in my questioning. I learned to become a better listener, and the end result was that more trust was developed and the dialogue flowed more reciprocally in the latter stages of the interview. Even so, I was sometimes frustrated after reading the transcripts and wondered why I had intervened/interrupted at certain points.

In the initial part of the interviews, I played down my feminist research interests, often waiting until near the end of the interview to raise direct questions about feminism. I found that by the latter stage of the interview most participants were more relaxed and comfortable with me and the areas of discussion. There was also more reciprocity between interviewee and interviewer in the dialogues with the three women who identified as feminist. I found their ideas fascinating as a researcher, but personally and professionally their concerns and joys about the industry resonated deeply with me. In them, I found journalistic colleagues with whom I shared a common interest and thoughtfulness about gender relations in the newsroom, and this opportunity was certainly new to me, and in many cases to them. Academic research, therefore, allowed me access to journalists who would share ideas with me in a way that I had not previously experienced as a journalist. It wasn't only the ideas about gender relations that were insightful. Overall, the interviews canvassed ideas that I had rarely had the opportunity to discuss while working in the industry.

Interpretation: How I Use the Interviews

It is clear that analysis of 17 interviews does not allow for definitive statements generally applicable to all Australian journalists or the industry as a whole. The research project was not set up to be a representative sample, but rather a small and diverse sample through which a close reading of the transcripts could allow for the exploration of key themes. De Bruin (2004) similarly notes the potential of in-depth interviews with a small number of journalists. Her aim, as was mine, was to collect stories, accounts, and narratives that would present her with experiences in newsroom production. Yet as she notes:

> The data from these interviews should be considered as descriptions of perceptions and not as descriptive facts. It is not important whether their statements are true or false: The texts provide an insight into how interactions with journalists at work are perceived. (de Bruin, 2004, p. 8)

My interpretation of the journalists' narratives focussed on their lived experience in the newsroom. I don't suggest that everything that the interviewees discussed with me can be understood as objective 'truth,' but I do understand it as part of their individual 'truth' within very complex organisations in the occupation of journalism. In many ways my interpretation of the interview material is directed towards understanding processes of taking up particular subject positions.

I am using the notion of subject positions in the way that McLean et al. (1997) have used it. A subject position is taken up by a person or group in response to a dominant person, group, or culture. For example, McLean et al. (1997) in their research of male and female students in a male-dominated university engineering course argue that a core group of (male) students set the norms and determine who and what is acceptable to that group. In response, female students take up one of three particular subject positions in response to the masculine culture of engineering—'traditional,' 'feminist,' or 'one of the boys.' In this way subject positions are taken up in a bid to either be accepted by the dominant group (by fitting in or mimicking the group's behaviour) or to resist the behaviour of the dominant group. Of course these are not definitive subject positions, because we all occupy multiple subject positions at various times in various situations.

So, how do journalists cope with conflicting subject positions? Which subject positions are preferable or more rewarded? What subject positions do female journalists take up, and why? How do journalists negotiate their changing/unstable subject positions in a changing/unstable industry? Why is there a preference for some subject positions over others and the rejection or denial of others? In asking these questions of the interview material, I acknowledge "that experience is both a cultural construct and an ongoing process out of which the subject is constructed as a particular type of individual and takes on a particular identity" (Mason, 2002, p. 25). I wanted to do more with the interviews then just use them to render visible the experiences of male and female journalists. It is, therefore, in the interpretation of their narratives that ways of thinking about how newsroom culture works are provided. Occasionally I have used some excerpts to reinforce a theoretical point or to illustrate a general observation or claims, rather than interpret what has been told to me, and in doing so the journalist's statement is assumed to be self-evident. On the whole, however, I have opted instead to interpret and analyse the material in a bid to discuss particular aspects of what is being told to me, rather than assuming it to be an objective 'truth' in any simple way. I have worked to explore how the interviewees came to particular subject positions in relation to a number of themes that related to understanding newsroom culture, unpacking the multiple ways in which various subject positions were rendered available to particular journalists. Consequently, I acknowledge that each of the journalists has come to the industry, and indeed the interview, with already established ways of being, experienced through particular fields of knowledge and shaped by a social and historical context.

As well as conducting interviews, I also utilised a professional journal during the first six months of this research when I was working casually as a sub-editor at *The Mercury* newspaper in Hobart, Tasmania. I noted particular events and discussions that occurred in the newsroom that may have been relevant to this project. To address ethical concerns, for one important anecdote that takes up a large chunk of Chapter Ten I requested, and was given, signed permission from the various journalists paraphrased to use the quotes in my research. This method provided a rich source of data and is one in which I acknowledge and analyse my own subject position(s) as thoroughly as those I write about.

Particular Issues in Researching the Production of Media

McRobbie (2000) argues that even though production studies require intense periods of immersion in the field, even simply interviewing media professionals is a "slow and unpredictable process" (2000, p. 257). She queries that though there are difficulties in gaining access to powerful people and then getting their time for an in-depth interview, this does not fully explain the eclipse of studies of media workers in recent years. "There are other reasons why what people say about what they do, and how they do it, has dropped down the agenda" (2000, p. 257). She cites Nicolas Garnham (1990), who also maintains that a good deal of research needs to be done on media production processes and organisations. Garnham's main concern, according to McRobbie (2000), is that existing work[1] often 'succumbs to the superficial glamour,' taking at face value what journalists say about the creative aspects of the work they do. This implies that research would need to dig more deeply, gaining familiarity as well as insight, so that the respondents would drop their professional images and speak more directly about the reality of their working conditions. When this happens, researchers are more able to focus on what he considers the point of production studies, which is to explore relations of power, decision-making, control, organisation, and administration.

Garnham is also aware of the limitations of traditional ethnographical studies (McRobbie, 2000), particularly those that adopt a microsocial approach in which analysis of the fine details of social interaction, such as compiling a news bulletin, fail to recognise the more structural constraints that dictate in advance the nature and shape of such a process. This emphasises human agency, but often at the expense of social structure. McRobbie (2000, p. 258) dismisses Garnham's fears and claims rather that the "need for work that shows the complexity of decision-making in contemporary, media and communication practice far outweighs the fear of disappearing into the minutiae of ethno methodological detail." She continues:

> I am therefore arguing for a renewed commitment to production studies, but from a position that acknowledges the scale of the changes that have swept through the culture and media industries to the point that working practices within this vast sector are almost unrecognisable compared to those that prevailed when sociologists talked convincingly about the routines and daily practices of media professionals as they worked alongside each other in a relatively stable TV newsroom environment. (McRobbie, 2000, p. 258)

This approach shows a "renewed interest in 'history from below,' and on how working people experience directly their own situation" (McRobbie, 1982, p. 47).

Within the industry itself, there is little scrutiny of newsroom culture by journalists or former journalists. Former Fairfax reporter and now freelance journalist Margaret Simons' (1999) account of the workings inside the press gallery in Canberra that covers federal politics is one recent Australian book that does expose the gallery culture. Yet the gallery is a very specific newsroom and contains a select and small group of journalists (who focus on politics in a hothouse environment). The book does, nevertheless, make some interesting and pertinent comments about the occupational culture of the gallery. Although Simons skirts around a thorough analysis of the gendered production of news,

---

[1] I suggest that Garnham is not talking about feminist or critical studies about the media.

she does acknowledge the "macho priorities" of the profession's culture. She sees gender inequality as one of many factors that "act against the education and inspiration of those who are making their way up" (Simons, 1999, p. 113). Simons' most recent book (2007) delves into the issues driving dramatic change in the Australian media. It's a broad-ranging analysis of media ownership and technological shifts and the impact these changes have had on the way journalists work. Simons' voice is typically strong throughout the analysis and in her interviews with key media players. The issue of gender and media production at first appears to have its own chapter titled "Ethics and the Boys," but it never really attempts to unravel the oppressive nature of the typical newsroom, even though examples of it are detailed in other sections of the book. Rather, Simons seems content to still be considered 'one of the boys' and to be privy to some key 'boys' discussion on ethics and the role of the Australian Press Council. It is a subject position that has allowed Simons exceptional access to some of the biggest players in the Australian media.

A few other Australian journalists, for example, Virginia Trioli (1996) and Virginia Haussegger (2005), offer a handful of newsroom anecdotes in their books that address other themes, and I draw on all of these later in the book.

In summary then, this book makes the point that the lack of focus on production issues has serious implications not only for understanding the gendering of journalists as occupational subjects, but for understanding news content. The problem in terms of production research, as noted by van Zoonen (1998a, p. 124), is that there is "next to nothing in terms of theoretical concepts or models that aim at a general understanding of the wide variety of practices and experiences that typify the day to day work of contemporary journalists."

Book Outline

Chapter Three draws on research in organisational and occupation culture and feminist theories of the body to ask 'What is the occupational culture of journalism in Australia?' 'What is a journalist and what does it take to embody a journalistic life?' 'How is newsroom culture embodied?' 'How does a woman's body fit with the profession's notion of the 'right body'?' From my analysis of the 17 interviews with male and female journalists in the Australian print media, I explore male and female embodiment in the newsroom and how 'femaleness' is constantly drawn to women's attention, while the white heterosexual male body stands normative and immutable. I analyse how the gendering of a worker's body is a key marker and product of organisational and occupational structure. Assumptions about, and practices of, gender are produced by, and underlie, many aspects of the structure and culture of the workplace, and the newsroom is no exception.

My investigation provides insights into the nature of gendered change and the impact of feminism. One particular feature of newsroom culture is sexual harassment. In Chapter Four, I analyse the interview material to reflect on how men's sexual harassment of women is remembered and explained to me, and how feminist discourses, government legislation, and company policies about 'sexual harassment' have limited benefits for female journalists. I argue that the term itself has been captured by liberalism and antifeminism to mean things that minimise and mock its original challenging potential. Analysis of the interviews I've conducted indicates that female journalists are less inclined to take up the discourse of sexual harassment because it will be used against them. Just as Cynthia Cockburn (1991, p. 167) found that women she interviewed in retail work, a public service department, and a trade union did not want to be associated with feminism because 'feminism has got itself a bad name,' female journalists similarly are fearful of the repercussions of the term sexual harassment because of its link to feminism and the negative discourse that has emerged from public debates about sexual harassment in the 1990s. Far from the euphoria of the mid-70s when naming 'sexual harassment' promised women freedom from it, it now taints them and ties them to a devalued subject position. 'Sexual harassment' describes a discursive object that feminists identify but which the majority of women in newsrooms, especially younger women, do not find useful. Perhaps it is that they do not dare to use it?

Chapter Five is concerned with how the changing nature and structure of the media industry through globalisation impacts on newsroom practices and specifically the gendered nature of the newsroom. I consider 'globalisation' and what it means, turning up a complex amalgam of change across individual, social, union, government, and industry dimensions. I discuss technological changes to news production, explore the gendered nature of production processes, and ask how the concentration of media ownership in Australia and the current neoliberal climate affects journalists. I consider how interviewees discuss these changes and how journalists accept/reject and negotiate/accommodate change in their day-to-day practices.

Chapters Six and Seven demonstrate the various sites of resistance to these trends, both within individual journalists' narratives of industry and personal change, and legal challenges by three senior female journalists to what some in the media now acknowledge as a discriminatory and 'blokey' newsroom culture. Consideration of global changes must consider the gendered nature of journalism and how gendered culture/structure do/don't change.

In Chapter Eight the interviewees reveal a very stringent assessment of feminism and feminists inside and out of the newsroom. This chapter sets the scene for Chapter Nine, which brings together my key themes about gendered production with its impact on news content (with an interesting outcome). The chapter uses as its pivot a series of brief discussions by journalists in *The*

Mercury newsroom about a to-be published picture of 36 women who stripped naked to demonstrate their antiwar sentiments in 2003. I use the image of the naked protesting women to explore broader themes about feminism and the media. Specifically, I'm interested in three areas: How feminism and ideas of feminism are deployed in the newsroom; how feminism variously shapes subjectivities of journalists; and how feminism shapes news content. The newsroom encounters indicate confusion about what feminism means and some dissent among its workers who took various subject positions on female nakedness and feminism. The disjuncture between the debate in the newsroom, in which many of the players are critical of feminism and the 'successful' news story is a complex, yet fascinating insight into newsroom culture.

The conclusion of the book summarises key points about how the interviewees in this research experience, negotiate, and discuss the massive changes that have occurred in the Australian news media industry in the past 30 years. While the book is broadly focussed on the gendered nature of the newsroom, in asking what impact has 'feminism' had on the experiences of journalists in the newsroom and on news content, it is also specific in teasing out the nature of industry changes and assessing how important globalisation is to these changes. I also consider my own professional changes during the process of writing this book in relation to the practice of journalism and academic study and suggest ways in which journalism courses in Australia can better incorporate feminist media studies into their curriculum. This, I hope, will better equip young journalists with the tools to survive, negotiate, and even challenge the gendered (raced and classed) practices in their workplaces.

Chapter Three

'Bowled Over by the Big Boys'

Female Embodiment in the Newsroom

I've always struggled because I'm a short woman. I used to get stomped on in press conferences. When there was a big press conference, I was literally bowled over by the big boys at the back and literally elbowed in the face, and come home injured—physically injured. (Susan)

When this senior female metropolitan newspaper reporter tells her story of being a short woman in a predominantly male and aggressive media pack, she is problematising her physical embodiment as a female journalist. Another senior female metropolitan reporter explains her slow promotional progress in terms of her nonconformity to traditional feminine bodily norms. She speaks to the creation of another type of gendered embodiment in the newsroom:

If I was to cut my hair tomorrow into a bob, and get my straightener, like the other girls do and straighten it every day and to maybe start wearing a few sexy clothes—like as in a bit of cleavage and stilettos—went out of my way to be nice to absolutely everyone, in a sort of a cutesy-pie way, you know 'darling' or 'sweetie' or, 'oh, that's wonderful,' and be really airy and light in my tone, and write stories about cane toads, crocodiles and models, I reckon that in six months he [the editor] would reconsider me for a management role. (Christine)

I'll return to the dynamics in these expressions of female embodiments, gathered from the interviews I've completed with Australian print media journalists, later in the chapter. For now these lead me into an exploration of the gendering of a worker's body as a key marker and product of organisational and occupational structure. Assumptions about and practices of gender are produced by, and underlie, many aspects of the structure and culture of the workplace. The newsroom is no exception. These include the sectors and the type of jobs in which men and women are variously employed, the tasks allocated, and the career progress of workers.

The lived experiences of differently gendered bodies can tell us much about how culture is embodied, and for the purpose of this chapter, how culture is embodied in the newsroom. The chapter draws on research into organisational and occupational culture and feminist theories of the body to ask 'how is newsroom culture embodied?' I take up Joan Acker's (1990) notion of the gendered organisation and explore the ways in which gender, sexuality, and the body are part of the processes of control in work organisations. The literature about occupational culture is used as a frame to which I put questions about embodiment using feminist theory about bodies. 'Physical capital'—a term coined by British sociologist Chris Shilling (1991) that refers to body shape and size, as well as stance, attitude and posture, and clothing—is a key term in my discussion of occupational culture. Here, I refer to the example of Susan, with whom I started this chapter, who struggles in the rough-and-tumble of the physical media pack, and Christine who indicates an awareness of the power of particular female bodies. Female journalists not only have to deal with contradictory attitudes and cultures; they are required to embody them. It is this requirement to enact certain gender norms, "which surface as so many styles of the flesh" (Butler, cited in Bartky, 1997).

Theorising about the body has been the centre of second-wave feminist theory, challenging ideas of women's 'naturalness'—of women's supposed connection with nature. Simone de Beauvoir's (1978) quest to answer the question 'what is a woman?' anticipates the lengthy debates within feminism about whether women have some essential shared characteristics or whether the idea of woman is a social construct. Australian academic Moira Gatens (1998, p. 1) argues that mainstream theories about institutions have failed to attend to the difference that sexual difference makes to how individuals "inhabit, act within, and are treated by the institutions which structure our lives." Sexual differences (as well as others such as race and class) are embodied differences that affect the way people are able to engage with institutions (Gatens, 1998, p. 1). Borrowing from Edna Ullmann-Margalit (1977), Gatens (1998) contends that gender norms support a status quo in which one party is placed in a position of advantage and power in relation to the other party, and that is presented as the 'natural order of things rather than an exercise in power. Her examples include laws prohibiting *any person* to procure an abortion, and the expectation that child care is a private rather than a corporate matter (1998, pp. 5–6). Another example could include legislation that defines sexual harassment as "an unwelcome sexual advance, unwelcome request for sexual favours or other unwelcome conduct of a sexual nature which makes a *person* feel offended, humiliated or intimidated" (www.hreoc.gov.au/ sexdiscrimination/index.html). Implicit in this carefulness about gender neutrality is not only the assumption that both men and women experience sexually harassing behaviour at the same levels but an ignorance of the cultural and social structures that privilege male power and masculinism. As

Gatens (1998) points out, gender norms construct specific forms of embodiment as socially meaningful. Consequently, it is possible to impartially apply norms that nevertheless impact differently on embodied men and women.

Organisational and Occupational Structure

There is a long history of scholarly research on organisations. Susan Wright (1994, p. 5) suggests that there were three periods where anthropologists made important contributions to organisational studies: the 1920s, when both disciplines were in their infancy; the 1950s and 1960s; and the 1990s onwards. Harrison Trice and Janice Beyer (1993), however, although noting that a steady stream of research occurred from the 1930s, view the 1980s as a key time in the changing reputation of organisational studies. They suggest that two major books, *In Search of Excellence* (Peters & Waterman, 1982) and *Theory Z* (Ouchi, 1981), brought the field into prominence. The first systematic attempt to understand modern work organisations, in cultural terms, occurred in the early 1930s at the Hawthorne Plant of the Western Electric Company in Cicero, Illinois, in the United States. The 'Hawthorne studies' explored the relationship between productivity and the physical work environment.

In the 1950s and 60s the American anthropological tradition continued, with the emphasis on studies of formal rules and technical efficiency. The best-known work of the time was Melville Dalton's book, *Men Who Manage* (1959). Also influential in mainstream organisational research was American sociologist Philip Selznick (1959), who described how institutions responded to changing circumstances. As Gibson Burrell and Jeff Hearn (1989, pp. 10–14) describe it, these studies were more interested in the 'organisation of production' than the 'production of organisation.' Issues of power—how organisational structures and processes might have assisted the reproduction of social inequalities—tended to remain marginal (Witz & Savage, 1992, p. 5).

All of these studies, however, neglected a critical analysis of gender relations, failing to account for gendered discourses and practices and men's power in the workplace. The 1990s heralded research on organisations that was increasingly informed by a critical analysis of gender relations. There are a number of reasons why this occurred. No doubt the increasing number of women in the workplace proved a catalyst, but of central importance is the rise of feminist academic critiques of the workplace that highlighted the dominance of men (see for example, Cockburn, 1983; Kanter, 1977b; Pringle, 1988; and Walby, 1986), critiques from gay liberation and gay scholarship (Plummer, 1992; Weeks, 1977), and some men who, inspired by feminist analysis, began to write critically on men and masculinity (Brittan, 1989; Connell, 1983; Kimmel & Messner, 1989; Morgan, 1992; Roper and Tosh, 1991) (cited in Collinson & Hearn, 1994, p. 5).

David Collinson and Jeff Hearn contend that: "Despite—and possibly because of—this frequently pervasive association between men, power and authority in organisations, the literature on management (and indeed organisation theory) has consistently failed to question its gendered nature (1996, p. 4). They note that feminist studies constitutes *the* major influence in developing an analysis of gender in organisations" (1996, p. 9).

Feminist scholars who study organisations generally argue that the gendered nature of the workplace is partly masked through obscuring the embodied nature of work (see, for example, Acker, 1990, p. 139). According to Acker, abstract jobs and hierarchies, which are common concepts in organisational thinking, "assume a disembodied and universal worker" (1990, p. 139). That disembodied 'worker' is still generally thought of as male. Consequently, as Carole Pateman (1988, p. 223) argues, women stand in an ambiguous relationship to the universal worker, who is "constructed from a male body so that his identity is always masculine." This understanding of the male worker as norm marginalises women and contributes to gender segregation in organisations. As Acker notes: "The concept of a universal worker excludes and marginalises women who cannot, almost by definition, achieve the qualities of a real worker because to do so is to become like a man" (1990, p. 150).

In terms of organisational theory these points I have just established were not explored by sociologists until the intervention of second-wave feminism (Acker, 1990). The first and probably most outstanding contribution to this area of research came from Rosabeth Moss Kanter (1975, 1977a, 1977b). In particular, Kanter's *Men and Women of the Corporation* (1977b) is held by both feminists and scholars of organisation theory as path-breaking,[1] because it seeks to show how gender differences in organisational behaviour are due to structure rather than the characteristics of men and women as individuals (Kanter, 1977b, pp. 291–292). In her study of women in a large American corporation, Kanter argues that women's structural placement in organisations—en masse in jobs at the bottom and exposed as tokens at the top—impedes women's advancement. Yet, as Acker (1990, p. 143) notes, despite Kanter's insights into the central problem of gender neutrality, organisational structure, rather than gender, remains the focus. For Kanter, gender stands outside of structure. But as Amy Wharton and Sharon Bird (1996, p. 100) remind us, inside the workplace high levels of gender segregation serve as a "pervasive and entrenched marker of gender difference." As a result, gender plays an important role in workers' classification of self and others.

---

[1]See, for example, Cliff Cheng (1996) who describes Kanter's book as a 'watershed effort' and Collinson and Hearn (1996) who consider it a 'path-breaking study.'

Masculinities and the Workplace

I want to turn my attention now to masculinities in the workplace because it is not possible to understand gendering practices without understanding both masculinities and femininities. Although there are many perspectives and debates about masculine identity, the overarching idea of masculinity identity, with respect to the workplace, is that it is socially constructed through work, which is embedded in an occupation and often within an organisation (Cheng, 1996, p. xiv). Work is the primary source of what Australian gender theorist Robert Connell (1987)[2] has labelled hegemonic masculinity, and hegemonic masculinity is what Cliff Cheng (1996, p. xiiii) considers to be the organising principle of modern workplaces, where it is contested, achieved and conferred. Connell bases his notion of hegemonic masculinity on Antonio Gramsci's (1971) analysis of class relations. His use of the term 'hegemony' thus introduces a conception of genders as both political and social constructions. " 'Hegemonic masculinity' is always constructed in relation to various subordinated masculinities as well as in relation to women" (Connell, 1987, p. 183). Within the dominant culture, this masculinity is embodied by men who meet the current socially, historically, and culturally specific definition of what it is to be a man. According to Michael Kimmel (1994), that (white, heterosexual, Western) man is successful, capable, reliable, and in control. That is, there are men in power, with power, and of power. It is axiomatic that what counts as masculine shifts over historical periods, during the lifetime of the individual and in differing spatial, social, and historical contexts (Kerfoot & Knights, 1996, p. 86). This raises the important point that it is not masculinity as such that is in question here but rather masculinities. Masculinities (or femininities) are by no means homogenous, unified, or fixed identities (Cheng, 1996, p. xiii; Collinson & Hearn, 1996, p. 10; Connell, 1987), rather they are plural—diverse, differentiated and shifting. Masculinity, then, is always 'becoming' (Kerfoot & Knights, 1996, p. 85) because it is not fixed, but rather constituted in and through practice, the ongoing process of inscription and re-inscription in a multiplicity of sites, not merely the workplace (Kerfoot & Knights, 1996, p. 85). So to talk of 'becoming' is to reject any notion of inevitability, universality, or constancy in what it means to be a man.

Hegemony is achieved in a state of play, where other patterns and groups are subordinated rather than eliminated. Connell (1987, p. 183) notes that although there is no equivalent femininity that is hegemonic, "at the level of

---

[2] I refer to Robert Connell as the male author of this 1987 book, but acknowledge that since 2006 Connell identifies as a transgender women. Her name is Raewyn Connell.

mass social relations, however, forms of femininity are clearly defined enough. It is the global subordination of women to men that provides an essential basis for differentiation." Compliance with this subordination to men and the acts of accommodating the interests and desires of men is what Connell labels 'emphasised femininity' (1987, p. 183). This form of femininity appears in reaction to male hegemony. As Acker (1990, p. 153) maintains, "women's bodies cannot be adapted to hegemonic masculinity; to function at the top of male hierarchies requires that women render irrelevant everything that makes them women."

For Acker (1990, p. 152), organisational structures are legitimised through the 'maintenance of a gender hierarchy' achieved partly through such often tacit controls based on arguments about women's reproduction, emotionality, and sexuality—assumed biological traits attributable only to women. Yet this is to simplify organisational structures. Even though I suggest here that gender is central to understanding these structures, other categories such as age, race, class, ethnicity, physical ability, sexuality, and religious affiliation play a part in the hierarchy of organisational structures and the control of its workers. More overt controls include sexual harassment (Acker, 1990, p. 152). Catharine MacKinnon (1979), for example, has argued in her study of legal cases that a willingness to tolerate sexual harassment is often a condition of the job. While 'women's bodies are ruled out of order' (in terms of their sexuality, ability to give birth, their pregnancy, breast feeding, child-care, menstruation, and 'mythic emotionality') in work organisations, 'men's bodies are not' (Acker, 1990, p. 152). Yet this gender hierarchy is also sustained through a focus on individual masculinity that is supported and verified by other organisational members. Laurie Teleford (1996, p. 135) argues that when masculinity is verified, the individual "who holds it feels that he can enact this masculinity and that others are aware of it and will support it." This norm of male hegemony in the private and social worlds has come to characterise organisations.

Issues around 'change' and 'control' are often explored in the literature around masculinities in the workplace. For example, Wharton and Bird (1996) argue that numerically dominant racial and gender categories react most dramatically to changes in the heterogeneity of the workforce. They suggest that men in the dominant category may perceive themselves with the most to lose from changes in the status quo and "thus, may be more sensitive to changing workplace demographics than other groups" (1996, p. 97). When the theory of male hegemony suggests that power and dominance is more important to male identity than it is to female identity, then it 'fits' that change in the workplace is more concerning for men's identity. Collinson and Hearn (1996, p. 3) in exploring men's historical and contemporary domination of the occupation of management, posit that preoccupation with work, discipline, and emotional control are indicative of highly masculine modes of thought and behaviour that "prioritize 'mastery' over self and other." They problematise the depiction of male executives, especially by journalists in the 1980s, as heroic, swashbuckling, and macho, which aided a widely valued and celebrated "masculine, abrasive and highly autocratic managerial style." They argue that " 'Man'-agement came to be defined in terms of the ability to *control* people, events, companies, environments, trade unions and new technology" (1996, p. 3). Control, it seems, is necessary when there is a state of flux or change that challenges male hegemony. In journalism, the introduction of sexual harassment grievance procedures by media organisations are an example of this changing environment, which sets up a challenge to male hegemony.

Unpredictability and uncertainty affects all members of an organisation, yet it is men, especially, who try to manage this by seeking to *control* social relations and particular notions of self (Collinson, 1992) through 'identity work' (Thompson & McHugh, 1995). In an attempt to find a stable and defined sense of masculine identity, men often seek to define masculine/hierarchical difference, status, and power through the subjective process of identifying with some men, while simultaneously differentiating themselves from other men and women (Collinson & Hearn, 1996, p. 14). Informal networks provide a basis for this control and power. Mutual identification occurs through sports, religious connections, kinship and the like, or even 'heterosexist joking relations' (Jackall, 1988, n.p.). In a complex, changing world, it would seem the struggle is in vain. Yet it continues, growing stronger as the fear of change intensifies.

Although the concept of masculinity is open to various interpretations, I take up Connell's (1995) explanation that the term 'masculinity' cannot exist except in contrast to 'femininity,' and both are culturally and historically specific. These terms importantly point beyond categorical sex differences to the ways men differ among themselves and similarly, how women differ among themselves, in matters of gender (Connell, 1995). I have adopted Connell's definition of masculinity (and by extension femininity):

> 'Masculinity,' to the extent the term can be briefly defined at all, is simultaneously a place in gender relations, the practices through which men and women engage that place in gender, and the effects of these practices in bodily experience, personality and culture. (Connell, 1995, p. 71)

Further to this, Connell (1987) acknowledges that there is a 'gender structuring of production.' "Elements of sexual character are embedded in the distinctive sets of practices sometimes called 'occupational cultures' " (1987, p. 181). Collinson and Hearn (1994) suggest masculinities' material features (combinations of behaviour, identities, experiences, relationships, practices, and appearances) and discursive features (language and relationship discourses) are related more to men than to women. When these elements are dominant in an occupation, it is appropriate to label this as occupational masculinity (Wright, 1996, p. 88). Professionalism is a case in point. Connell suggests: "The masculine character of professionalism has been supported by the simplest possible mechanism, the exclusion of women" (1987, p. 181).

Organisational and Occupational Culture

Cultures are "collective phenomena that embody people's responses to the uncertainties and chaos that are inevitable in human experience" (Trice & Beyer, 1993, p. 2). Trice and Beyer (1993) suggest that occupational cultures consist of both ideologies and cultural forms. Ideologies tell members of a profession the taken-for-granted beliefs about what they ought to do and how they should behave in order to be included in a given group; cultural forms are mechanisms for expressing and affirming these beliefs. People in organisations develop cultures because of uncertainties about a range of phenomena including job loss, social status, and self esteem (Trice & Beyer, 1993). Cultures, therefore, provide organisational members with sets of ideas that help them individually and collectively to cope with various kinds of uncertainties and ambiguities (Trice & Beyer, 1993, p. 2). Australian researcher Sue Lewis (2000) notes that these forms are not fixed, but emerge over time, are constantly reconstructed, and open to disruption. Cultural forms include occupation-based stories, myths, ceremony, symbols, legends, rituals, languages, gestures, physical artefacts, taboos, and rites (Trice, 1993). Most scholars of organisational and occupational theory agree that organisational cultures have six characteristics. Trice and Beyer (1993, p. 5) assert that cultures are: collective (cannot be produced by individuals acting alone); emotionally charged (because cultures help to manage anxiety, they are infused with emotion as well as meaning); historically based (cannot be divorced from their histories and do not arise quickly); inherently symbolic (expressive, rather than only the technical and practical side of human behaviour); dynamic (are not static and are always changing); and inherently fuzzy (cultures are not monolithic single sets of ideas, but incorporate contradictions, ambiguities, and confusion).

When exploring how culture is embodied in journalism, it is helpful to see how it has been analysed in other industries, with a similar dominance of men in positions of authority. Judith McIlwee and J. Gregg Robinson (1992), for example, found that there were two major components of engineering culture that could be applied to all occupational cultures—ideology and interactional style. Ideology in engineering emphasises three things: the dominance of technology over people, engineers as producers of the technology, and organisational power as the basis of engineering success. Engineering interactional style requires looking, talking, and acting in particular and masculine ways: aggressive displays of technical self-confidence and hands-on ability for success; defining confidence in dominant masculine terms; and devaluing the gender characteristics of women (McIlwee & Robinson 1992, in Lewis, 2000, n.p).

Perhaps in journalism this interactional style is best exemplified in a newsroom where 'breaking news' epitomises success and power for an editor. Ian McCausland, the former editor of Hobart's *The Mercury*, demonstrates a form of masculinity that symbolises success in dominant dynamic masculine terms and is focussed on power. The day that 35 people were shot dead by Martin Byrant at Port Arthur, Tasmania, in 1996, a reporter recalls McCausland shouting across the newsroom "We are the centre of the fucking universe today" (Altmann, 2006, p. 103). This is a masculinity that is preoccupied with the power of news and its seductive power of increased readership and peer kudos. It also illustrates many of the characteristics that Trice and Beyer (1993) define as aspects of organisational culture—emotionally charged, inherently symbolic, and dynamic.

It is not necessary to be an insider to gain an insight into this type interactional style. *The Australian* newspaper's Media section regularly publishes industry anecdotes that valorise a dominant and aggressive masculinity. Here are two recent examples:

> Veteran *Daily Telegraph* sports journo Bob Cooper is retiring and made sure that all who went to his send-off last Thursday, including News Limited chief executive John Hartigan, could witness his notorious party trick. Cooper, 61, enjoyed a few hours in the company of about 50 well-wishers at the Aurora Hotel, in Sydney's Surry Hills, before stripping off his shirt and, as he has done countless times before, lighting his chest hair. A flash of flame has the assembled throng reeling, especially as the smell of singed hair permeated the room. (Meade, 2007a, p. 40)

A month later 'The Diary' column reported that the newspaper's chief political reporter Dennis Shanahan's son Leo, a newly appointed cadet journalist at rival newspaper, *The Age*, punched a government minister advisor after he was heard to be making derogatory comments about his father (Meade, 2007b, p. 36).

The Embodied Worker

It is important to consider a number of different dimensions in the interaction among people in organisations. There are many ways in which the authority and status of manager, for example, can signify 'men' (Collinson & Hearn, 1996, p. 11) and indeed vice versa. The cultural processes of signification include: size and position of offices; office furniture; display of pictures, paintings, and plants; and the choice of clothing (Collinson & Hearn, 1996, p. 11). In journalism this signification is embodied in a number of ways. For example, there exists a clear separation between the reporting staff and the sub-editing staff in most newsrooms, along the lines of gender, spatial office geography, dress code, and, to a lesser degree, age.[3] A study compiled by the industry union the Media, Entertainment and Arts Alliance (MEAA) and the International Federation of Journalists (IFJ) (MEAA and IFJ, 1996, p. 31) showed that of the 368 female respondents the majority were reporters (35 percent, compared to 12 percent in sub-editing) in the print, radio, and the television sectors. Anthony Delano (2003) also notes the dominance of men in editing and women in reporting roles in the British newspaper sector. It is here that a gender divide is established in journalism, although this has changed over time, in which men dominate in the editing positions and women in the reporting. But it is not just the tasks that decides sex segregation in the newsroom, it is also the time of the day and night during which those tasks are completed. Reporting is essentially a day-time task, whereas sub-editing (especially general news editing) is a night-time task on metropolitan daily newspapers, where the most senior sub-editors are located. It is also common industry knowledge that most of the sought-after senior and influential positions such as chief-of-staff, deputy-editor, and editor are almost always selected from those workers in sub-editing (male dominated) positions, rather than the reporting (female dominated) side of the occupation. The act of reporting (female dominated) has a clear emotional labour content, whereas sub-editing (male dominated) has more of a need for technical, analytical, and computer expertise, while also being removed from news events.

Sexuality in the Workplace

Sexuality is central in workplace interaction, yet it was only in the late 1980s that contributors to organisational theory, inspired by feminism, began to explore the significance of sexuality in the selection of workers (Cockburn, 1991, p. 148). In 1987 Jeff Hearn and Wendy Parkin studied the sexualised social relations in public sector organisations (local councils, hospitals, and universities). They concluded that there is a world of sexuality in most organisations (Hearn & Parkin, 1987, p. 3). The 'sexual regime,' as Hearn and Parkin label it, sustains the male power system in most organisations. For Cynthia Cockburn (1991, p. 149) "The heterosexual construction of certain relationships, such as that of

---

[3] I base this claim on my experience working in many regional and metropolitan newspapers and news agencies in the past 19 years, as well as anecdotal evidence that has arisen from my conversations with industry colleagues and from some of the interviews conducted for this research.

boss and secretary, the management of spaces and movement, the deployment of imagery, language and dress, all foster a male authority."

Here I draw from the interview material to flesh out one of the female interviewee's experience of being sexualised in the workplace. Christine is a 36-year-old senior journalist on a metropolitan newspaper. The following excerpt exemplifies just one of the elements that foster male authority in the newsroom—the heterosexual construction of boss-worker relationships. Christine describes the type of embodied female that she believes her male editor wants on staff, and how she doesn't fit the desired model. This was raised in the interview when I asked what occurred during her telephone interview to secure a job at the newspaper where she is employed. Christine laughs and says:

> Christine: Over the phone, and he [the editor] asked me quite a range of the normal questions—20 minutes. But I often wonder if they had seen me . . . because when I walked in and the editor saw the size of me, he looked me up and down and I thought, 'you fucker.' But that's OK, yeah.

> LN: What do you mean by that? What do you think he would have expected or wanted?

> Christine: More of the same girls that were already in the newsroom.

> LN: And what are they?

> Christine: They're like . . . I'm a size 16, they're a size 8, right. They wear midriff clothing and straighten their hair and lots of makeup, and everyone else in the newsroom wears stilettos, I'm the only one that wears flat shoes. They get ahead by engaging in eye contact, and certain mannerisms, sort of subordinate mannerisms, and they play up to the male ego. I walked in straight away and shook his [the editor's] hand and looked him straight in the eye and he sort of backed off and looked me up and down a bit, and I just thought 'right, you're a sexist pig.' That was [editor's name]. At his farewell one of the girls that wears the midriffs and all of that, she actually said 'oh [name] did you enjoy your time here?' and he said 'yeah, looking at your tits was the best thing.'

Sexuality is also the focus of Gillian Rose's (1999) essay on women and their use of public spaces (rather than private spaces, such as the home). It provides a background from which to explore how newsroom culture is embodied and how some women may experience it. Rose probes violence against women and women's unease in, and fear of, public spaces. Women's sexuality is still perceived by many men as partly defined by their location (Rose, 1999, p. 363). This perception of women as primarily suited to the 'female' functions within the home makes its binary opposite, the public sphere, one where men primarily order. Jalna Hamner and Sheila Saunders (1984, p. 39) also suggest, like many feminists, that "women's sense of security in public spaces is profoundly shaped by our inability to secure an undisputed right to occupy that space." Gill Valentine (1992) notes that the connection between the public and the private spheres underlies a masculinist perception of women's place. The construction of the public space as masculine is not, as Rose (1999) points out, without contradictions. Dorinda Outram (1989, p. 164), for example, suggests that the masculine claim to public space is fragile because what it excludes can erupt into it. Its masculinisation through a policing of bodies means that every new body requires disciplining in order to guarantee its reconstitution. Yet when that body rejects 'reconstitution,' some women and some men are then the subject of other methods of integration and organisational culture.

This surveillance of women's bodies is evident in Byerly's description of her embodied experience in journalism: "I found myself first prey to the advances of male supervisors and others who seemed more amused and attracted by my physical presence than impressed with my professional assets or potential" (Byerly, 2004a, p. 115). Further, she recalls being backed up against a filing cabinet by one newspaper publisher trying to kiss her, being asked by a Pulitzer-prize winning journalist whom she was interviewing to spend the night with him, and being told by a male editor to buy some new ('presumably more feminine') clothes for an interview with a male politician. This type of demand on women to wear clothes that emphasise their bodies and femininity is common in all occupations. For example, Margaret Whittock (2000, p. 204) similarly notes that a young female researcher, speaking of her work in the House of Commons, told *The Daily Mail* "I was told to emphasise my assets as a woman and complimented when I wore short skirts and tight tops." Consequently, if 'emphasised femininity' is a prerequisite to being a female journalist it has to be maintained in a way so that other models do not gain cultural ascendancy (Whittock, 2000, p. 204). This point is clearly evident in Christine's comment, which started this chapter, where she acknowledges that if she were to conform to a known feminine ideal, then her chances at promotion would be significantly better.

Gendered Occupations

Although Acker (1990) laments that of the scholarly work on organisations and organisational theory little has included a critical and thorough consideration of women and gender, the past decade has seen an increase in analysis of gendered occupations. From the 'rambo litigators' who Jennifer Pierce (1995) describes in her tract on men and women's varying experience within the legal profession, to the ways that women's authority as legal knowers has been diminished (Thornton, 1996), the 'boys club' of engineering (Lewis et al., 1998; McLean et al., 1997), and the gendering of occupations such as secretarial work and the medical profession (Pringle, 1988, 1998)—the gendered occupation has been increasingly documented by feminist scholars (see also Cheng, 1996; Eveline, 1994, 1998; Whittock, 2000; and Wright, 1996).

Australian feminist sociologist Rosemary Pringle's broad[4] and well-known study of secretaries (1988) led the way for a more comprehensive understanding of gendered occupational culture. It moved from earlier feminist work, which tended to just 'add women' to the existing framework. There were exceptions to this, and those researchers who did more than just make women visible did show concern with gender as an organising principle of work relations (Pringle, 1988, p. ix). These included accounts of masculinity and sexuality in the workplace (Cockburn, 1983, 1986; and Hearn & Parkin, 1987), which drew to attention the idea that gender is not merely created in the private sphere, but that work is one of a number of sites of gender construction.[5] Pringle's book (1988, p. x) did, as she says, "bridge the gap by locating 'work' in the context of debates concerning culture, sexuality and subjectivity." For Pringle, gender and sexuality saturate all workplace power relations, yet most organisational theory had treated the two as incidental or marginal to the workplace. 'Work' and 'sex' are not separate spheres, rather they are thoroughly intertwined.

> Far from being marginal in the workplace, sexuality is everywhere. It is alluded to in dress and self-presentation, in jokes and gossip, looks and flirtations, secret affairs and dalliances, in fantasy, and in the range of coercive behaviours that we now call sexual harassment. (Pringle, 1988, p. 90)

Importantly, however, Pringle contends that women are not always 'victims' of male power, but in the Foucaultian sense, necessarily engage in acts of resistance. This is not to say that secretaries constitute a revolutionary group, but Pringle asserts that neither are they totally powerless. An aspect of Pringle's research that is particularly of interest to this and the following chapter is her acknowledgment that while sexual harassment draws attention to the centrality of sexuality in workplace organisations, many feminists have consequently restricted understanding of sexuality to its coercive or unpleasurable dimensions. The radical feminist and rational bureaucratic perspective that suggests that sexuality has no place at work is not an adequate position for Pringle. Attempts to see sexuality as an 'intruder' create a negative representation of women and sexuality. Rather, Pringle (1988, p. 96) contends that an opposition to sexual harassment in the workplace needs to be "supplemented with analyses of the ways in which sexual pleasure might be used to disrupt male rationality and to empower women." "It is by insisting on its presence, making it visible,

---

[4]A total of 400 interviews were conducted for the book.
[5]Pringle's earlier work with Ann Game, Gender at Work (1983), also attended to these concerns.

asserting women's rights to be subjects rather than objects of sexual discourses, that bureaucracy can be challenged" (Pringle, 1988, p. 100).

Finally, Pringle argues that it is not only important that there be recognition of female subjectivity in making visible sexuality in the workplace, but also to expose the masculinity 'that lurks behind gender-neutrality' (1988, p. 102). Men are not asexual in the workplace, and as such masculinity needs to be made visible as much as femininity.

Pringle's later work on medicine (1998) is also of interest because it studies an occupation that has some similarities to journalism. Medicine is an occupation in which women are making inroads, numerically and in positions of authority, and challenging the traditional masculine dominance in the occupation, arguably to a greater degree than is the case in journalism. The story of Western medicine's resistance to women and of women's struggles to gain entry has been told (Pringle, 1998). She highlights that part of the 'trouble' with medicine has to do with gender. The basis for the research is 150 semistructured interviews with women doctors from Australia and England. Pringle moves away from focussing on male medical power in search of its 'vulnerabilities and cracks.'

This shift is similarly evident in some recent feminist media research on production. In the United States, Byerly (2004a) is the predominant exponent of this school of thought, which seeks to explore feminist intervention in the newsroom. She explores the changes feminist journalists and feminist politics and/or the movement in general have brought to the newsroom, its culture, and the news it produces, selects, and publishes. Her focus on feminist intervention importantly refocusses a debate that is often weighed down by a singular focus on a 'misogynist media,' a similar move to Pringle's (1998) proposal to not concentrate exclusively on male power. Byerly has called for feminist media scholars to move on from this simplistic 'misogynist media' position and instead unpack how feminism has shaped news content and newsroom culture (for example, see 1999). This is, in effect, the same position that Pringle takes in wanting to reveal the 'cracks and vulnerabilities' of male power in medicine.

Australian scholar Catharine Lumby's interest in the importance of 'human interest' stories and the breakdown of the public/private divide in the value of news stories demonstrates another way of looking at the 'cracks and vulnerabilities' in Pringle's terms. Anxiety about the media's propensity to invade privacy and entertain the public with 'tabloid' or sensational stories is nothing new, according to Lumby (2002). There is a common assumption that a tabloid/or human interest focus 'appeals to immature and ill-informed sections of the community' (Lumby, 2002, p. 321), and that this focus blurs the lines between entertainment and information, between quality news and tabloid journalism, and, importantly, between objectivity and subjectivity. In Gotcha (1999) Lumby explores tabloidisation through the media representations of Princess Diana, the sexual predilections of former U.S. president Bill Clinton, the murder trial of former U.S. footballer O.J. Simpson, and the rise of former Australian politician Pauline Hanson. Lumby argues that apart from ethical considerations, the tabloid-driven media scandals that surrounded each of these four people brought other issues to light that might not have otherwise been raised. In a 2000 interview Lumby highlights how gender politics, for example, can have an increased visibility through tabloidisation: "The O.J. Simpson case is sometimes dismissed as just a voyeuristic story about a terrible killing. This is also a very important case about race relations in America, domestic violence, gender politics" (2000, n.p).

However the debate about tabloidisation and its impact on the representation of women in the media, in particular, is questioned by one of my interviewees. Janet, a former metropolitan reporter, interrupts our interview to retrieve a recent edition of the state's daily newspaper when I asked her about this trend. The front page (*The Mercury*, October 22, 2003, p. 1) uses head shots in the 'pointers' to accompany stories of four women—the women's first names large in each headline: 'Diana's Secret Letter' (the late Princess of Wales), 'Mary's Special Night' (former Tasmanian Mary Donaldson who was revealed as the girlfriend of the Danish Prince Fredrick), 'Brave Delta on a High' (Australian pop singer Delta Goodrem who was battling cancer), and 'Search for Key Ruth Letter' (Tasmanian schoolgirl Ruth Cruz Mendoza facing deportation and hoping to secure permanent residency) (see over page).

> Janet: Here are all the girls. Their first names on the front page—Diana, Mary, Ruth, and Delta. They are all presented as victims, all first names, and they're all kind of 'girlified.'
>
> LN: Some people would see this as the feminisation of newspapers.
>
> Janet: Well I see it as a very masculine take on trying to get more women (inaudible) a very unprocessed, immature attempt to capture the women's market. They don't really care at all. It's just about the man.

Those 'cracks and vulnerabilities,' where women can often make inroads into male-dominated occupations at various levels, don't appear to resonate with Janet in this particular case. (In Chapter Nine, I discuss how women, as news producers and news sources, can indeed shape and arguably control or manage some news output.)

In line with Pringle, Margaret Thornton's Australian study of women in the legal profession is based on 100 semistructured in-depth interviews, which she says 'give voice to those who have been long silenced' (1996, p. 4). Although a theme of gendered embodiment does not flow through the entire book, a chapter has been dedicated to what Thornton labels 'body politics.' Here she explores dress codes and personal style, marital status, motherhood,

The feminisation of newspapers? The front page of *The Mercury*, 22 October, 2003.
Reprinted with the permission of *The Mercury*.

discrimination, and sexual harassment. Thornton (1996, p. 8) demonstrates
how body politics are deployed to "affirm and reconstitute the feminine so as
to diminish the authority of women as legal knowers." Corporeality, then, is
highlighted by Thornton as one of the ongoing sites of contestation (along
with clubs and corporatism). Her discussion on motherhood and issues around
sexual harassment parallel the experiences of the female journalists whom I
interviewed. Thornton (1996, p. 230) argues that the most familiar way of
marking a woman as 'other' to the claimed norm of masculine neutrality is
to construct her identity reductively in terms of motherhood. The structure
of the legal profession and the animus towards motherhood in the workplace
discourages women in law, she argues, from having children.

Similarly, in journalism those women who do have children often return
as part-time, and less-senior workers, because they know that a career in mainstream journalism means long hours and identification with masculine norms.
All of the female journalists whom I interviewed who had children noted this
as an impediment to their careers, or at the very least as creating a struggle

to maintain a career in journalism and raise children. The major employers of print journalists in Australia—News Limited and Fairfax—have offered both full-time and part-time female editorial staff six weeks' paid maternity leave in the available 52 weeks unpaid leave (after one year's service) for at least the last 20 years. Both companies also publicly claim to abide by equal employment opportunity (EEO) principles, for example on their employment advertisements and in-house literature. It appears, however, that EEO principles seem to evaporate within newspaper organisations where the possibility of children-rearing is cited as a measure of women's unreliability as employees.

A senior metropolitan section editor, Nicolas, links women's absence from the senior positions in the industry as a biological issue and therefore one that, for the most part, is fixed. I had asked Nicolas about whether he saw a gendered divide in the newsroom.

> LN: Do you look around the newsroom, and think 'oh, there's a lot more men in this section, or there's a whole lot of men in the subbing section'? Is it ever a consideration in decisions you make about employment practices?
>
> Nicolas: Now I don't think it matters. You are either a good journo or you're not a good journo and they [management] judge you like that. And they judge you very harshly like that too. You're crap, or you're really good, or you're average. It doesn't matter what gender you are. We have done surveys and there are pay issues, women are still underpaid. I don't remember the details of it, and I'm not sure if it's a function of women going in to work doing really very, very well and then taking maternity leave and having to start not quite all over again, but you know, a year or two back from where they might be or should be and never making up that ground. Or the vagaries of working part-time and not being in the newsroom when the big stories happen, it's a very complex issue.

A senior female section editor, Nicola, who is also a single mother, knows that her connection with her child has been hampered by the time demands of journalism. She breaks down at her desk in a busy newsroom where we are conducting the interview and cries when I ask:

> LN: To be able to work those long hours you need—if you have a family—you need to have a wife at home to look after the children?
>
> Nicola: You do, you do.
>
> LN: And that's a big support to men going up a career ladder, isn't it?
>
> Nicola: Yes. I would not have got where I have unless my mother—my mother is dead now—but if she hadn't been around in those early years . . . because when I was coming through the system women hadn't got these jobs, hadn't got many senior jobs. There was one editor I worked for a long time ago here—this was a Sunday paper—he liked the chief-of-staff to be there from eight o'clock

Saturday morning till midnight. Now, I did that for two or three years, at what cost to my daughter I don't know.

Nicola, although on reflection lamenting the difficulties of her career combined with raising a child, has still managed to find a niche that works for her today. Her daughter is older and she has a more time-structured job, although a senior role within the newspaper.

Janet, however, who has three children, describes her experience of having children and working as a journalist, as incongruent. I asked if having children had been a good for her career:

> *Janet: They've been good for me, terrible for my career. I couldn't do the rounds I'd done before I had children. A lot of the areas that I was working in, even in feature writing, wouldn't sustain broken shifts. Those sort of stories I couldn't do with children. It wasn't that I couldn't do the stories, it's just it wasn't their way, they were very anxious. The other reasons were logistics. I had a 10am to 6pm day and childcare centres don't, you know they run from 8 to 5.30. I would have to leave the city at you know 5o'clock to pick up three children from two childcare centres, you just can't manage it, half an hour in traffic, very, very stressful.*

> *LN: When you have been hired by various newspapers do you think that . . . obviously you thought having children was a little bit of a limitation to your career, do you think others saw that as limiting you as a professional?*

> *Janet: Well, look they may have. It might be very naive, but I've always felt that in certain interviews if it has been raised—it is almost as if they want to be reassured, that you can cope and once you reassure them, even if it's an outright lie, that's all they want. They are not interested in complexities or problems with children, they want to be reassured.*

Clearly Janet experiences raising children and working as a journalist as incompatible. She takes on the 'problem' of having children as her responsibility rather then one that the newspaper management, or possibly her partner, may want to address. The newspaper managers want to be 'reassured' that she can 'be a journalist' in the same way presumably as an unencumbered female or male journalist. When Janet applied for jobs she says that all the editorial mangers wanted was to be reassured that she could do the job, yet when it came to the crunch the editorial mangers were 'very anxious' that she may not be able to complete stories. That culmination of stress from having to work within the set confines of what it is to 'be a journalist' led Janet to leave the industry after 14 years.

American scholar Jennifer Pierce's excellent 1995 book about the U.S. legal profession explores the gendering of the occupation and how an under-standing of particular positions within a law firm is viewed as appropriate for men or women. For Pierce this also constructs gendered expectations about the emotional dimensions of the jobs. Naturalising the division of labour (who is best in what work roles based on gender) conceals the extent to which the gendered assignment of work creates and reproduces the asymmetrical distri-bution of power and resources between men and women (Pierce, 1995, p. 2). Her research demonstrates how sex segregation is maintained and reproduced through case studies of two American law firms. She also explains how the gendered division of labour is maintained. Her central thesis is that the gen-dered structure of law firms shapes legal workers' practices at the same time that legal workers participate in the reproduction of gender relations. Rather than seeing occupational sex segregation through only an analysis of structural characteristics, or specifically focus on social actors to explain the gendered division of labour, Pierce bridges the two sociological explanations. Her study, then, considers the structural characteristics of law firms and the role of legal workers, but she also considers emotions, or 'emotional labour' (Hochschild, 1983) as a site for the reproduction of gender. Pierce finds that in contempo-rary law firms, emotional labour takes the form of caretaking and deference for female paralegals. She offers the example of when trial attorneys lose their tempers and "their paralegals are expected to stay calm, and be comforting and deferential in the face of such outbursts" (1995, p. 3). For Pierce the embodied worker is central to her understanding of law firm culture. Her observations about emotional labour in the law firm apply similarly in the newsroom; for example, the distinction between the position of reporter and sub-editor, as previously noted. Sub-editing entails a high level of technical expertise, and the positions are generally filled by a disproportionate number of older men. Reporting, however, involves much more 'emotional labour,' and those jobs are often filled by younger women. Reporting also involves spending emotional energy maintaining news contacts and being available at all times of the day and night to answer queries from sub-editors, as well as responding to tip-offs or story ideas from senior staff and sources.

Australian researchers Christopher McLean, Sue Lewis, Jane Copeland, Sue Lintern, and Brian O'Neill (1997) demonstrate in their study of under-graduate engineering students that engineering is dominated by a particular type of masculine culture that is characterised by a set of beliefs, behaviours, and assumptions. It is a culture that excludes women (and some men) from full participation in the occupation. McLean et al. (1997, p. 147) note that certain rituals of a dominant group, in this case male engineering students, enforce adherence to the rules, making it clear who belongs and who doesn't. These masculine bonding rituals include binge drinking in groups, risk taking, misbehaving, and shared jokes at the expense of women, homosexuals, and marginalised racial or ethnic groups. "There were a range of attitudes towards women expressed in the project interviews which clearly indicated that girls were regarded as outsiders, and as somewhat inferior" (McLean et al., 1997, p. 148). In other words, the 'boy's club' culture was strong.

I'm not suggesting that male journalists are all, or always, involved in such an unsophisticated and obvious exclusion of female journalists—although this has been noted by some as being the case—but rather I am interested here in the similar ritual models of joking, exclusion, and drinking that is a part of newsroom culture and how it defines 'insiders' and 'outsiders.' In the following chapter I explore Susan's recollection of sexually harassing behaviour by men increasing at social occasions during which alcohol was consumed. This also raises the question of how women respond to this type of hegemonic masculinity. McLean et al. (1997, pp. 152–153) suggest that there are three main ways in which female engineering students respond to the masculine culture. They identify three available subject positions: to merge with male students through mimicking male behaviour (become just *one of the boys*); to take up a traditional female gender role that reinstates a conventional heterosexual male-female relationship (*traditional femininity*); or, to lastly take up a *feminist* response that could be viewed as the main point of resistance to the dominant student group. Margareta Melin-Higgins and Monika Djerf-Pierre (1998), through in-depth interviews with journalists, have documented the types of strategies that female journalists develop depending on the type of organisation in which they are employed. How women deal with a hegemonically masculine newsroom depends on any number of personal, professional, and experiential factors, but what they found resonates with McLean et al. (1997). Melin-Higgins and Djerf-Pierre (1998) identified three strategies including: *incorporation* (one of the boys), which requires women to take on so called masculine approaches and values such as objectivity; *feminist,* in which journalists make a conscious decision to provide an alternative voice; and *retreat,* in which women choose to work as freelancers rather than continue to fight battles in the newsroom. A 'feminist' approach was perceived as having developed a female 'counter-culture' in the newsroom, where capabilities were frequently undervalued and promotional difficulties were encountered. The 'opt out' group tended to do so because they wanted to combine child care with work. Melin-Higgins writing in 2004, however, reassesses her use of the term 'strategies,' following Michel de Certeau's (1984) understanding of 'strategy' to explain action in relationships. For de Certeau strategy is for the strong and powerful, whereas 'tactics' are used by the weak. Melin-Higgins prefers to use the term 'tactics' because female journalists, she says, have no place or power to employ 'strategies'; therefore women can only use 'tactics.' *One of the boys* is still there. The two new 'tactics' she identifies are *woman journalist* (nonthreatening to the dominant culture and covering 'soft news' and 'kept' in lower-status ghettoes); and *one of the girls* (attempts to make journalism more feminine, for example, by raising the status of feminine subjects) (Melin-Higgins, 2004, p. 199). Melin-Higgins (2004) reads the subject position of being 'one of the girls' as emancipatory, and in this way is similar to McLean et al.'s (1997) *feminist* response in the occupation of engineering. *One of the girls* is a significant and enabling subject position, because it is available to women in an occupation where there are a large number of women (unlike engineering), and this can be read as a position of resistance to a hegemonically masculine newsroom.

Theories of the Body

There has always been a "tension between women's lived bodily experiences and the cultural meanings inscribed on the female body that always mediate those experiences" (Conboy, Medina, & Stanbury, 1997, p. 1). In this way gender is not fixed, but as Judith Butler (1997) has noted, 'performed.' Butler suggests that gender can be treated as a 'corporeal style,' an act, which is both intentional (partly) and performative (1997, p. 404) and that the body is a site for play with categories. Gender, she argues, "is not passively scripted on the body" but rather "put on, invariably under constraint, daily and incessantly, with anxiety and pleasure" (1997, p. 415). Yet, wrongly performing one's gender "initiates a set of punishments both obvious and indirect, and performing it well, provides the reassurance that there is an essentialism of gender identity after all" (Butler, 1997, p. 412). Similarly Sandra Lee Bartky (1997, p. 148) argues that the disciplinary techniques through which the 'docile bodies' of women are constructed "aim at a regulation which is perpetual and exhaustive"—for example, the body's size and shape, its posture, gestures, and general comportment in space. Yet, as Bartky makes clear, resistance to feminine bodily 'norms' (and therefore a loss of the rewards of compliance) is neither always constraining nor always pleasurable.

What these contemporary theorists argue is that our bodies are not just mechanical vessels that we are trapped within and inhibited by. Rather they are means through which we build and experience our world. It is in relation to other bodies that we come to know our place in the social world. Entry into various social communities is dependent on the hairstyle we have and the colour of our hair, our clothing, how much flesh we choose to expose, how we hold our body, our stance—our physicality. The publicly 'presented' body, therefore, creates our cultural identity as we speak to another person, as we say what we do for a living or where we live. Gail Weiss (1999) finds 'embodiment as intercorporeality,' that is, we can only come to know and understand our bodies through encounters with others. It is through these encounters with others that social meaning and cultural values become inscribed on the surface of the body (Colegate, 2004, p. 62).

The social and cultural meanings that male bodies embody differ from those of female bodies. Although drawing attention to female embodiment, I do not assume biological or universal imperatives—that all women are 'naturally' embodied in particular ways. In this book I focus on gender, but acknowledge that other categories of embodiment such as race, class, physical ability, and age, for example, are equally important. Further, there is no clear separation between these social and cultural categories and how they are represented and how we live them. Race, for example, isn't a quality that pre-exists its embodiment in socially and culturally specific ways; rather it is continuously created through intercorporeality and, like gender, through history.

Shilling (1991) argues that a social analysis of the body is central to understanding the production of gender inequalities and that sociologists should take more seriously the multiple ways in which bodies enter into the construction of social inequalities. At various periods in history some bodies have been socially constructed as more desirable than others. The term Shilling uses to describe this is 'physical capital' and is derived from Pierre Bourdieu's (1986) concept of embodied capital. Bourdieu expands the notion of capital beyond its economic conception, which emphasises material exchanges, to include 'immaterial' and 'noneconomic' forms of capital—specifically cultural capital. He distinguishes three forms of cultural capital: objectified in cultural goods; institutionalised as academic credentials or diplomas (1986, p. 248); and the embodied state, directly linked to and incorporated within the individual, representing what they know and can do. As embodied capital becomes integrated into the individual, it becomes a type of habitus.[6] How bodies take up space is thus an important aspect of gendered embodiment. Physical size is an issue that was raised in my interviews with female journalists.

I had been discussing with Christine the stories she had written in her career that she felt had had the most impact on her or her sources. Christine detailed a story that when published had helped the Aboriginal community where she was living and working at the time. This led her to express concerns about the large size of her body in this way. She identifies and comments on a notion of dominant femininity:

> Christine: I think I identified with them [Aboriginal people] because they are oppressed and disadvantaged, and I have always been a big girl and well, fat

---

[6]Bourdieu has described the habitus as a set of dispositions; the basic beliefs, values, norms, and ways of being in the world that are taken into the body at a very deep level and will reproduce class domination as apparently natural and effortless (Pringle, 1998, p. 22).

women are the Jews of the 20ᵗʰ Century. I understand racism from the point of view that people make assumptions about me because of my size, so people make assumptions about indigenous people because of their colour, so I know what it is to be picked on.

That Anglo-Saxon Christine compares racism and Aboriginal inequality to her personal weight concerns begs belief. Nevertheless, it provides a pertinent example of the pervasiveness of a liberal perspective.

Having a small female body is problematic for Susan, as noted at the beginning of this chapter, and it's a theme that runs through her interview. She points to the difficulty for women of embodying hegemonic masculinity:

Susan: I guess getting back to what I was saying, experiences I have had from thinking I was a small person in a news conference situation and I got you know stomped on, through to getting slightly intimidated with the big man behind the desk.

Susan has become a 'small woman' through the socially constructed nature of bodies (and in this quote it's a relative construction—versus the 'big boys') and, indeed, the occupationally specific social construction of bodies. What then are the social practices and cultural norms that have created Susan in this way and make this relevant in relation to 'the big man'? What gendered bodies are implicit in and created through the occupational culture of journalism?

There are two areas to address here, firstly the prevailing mythology that women are unable to transcend their bodies or their personal involvement with others (Steiner, 1998, p. 147). Essentially this involves the alignment of the political, the rational, and the public with maleness—and the corollary, the female body, with the private, embodied, domestic realm. Secondly, and specific to the occupational culture of journalism, is the well-known philosophical (or ideological) notion of objectivity. Objectivity is often viewed as a central tenant of 'good' journalism, although this has been challenged by some in the industry and feminist media scholars. Being objective implies someone's capacity to act as an independent, disinterested, impartial observer (Steiner, 1998, p. 147). Yet as Joanna Hodge (1988, p. 166) points out: "The subjectivity attributed to women is not convertible into objectivity." An objective, rational, and impartial journalist therefore involves being male and having a male body.

Susan's physical experience in the media pack is a reminder of her femaleness and her smallness—of lacking what Shilling (1991, 2004) calls 'physical capital.' Body size and shape, as well as stance, attitude and posture, and clothing, are gendered embodiments. A comparatively small, female body struggles to demonstrate an embodiment that is consonant with a journalists' body. This raises the question 'would some women not be "small women" no matter what their size?' The answer, I think, is yes. There are varying subject positions available for women in journalism, just as McLean et al. (1997)

found in engineering. However, Cockburn's (1991, p. 141) thesis that sexual harassment is a method in which potentially powerful women are 'cut down to size' is an important aspect of Susan's willingness to accept her smallness as problematic. In the next chapter Susan details her experiences of sexually harassing behaviour. The subject position that Susan occupies as a journalist is that of 'one of the boys,' but in the context of normative physically aggressive behaviour her physical capital (smallness) is not worth much. To be a success at 'one of the boys' it appears that Susan needs a large body and/or a body practised in aggressive physical contact.

Jodie, a 45-year-old former metropolitan journalist and now a freelance journalist, similarly notes that being short and not having a beautiful body is a disadvantage in journalism:

> Jodie: I was never beautiful or tall. I just had an outgoing personality and I was slim and blonde. I guess it's better than being dog ugly. That's a terrible thing to say, but I think it can play a part. I think you can charm people. I think people are more attracted to attractive people than ugly ones.

Jodie seems somewhat invested in her own beauty. Her use of the words 'dog ugly' suggest an investment in a cruel and masculinised assessment of women's bodies. Jodie's excerpt also demonstrates the resolution of issues raised previously by Christine and Susan: a third position. Jodie is 'pretty' (in the femininity stakes), but small (bad in the masculinity stakes). So the (ideal compromise) position for Jodie is to accept all this and adopt a 'woman journalist' position. That is, success via 'charm,' not the aggression needed in the media pack.

In summary, Christine suggests that her physical size—being big—is an impediment to her career. Susan's small size caused her to be 'bowled over by the big boys' in the news pack, and intimidated by 'the big man' behind the desk. For Jodie, beautiful (slim) and tall bodies have more success because they can be used to 'charm' or disarm people.

Insiders and Outsiders in the Newsroom: Who Is a Journalist?

Distinct occupational cultures arise that are often normalised and therefore not obvious to insiders (Lewis, 2000). The notion of 'insiders' (and by connection 'outsiders') is important to understanding 'who is a journalist.' I argue here that female journalists are often considered 'outsiders.' Women's lack of representation in positions of authority is often viewed by my interviewees as a problem for and about women, rather than a problem of entrenched masculine norms that work to exclude women as authoritative knowers. Consequently, gender becomes a clear maker of division between 'outsiders' and 'insiders' in journalism. Australian journalist and author Margaret Simons (1999, p. 6) describes how having 'insiders' within journalism stifles change in the industry because they exclude outsiders, those who do not bond with their colleagues or do not fit the required ways of being. To be part of a community one must make alliances and compromises, and journalism is no different, says Simons.

> Just as in any other office there are all the minutia, the unexamined bonding that come with shared space and shared lives. There are notices in the tearooms for people to wash up their mugs. There are photos of parties on the wall. There are shared jokes, shared views. There is all the trivial knowledge of how the office works—the length of time it takes after selecting your floor before the lift doors will close and when the queues will be shortest at the coffee shop; knowledge of who is in and who is out, how any particular person is to be regarded, and whose blood is in the water; what it means, and what you should do, when a bell rings in the corridors, or when a certain person appears by your desk; how to behave, and the limits of acceptable eccentricity. These are the things that define who is an insider and who is not. This is what makes a community work, what makes it strong and effective. It is also what excludes outsiders, and inhibits change. (Simons, 1999, p. 6)

Simons does not note gender as a characteristic that defines an insider and outsider, but I see it as implicit in her description.

All male journalists interviewed agree that men hold nearly all the powerful and high-status positions in the industry; only some see this as problematic, or acknowledge that their tacit condoning of such numerical inequity is highly consequential for women. Female journalists, too, were all aware that men dominate numerically in senior editorial positions. Not all see this inequality as problematic or an issue of personal or political concern. Many subscribe to the view of the liberal individual being genderless and promoted on merit. Those women who do digress about why they are so few in number in the upper ranks take on an acceptance of the social construction of the workplace that naturalises and reinforces the social structure of child rearing. The majority of senior male and female journalists note that child-rearing is not generally compatible with being a senior journalist. Expectations of long hours at the office and being available outside office hours took its toll on relationships and were understood as not generally sustainable with children. Some senior female journalists suggest that discrimination on the basis of gender has never been a problem, and that all women have the same opportunity to succeed as men.

Pat is a 55-year-old regional editor who has been in the role for more than 15 years. She sees the lack of women in senior roles as more a problem for metropolitan newspapers rather than in the 'family' atmosphere of regionals.

The work 'family' then, in Pat's mind, is a happy and equal mix of men and women in positions of authority. She is therefore able to interpret her own success via a separation of metropolitan and regional newspaper cultures. In this way she doesn't have to acknowledge her difficulties in a male-dominated environment, although she does give long accounts of situations, past and recent, that have been discriminatory, but that she experiences as humourous. I also find it interesting how Pat is able to articulate the idea of 'insiders,' not in terms of gender, but rather via making a distinction between metropolitan and regional newsroom cultures.

> LN: When you took on that role [editor] did you see it as being a good thing for women, that this was great for newspapers, to have a woman at the top?
>
> Pat: I guess I did but I wasn't too concerned. I never had any occasion to be worried about sexism or discrimination or anything like that. [Later in the interview, however, Pat offers various descriptions of discrimination; see Chapter Eight].
>
> Pat: I think the regionals are so far ahead of the metropolitans in terms of accepting women as pretty much equal.
>
> LN: Why do you think that is?
>
> Pat: I don't think they're as threatened as much as they are in the metropolitans. If you look in the regionals, maybe the competition isn't as fierce or maybe everything is a lot more clear-cut than it is in the metropolitans. I think in the metropolitans you tend to occasionally lose sight of merit and it becomes very much an in-house, in-club thing and you're either in the inner circle or you're not in the inner circle. I think there's much more respect for everyone who works on a [regional] paper regardless of whether they are young, old or female, male, or whatever because they have to do so much more whereas I think the bigger papers can get very dismissive of people. I guess it's the old story; it makes you feel stronger if you can put somebody down, doesn't it?
>
> LN: There is a sense of family in regional newspapers, do you think?
>
> Pat: Yes, and I guess sometimes you can come across the same feuding as you have in families.

Pat's downplaying of gender as in any way significant to the opportunities of women in the industry is an example of how her own success is used as a means by which to refute the suggestion of sexism in the industry. This strategy has been previously found in research about female metropolitan newspaper journalists in South Africa (Gillwald, 1994) and more recently in a small-scale project by Karen Ross on female journalists in the British media. Ross (2004, p. 146) found that "this strategy of self-deception or, at best, a refusal to empathise with the lived experiences of other women" was mirrored in the responses of some of the women in her study. This, she argued, "neatly exemplified internalized sexism by placing the blame for women's subordination squarely back in the hands of women themselves" (Ross, 2004, p. 146). Although it is possible that some women do not experience discrimination based on their gender in their working lives, to dismiss it as not a behaviour that other women do experience is naive. This works to reduce those very real experiences "as mere excuses for special pleading" (Ross, 2004, p. 146). This kind of playing the game by male rules results in what Anne Phillips (1991) labels 'domestic feminism'; that is, striving for equality of opportunity within the existing structures of patriarchy rather than challenging the structures themselves (Ross, 2004, p. 146). It could also reveal what American journalist Marlene Sanders says is the 'problem we don't like to talk about':

> Not all women in power are our friends. The need to be 'one of the boys' does exist. Some women are simply afraid to appear to tilt towards other women, afraid to be labelled feminist. As a result, they therefore fail to make their presence count. (Sanders, 1993, p. 171)

An example of this 'fear' of supporting other women is evident during my interview with Jodie, a freelance journalist. Jodie remembers with bitterness how women in the newsroom treated her at her first and only job that involved working in the newsroom. She details how she requested an interview with the editor, how he created a position for her at the newspaper, and how she was quickly promoted out of her cadetship. This discussion arose after I asked Jodie if there had there been an equal number of men and women working in the newsroom:

> *Jodie: It was equal but the women were vicious. I remember the women most particularly; they were jealous, they were vicious, they made my life hell. I was unused to that sort of behaviour because I didn't understand why they were doing it.*

Jodie tells of her experience through a discourse of women's bitchiness. There was clearly a gendered and divisive dynamic occurring in that newsroom. She explains that a senior woman took the staff out on strike over Jodie's appointment. But Jodie proudly recounts how she was told by one male journalist that she had the support of 'the men.'

> *Jodie: He said, 'she's got the knives out for you, so watch out.' I said, 'yes, I've noticed that. Thanks.' 'Look, the men are behind you [Jodie]. You've got our full support. The girls hate you.'*

Jodie resigned from that job, but again encountered the same animosity from female journalists working in women's magazines. Jodie says the women were:

> Jodie: Bitchy. They're ruthless. They're ambitious. They don't care what they
> do to get a story at all. They all hail to the queen who was [editor].

Jodie seems unaware of or unconcerned about numerical gender disparity in newspapers. I asked how many women worked at the first newspaper in which she worked and she replied that it was 'even,' but this was not the case, according to journalists I interviewed who had worked at that newspaper at the time of Jodie's appointment. Those interviewees acknowledge the newspaper's history as male centred and male dominated.

The male interviewees demonstrate an awareness of numerical gender inequity, but say that it is a 'problem' nearly impossible to address to the satisfaction of both men and women in the industry. All of the men interviewed offer rational reasons why men dominate in positions of authority. Some suggest that femininity is at odds with the necessary rational, unemotional, behaviour needed to succeed in the industry and that due to the long hours of the job a 'journalist' needs to be free from family responsibilities. This perspective assumes and naturalises men's freedom from family responsibilities. While there is an acceptance of a level of inequality, this doesn't extend to an acceptance of women in positions of authority. Mark, a senior metropolitan male reporter who had a deal of influence in management decisions, espoused a very liberal, and typical, view of equality for women at work:

> Mark: Today, what we haven't done to a large extent is actually acknowledge
> that those of our peers who are female are as equally capable of managing
> newspapers.

Yet, this still sets up a division between male and female. The 'those of our peers' comment sets men and women apart, male as norm and female as outside the dominant peer group. Mark followed this by implying that the women who did make it to the top were tokens and a product of EEO policy, rather than promoted on merit:

> Mark: [Newspaper name] has had to actually create positions to elevate women
> to get some sort of gender balance at the top. We had, until late last year, two
> deputy editors who were female. The women they chose for those jobs hadn't
> got the respect of not only the blokes,[7] but their own gender. One of these

---

[7] The term 'bloke' is an often used word by both men and some women in Australia to describe men who display normative masculine traits. For example, 'he is a good bloke' is a positive use of the word, but alternatively it can be used to highlight a hegemonic masculine culture, for example 'blokiness.'

people has moved on, but the other one is there and is just a pain in the arse to everybody and literally just gives the idea of that approach [equal employment opportunity].

Mark's comments contain conflicting discourses of 'who is a journalist' and of gender—gender keeps slipping out from his liberal framework. The gendered identity categories are what interest me most here. 'Gender balance,' according to Mark, is about getting women to the top rather than calling into question the practices that infer superiority of the male body for these positions of authority. He also fails to elaborate that there is no established merit-based protocols in place for promoting journalists in Australia. News Ltd tried one scheme of 'annual reviews' in the late 1990s and it failed dismally, never to see the light of day after two outings. Promotion in journalism is ad hoc, at best, and jockeying for promotion with senior players is part of your job description. Under this scheme, favourites win. Mark's reference to 'female' deputy editors establishes how rare indeed these positions are for women. Drawing parallels between 'women' and 'blokes' indicates to me how comfortable he is with 'blokes' as bosses and his ability to communicate with them because he is one of the blokes. Yet, when he is critical of one of the female deputy editors, he does not use the term 'woman' or assign any gender—rather the disembodied term *'people,'* and in this way (female) gender becomes invisible. The notion that women are 'naturally' more suited, relative to men, for less-desirable jobs is well documented (for example see Cockburn, 1986; Martin, 1996). The idea that men's 'innate' traits and capabilities make them better equipped for journalism than women is often noted in interviews conducted by feminist researchers as one reason why women succeed less than men in acquiring jobs in position of authority. According to Patricia Yancey Martin (1996, p. 201), when men invoke such essentialist frames "they depict men's talents and capacities as more *consonant with more valued* jobs and opportunities" (emphasis in original). Mark continues:

Mark: [Newspaper name] was so behind in having women in senior positions that we appointed a lot of women into senior positions, or middle ranking positions, where a bloke could have done the job. OK, a bloke could have done the job but at the end of the day we've got another professional journalist doing it.

Here we can see Mark reluctantly giving up his view that senior positions are naturally for 'blokes.' He moves to the language of liberal rational professionalism to allow that anyone (including a woman) can perform the role.

The narrative around women, the number of women, and positions women hold in journalism is almost always understood through a liberal framework. Nicolas noted management's attempt at addressing the issue of the lack of women in positions of authority:

Nicolas: I must say in fairness, management has been, over the years, piling on extra money for women, they have been trying to rectify it [numerical gender inequity]. They have been looking in a genuine half-hearted sort of way making really genuine half-hearted efforts. They see it as an issue and something that must be addressed, but they perhaps don't see it as the number one issue, but it's still something that they are trying to back. There are women in seriously senior positions, but not, to my knowledge at a Deputy Editor level.

Management, here, is understood as male, although not explicitly stated, and because management is 'fair' it has been *'piling on extra money'* to rectify the problem. Again, women's lack of representation in positions of authority is viewed as a problem for and about women, rather than a problem of entrenched masculine norms that work to exclude women as authoritative knowers. Consequently it is women's disadvantage that is understood as the problem and requires research and money to address, rather than men's advantage that is the problem and that warrants research and money. It is money that is understood as the key to solving the problem, or perhaps, the act of spending can absolve men of their entrenched and acknowledged numerical and hierarchical dominance.

Being a 'Journalist'

Thornton's (1996, p. 1) study of women in the legal profession is concerned with the issues pertaining to the conditions under which women have been 'let in' to the profession. Thornton (1996, p. 2) argues that women are constituted as 'nonmen,' as 'others' to the benchmark man, "the paradigmatic incarnation of legality who represents the standard against whom others are measured and who is invariably White, heterosexual, able-bodied, politically conservative, and middle-class." The equivalent of the masculinity of legality in law is the standard of objectivity in journalism.

Jessica, who had been in the industry for two years at the time of interview, demonstrates the difficulty of adopting the appearance of being a 'journalist.'

Jessica: Sometimes I feel like I have to put on a front to go out and be a journalist. I feel like I have to get up in the morning, put on my journalist face and my journalist outfit and go out. I think it gives me the confidence to talk to people that I would never speak to otherwise. Because you have to, it forces you to do things that you are not always comfortable doing, which sometimes is good, but then sometimes you find yourself doing things and you think 'God, I would never do that, as a person.'

For Jessica maintaining the persona of 'journalist' is a tiring and constant performative act that works to create a division between the ethics of a 'person' and the ethics of a 'journalist.' In this way she understands a 'person' as free to choose their actions and a 'journalist' as constrained by their position.

Susan, a 38-year-old senior metropolitan reporter, explains the blokiness of journalists. It's a norm that is not a rational professionalism, rather a norm that is overtly a blokey culture:

> Susan: It seems to me that guys can get away with more of that camaraderie that they share, you know that 'hey mate,' and it's sports and it's beer and it's pub talk, and it's a sort of a secret society. I even notice just how they talk to each other on the telephone. I can see the guys talking on the phone and it's an entirely different conversation than I would ever have with that very same person. It's not because I don't know them, it's just that I wouldn't be able to say, 'oh fucking hell, the fucking football is fucking great, hey, you know.' If I did that guys would think goodness gracious, she's a shocker isn't she. You know she's a slapper. You can imagine. Oh, she's dreadful. Yet to guys, what is camaraderie, to me would be seen as I'd just be unprofessional.

The possible effect of being a 'journalist' in this blokey culture is perhaps most evident in her narrative around emotional stress caused from the maintenance of, and adherence to, journalistic (male) norms. Susan articulates here her inability to cope with the defined role of 'journalist':

> Susan: Before Christmas I was going through a particularly bad patch and terrible things were happening, and it was just stress, stress, stress with the job generally. I sort of raised this email [to a more senior journalist at head office who decided her daily workload] saying 'I'm not coping very well at the moment, is there someone I could talk to.' Of course there was no response, and I just thought, 'geez, I've just laid my heart out here and now I feel really embarrassed, oh my goodness now they know I'm not feeling too good, and they haven't said anything.' I'm exposed. And then you start to feel like perhaps that's a weakness. Don't show your weakness, you know.

Conclusion

From these interviews it could be argued that many male journalists, particularly those in positions of authority in newsrooms, often don't experience a 'newsroom culture' as such. Rather, they are the 'culture,' the newsroom is 'theirs' and they guard the parameters from 'outsiders,' allowing some in, but rarely to the core, where power is experienced, wielded, and often homosocially[8] shared. This occurs, in part, because these roles historically and traditionally have been occupied by

---

[8]Roseabeth Moss Kanter (1977b), for example, points out that men 'homosocially' reproduce themselves in workplace selection processes.

men and are thus normalised as 'male' jobs, and because men actively continue to enforce masculinist culture. Men can be understood as insiders because they are more often in positions of authority than females. One repercussion of this dominance in positions of authority is that men's superiority to women is asserted and women are viewed as and experience the workplace as outsiders, as inferior others. Martin (1996, p. 190) thus notes that one consequence of the conflation of masculinities and working activities is women's relegation to the 'status of other or outsider.' Yet those on the 'outside'—some women and some less strategically placed (non) men (for example, gay men and men not supportive of male sport)—do understand they are in a culture that rejects them in various ways. Consequently, a focus on embodiment was a central theme in this chapter. I was interested to tease out the difficulties for some female interviewees in embodying hegemonic masculinity and how some identified a dominant femininity, equally difficult to embody. I also explored how some male interviewees responded to women's increased presence in the newsroom. As Martin (1996) points out, not all men at work enact masculinity and neither do all of men's actions at work entail masculinism or masculine enactments. Rather, some actions by men activate masculinism and masculinities, and these actions are consequential to women and men when done by those in hierarchical power and gender-based power. Although the interviews provide only a slice of organisational and occupational reality and an analysis of stories told to me, they do shed light on how newsroom culture is embodied and how men and women experience newsroom culture. This chapter posits that the gender of a worker's body is a key marker and product of organisational and occupational structure. The sectors and the type of jobs in which men and women are variously employed, the tasks allocated, and the career progress of workers expose assumptions about, and practices of, gender.

Chapter Four

Discourses of Power
and Sexual Harassment
in the Newsroom*

This chapter is concerned with how Australian print news media journalists, male and female, remember, talk about, experience, acknowledge, condemn, and/or deny sexually harassing behaviour in the newsroom. The interviews were not set up to specifically discuss sexually harassing behaviour in the newsroom. It was, however, a theme that arose in seven of the 17 interviews conducted. On reading the interview transcripts I became interested in how male and female journalists variously experienced this behaviour and how they discussed it with me. During my journalistic career I had also experienced sexually harassing behaviour but, at the time, had little support and opportunity to discuss it with colleagues. The fact that this was raised in the interviews made my experiences seem more real and, perhaps, in my analysis of the interview material in this chapter there is some unravelling of my own experiences. The female interviewees make clear that their encounters are constant reminders of how their bodies do not 'fit' and/or where and how they do fit in this occupation. This is the case, even though some women do not use the term 'sexual harassment' to describe the behaviour that under Australian government legislation clearly constitutes it. The two male interviewees who mentioned harassment talk about it in defence of accepted office behaviour or in passing about procedural business policy. I suggest that the use of the term 'sexual harassment,' or lack of its use, also tells us about the place of feminism and/or feminist inspired government legislation in journalism's occupational culture.

The interviews indicate that sexually harassing behaviour is a major feature of newsroom culture for many women. Sexually harassing behaviour by men occurs in newsrooms worldwide (see for example, de Bruin, 2004; Gallagher, 1995; Ross, 2004; Walsh Childers, Chance, & Herzog, 1996; Weaver, 1992) and is an established part of occupational culture that has been widely

*An article based on this chapter can be found in *Feminist Media Studies*, 2007, 7(1), pp. 81–96.

acknowledged by feminist media researchers, yet in Australia, researchers have so far failed to thoroughly explore this crucial aspect of newsroom culture. The communication and journalism literature suggests that relatively little research has been done on sexual harassment as a problem facing women journalists. International feminist media researchers, however, have addressed the issue. Carolyn Weaver (1992) found in her interviews with American newspaper, magazine, and television journalists that between 40 and 60 percent of female journalists had experienced sexual harassment. Weaver (1992) maintains that U.S. news organisations confronted with allegations of sexual harassment in their workplaces have tended to deny and discount them. Moreover, when faced with a lawsuit, they frequently propose confidential settlements that gag all parties involved. A special report for the United Nations (Gallagher, 1995) also details harassment. Kim Walsh Childers, Jean Chance, and Kristin Herzog's (1996) survey of American female newspaper journalists finds that of the 227 participants 60 believe that sexual harassment is a problem for women in the industry. More recently, Karen Ross's (2004) study of 22 female British journalists found that more than 75 percent of respondents said they had experienced some form of sexual harassment in the newsroom. Ross found that some women spoke of an underlying 'sense' of inadequacy, or of having to prove themselves as a woman as examples of low-level harassment, and that the respondents viewed such behaviour "as the price they have to pay to work in a male-ordered environment" (2004, p. 147). Marjan de Bruin (2004) has also researched sexual harassment in interviews with 10 male and 10 female Caribbean journalists. Her preliminary findings suggest that men don't use the term 'harassment' whereas women describe the experience "as coming in many shapes and forms" (2004, p. 9). Emerging scholarship from non-Western countries also notes the prevalence of sexual harassment. For example, Aida Opoku-Mensah (2004) posits that sexual harassment is a rarely discussed problem that often characterises and shapes working relations in African newsrooms.

In Australia, there is anecdotal evidence and emerging autobiographical accounts by Australian female journalists of the experience of sexually harassing behaviour in the newsroom (see, for example, Haussegger, 2005; Trioli, 1996). However, from my reading, there is no academic research that explores and analyses discourses and practices of sexually harassing behaviour in Australian print news media newsrooms. In 1996 a groundbreaking industry report in Australia statistically accounted for its presence (MEAA and IFJ, 1996, p. 14), yet there has been no follow-up report that expands on, or further examines the problem.[1] In that study, of the 368 female respondents from print, radio, and

---

[1]Emails to the MEAA requesting information about the possibility of a follow-up survey more than a decade later have gone unanswered.

television, 51 percent said they had been sexually harassed in the workplace. My research does more than just reveal sexual harassment as a 'problem' in Australian newsrooms. It aims to identify and flesh out the discourses through which sexually harassing behaviour is experienced in the newsroom and to explore available discourses around sexually harassing behaviour by analysing how it is remembered and told in interviews. How do the feminist discourses of government legislation, company policies, and newsroom culture concerning 'sexual harassment' currently shape Australian newsrooms?

Of my 17 interviews, seven participants—two men and five women—mention words or detail experiences that could arguably describe sexually harassing behaviour by male journalists. As I have indicated in the Introduction, all the interviewees were aware that I was a working journalist, and in all cases the interviewees drew attention to my own work history during the interview in order to elaborate points and establish a common understanding about working in the industry. As I have also mentioned, this acknowledgment as an 'insider' certainly did help in gaining access to, and quickly experiencing camaraderie with, the interviewees in general. I am mindful, however, that some narratives about sexually harassing behaviour may have been precluded. Some men, for example, may have felt less comfortable, and therefore less forthcoming, discussing this subject with a female interviewer, and some women may have said different things if I had been a different kind of woman. Also, I may have identified knowledge of the subject that may have worked to exclude, or negate, some comments. If the men had been interviewed by a male interviewer, perhaps they might have been more forthcoming about their personal experiences rather than their professional obligations. As well, there may have been more discussion by both men and women of sexually harassing behaviour had there been specific questions in relation to it. Nevertheless, I think the following excerpts provide an important and specific glimpse into this one aspect of gendered newsroom practices.

In reviewing the transcripts, I wondered why the two young women who had clearly experienced and talked to me about harassing behaviour by men involving sexual meanings never used the term 'sexual harassment'? Why did the only two men who mentioned harassment do so in defence of 'normal' and accepted office behaviour, or in passing about procedural business policy? And what was it that enabled three older female interviewees, who all identified as feminists, to articulate *and* link the term 'sexual harassment' with the experience—albeit tentatively and indirectly? These narratives about sexual harassment—whether the interviewees actually use the term or not—are pertinent, because they articulate what is common knowledge among, particularly, female journalists but is rarely exposed in academic scholarship about the industry in Australia.

History of Sexual Harassment

Sexually harassing behaviour by men first became a political issue in the United States in the mid-1970s (Bacchi, 1998; Tiddy, 2001). The term 'sexual harassment' had sufficient currency in 1975 for the *New York Times* to assume its readers would be familiar with it (see Nemy, 1975, p. 38). The first feminist book on the subject was by Lin Farley in 1978 (*Sexual Shakedown: Sexual Harassment of Women on the Job*). This was followed in 1979 by U.S. scholar Catharine MacKinnon's *Sexual Harassment of Working Women*. Since then the literature on sexual harassment, especially by feminists worldwide, has grown considerably.

According to former Australian Commissioner Josephine Tiddy, sexual harassment first became a public issue in Australia in 1979 when it was highlighted at a conference of Equal Opportunity Commissioners (Tiddy, 2001, p. 67). By the early 1980s sexual harassment was emerging as a significant workplace problem. It was being exposed and theorised by feminists, but general attitudes about what was appropriate behaviour remained much as it had for decades (Tiddy, 2001, p. 67). The federal Sex Discrimination Act (SDA), introduced in Australia in 1984, makes sexual harassment in the workplace unlawful. In that year, laws were also passed by the South Australian, Victorian, and Western Australian parliaments making sexual harassment unlawful, although it wasn't until 1997 that sexual harassment laws were passed by all Australian parliaments (Tiddy, 2001, p. 73). Institutional responses then, and now, are generally in line with government directives, typically in the form of establishing a grievance procedure. The SDA, as it stands today, gives effect to Australia's obligations under the Convention on the Elimination of All Forms of Discrimination Against Women (CEDAW) and parts of International Labour Organisation Convention 156. The term 'sexual harassment' is not easily definable, and not everyone agrees with the definition given in government Acts. The federal SDA (1984) defines sexual harassment as "an unwelcome sexual advance, unwelcome request for sexual favours or other unwelcome conduct of a sexual nature which makes a person feel offended, humiliated or intimidated, where a reasonable person would anticipate that reaction in the circumstances" (HREOC, 2002, n.p.).

But what behaviour is defined as 'unwelcome' has been open to constant re-evaluation, criticism, and challenges. Indeed, the Act instates a subjective dimension in the definition. The term has, and continues to be, contentious—a changing idiom shaped by societal, cultural, and historical norms and, importantly, the definition the government of the day provides. Currently, the SDA lists those unwelcome acts as including: touching, hugging, cornering, kissing, or unnecessary familiarity. Nonphysical types of sexual harassment include staring or leering; sexually explicit pictures, posters, or emails; intrusive questions about a person's private life or body; or insults or taunts based on sex (HREOC, 2003, n.p.). Yet 'unwelcome acts' change as societal norms or expectations change. Changing technology has meant that the SDA now lists unsolicited sexual SMS messages as sexual harassment. More broadly, societal norms also shape how different people interpret sexual harassment. For example, how a white, middle-class, male newspaper editor defines and interprets sexual harassment may vary from the interpretation of his staff based on a raft of differences, including race, class, ethnicity, gender, age, and education. I do not propose a definitive definition of 'sexual harassment'; rather, I am concerned here with discourses available about sexually harassing behaviour by journalists and what 'sexual harassment' means for them.

The Human Rights and Equal Opportunity Commission (HREOC) website states that the SDA's major objectives are to:

> Promote equality between men and women, eliminate discrimination on the basis of sex, marital status or pregnancy and, with respect to dismissals, family responsibilities; and eliminate sexual harassment at work, in educational institutions, in the provision of goods and service, in the provision of accommodation and the administration of federal programs. (www.hreoc.gov.au/sexdiscrimination/index.html)

Those objectives are admirable, and ones that all feminists would hope for, yet for women in the workplace—by the government's own admission and even in the published material of major media companies such as News Limited[2]—sexual harassment is a continuing 'problem.'

Statistics provided by the government demonstrate the prevalence of sexual harassment. In 2003 HREOC, the federal body that receives complaints about sexual harassment in the workplace (under the SDA), reviewed complaints in employment finalised in 2002. The report, its most recent, found that complainants were more likely to be women under the age of 45, relative newcomers to the workplace, in a subordinate position to their alleged harassers, that the harassing behaviour typically occurred over a period of at least six months, and that most complainants left the place of employment where harassment occurred. That report was then followed up by a national telephone survey of just over a 1,000 randomly polled adults and found that:

> 41 per cent of Australian women aged between 18 and 64 years and 14 per cent of men have experienced sexual harassment. Two-thirds of this sexual harassment occurs in the workplace, with 28 per cent of Australian women and seven per cent of Australian men having experienced sexual harassment at work. (HREOC, 2003, n.p.)

---

[2]News Corporations (2004, 9) "Standards of Business Conduct" brochure to employees states that "the company wishes to emphasize the special problems of sexual harassment." This was in comparison to other discrimination, such as that about race or ethnicity.

More than half of the sexual harassment experienced in the workplace involved physical forms of sexually harassing conduct, including unwelcome touching, hugging, cornering, kissing or unnecessary familiarity. Nonphysical types of sexual harassment, however, such as suggestive comments or jokes, staring or leering, sexually explicit emails or SMS messages, and sexually explicit pictures or posters were frequently experienced.

Feminist Critiques of the Implementation of Sexual Harassment Policy

Early second-wave feminists saw the establishment of a grievance procedure as a 'win' for women in the workplace, yet contemporary theorists have problematised this position and provide a more sophisticated analysis. Australian political scientist Carol Bacchi (1998, p. 76), for example, suggests that there are limitations to this type of approach, as it is based on seeing sexual harassment as a problem for institutions "as something exogenous to them in a sense, and hence something 'they' must manage." Rather Bacchi sees institutions as the problem and sexual harassment as a symptom of the problem. Yet in 1994 Bacchi, writing with Jim Jose, was prepared to include men, as well as institutions, as equally imbued with the power that allows sexual harassment to take place. "Men can and should be held responsible for their part in reinforcing and reproducing the structures integral to the oppression of women" (Bacchi & Jose, 1994, p. 6).

In Australia equal employment opportunity legislation is at the core of liberal feminism, yet it is also notoriously weak in exercising power. Legal theorist Margaret Thornton (1994) has critiqued the individual complaint basis of equal employment opportunity (EEO) legislation, bringing to attention the structural limits of liberal legalism. Thornton observes that direct discrimination complaints are the least efficacious way of achieving gender justice, and that this liberal doctrine lets in a few women, those most like benchmark males but less assertive (1994, p. 217). She concludes that "we should not ignore the psychological desire of benchmark males to subordinate others" (1994, p. 224). Thornton has also maintained that the lodgement of a complaint of discrimination requires:

> Both perspicacity and fortitude: perspicacity on the part of the complainants to recognise that an act of discrimination has occurred against them (after all, what has happened could just be normal life!), and fortitude to persevere in an adversarial relationship with a respondent who could be their boss. (Thornton, 1994, p. 219)

Harassment is generally understood in feminist theory to be an expression of men's power, rather than of men's 'unbridled' sexual desire. Thornton (1996, p. 262), for example, views sexual harassment as "a disciplinary tactic designed to keep women docile within traditionally masculine spheres." For American feminist scholar Cheris Kramarae (1992, pp. 100–101) sexual harassment is about efforts to maintain difference and dominance—"an expression and enforcement of power and a binary gender hierarchy." As Cynthia Cockburn notes:

> Hierarchies are expressions of differential power, maps of distribution of authority and subordination in an organization. Though conventional organisation theory represents this power-tree core as neuter, it is in fact a structure of gender power. (1991, p. 141)

Studies show (for example, Cockburn, 1991; and Yount, 1991) that sexual harassment is used for a variety of reasons. In line with organisational theory, Kristen Yount (1991) argues that harassment is often used to exceed the target's threshold of manageable distress and to designate the person as an outsider. Yount (1991) explains that young single women are more prone to receive 'come-on's' whereas women in higher positions were more likely to meet with harassment designed to exclude them. Yet, it seems to me that whatever the type of harassment, and whoever it is targeted at, the action is meant to exclude, or perhaps 'locate,' the victim. Cockburn (1991), for example, finds that sexual power is at the core of harassment aimed at young women and more senior and potentially powerful women. She describes a senior woman in a position of authority who was pinched on the bottom by a senior male colleague. This, she argues, shows "how emergent and potentially powerful women too must be cut down to size by sexual means" (Cockburn, 1991, p. 141). A younger female office worker had her breasts leered at nearly every day by a senior male who encouraged other men to do the same. This treatment of a junior woman is also a clear example of the exercise of sexual power (Cockburn, 1991, p. 141).

Despite Rosabeth Moss Kanter's (1977a) early assertion that harassment will decrease as women employees increase in number, the opposite appears to be the case. Sexually harassing behaviour by men is more overt the more women find places of authority.[3]

---

[3]Others too have concluded that as the number of women increases, they represent a greater threat to men, and this leads men to tighten boundaries and to increase their opposition and harassment (see Whittock, 2000).

The Changing Meaning of Sexual Harassment in Australia

There have been three major public debates in Australia that have shaped an understanding of sexual harassment since it was first acknowledged through legislation: the 1985 Lynette Aldridge case, the Einfeld judgment in 1988, and the 1995 debate over Helen Garner's book *The First Stone: Some Questions About Sex and Power*. All three debates serve to remind us that sexual harassment does not have a fixed meaning but, rather, in the process of public debate, among other things that I have previously mentioned, it is reconstituted and reshaped. Consequently, in the wake of these three major debates, sexual harassment began to mean something different than it had before. I am observing a different register here—not feminist definitions and theories of what sexual harassment is; not government legislation and reporting; not feminist critiques of the liberal approach to its censure; but how the meaning of the term and its deployment is shaped by public debate. These debates bring to attention the constancy of the political and public challenges to how sexual harassment is defined and experienced. The debates also highlight the mainstream media's general stance in the reporting of sexual harassment. I make this point because of the relationship between newsroom culture and news reporting of sexual harassment. The media, of course, is integral to making sexual harassment 'news' and shaping the tone of public debate, as indicated by the Garner debate. I describe the cases in detail here because they mark an escalating public awareness of 'sexual harassment,' but also describe an arc of its ascendancy from a feminist point of view, then its downturn and demonisation via the Garner debate.

In the first case, in 1985, 19-year-old Brisbane shop assistant Lynette Aldridge resigned from her job at the Tasty Morsel cake shop after claiming that her boss, Grant Booth, had sexually harassed her (Tiddy, 2001, p. 77). She had been unemployed for a year, so Aldridge was thrilled to secure her first job. After nine months of being sexually harassed by Booth she resigned and complained to the Queensland branch of HREOC. By 1987 her complaint has still not been conciliated, and it was the first in Australia to go to a public hearing. Tiddy (2001, pp. 77–79) details the case, in which Aldridge said that her boss had forced her to have sex on more than 20 occasions and that she had endured daily attacks in which Booth would slap her bottom, rub his hands up and down her dress, and twist her arm until it hurt. Aldridge was awarded $7,000 in damages, but Booth refused to pay, and so the case had to be reheard in the Federal Court. Once this occurred, Aldridge became the public face of the 'Tasty Morsel test case'—and intense media, and public, scrutiny. She was awarded the same damages of $7000. "Radio talkback shows ran hot with debates about every detail of her case. Press articles appeared in all newspapers across the country" (Tiddy, 2001, pp. 78–79). The effect of this intense media coverage was that national debate started to a degree not seen before.

In the second case, feminist scholars in this field often refer to the 1988 judgment by Justice Marcus Einfeld (see Bacchi & Jose, 1994; and Tiddy, 2001). This case, presided over by Justice Einfeld, the then president of the HREOC, raised media and public scrutiny of sexual harassment to a higher level. A case was brought by three female medical receptionists who lodged a complaint of harassment by their employer, Dr Atallah Sheiban (Tiddy, 2001, p. 79). All three women told the HREOC that their boss had squeezed their breasts, had attempted to kiss them, had made comments on their legs, and were told to wear dresses. Justice Einfeld, in verbally summing up the case, said that this did not constitute illegal sexual harassment. In his written judgment a week later, Einfeld found that the women's employer had unlawfully sexually harassed them, but refused to award compensation because the employer's acts were 'mild,' 'insignificant,' 'minimal,' and 'sporadic' (Tiddy, 2001, p. 80). Many influential media columnists were critical of Einfeld's conclusions and there was vocal public support for the women. After intense public pressure and media scrutiny, the decision was overturned by the Federal Court and compensation granted. The significance of this case is noted by Tiddy: "The decision by the Federal Court had far-reaching implications. The revolution in the rules of public behaviour between men and women had been firmly underpinned by the law" (2001, p. 81). This case set the scene for the turnaround effected by Garner.

The third, and most public and influential debate around sexual harassment in Australia since the Act came into place was sparked by former journalist and prominent feminist author Helen Garner. In *The First Stone* Garner (1995) traces the case of two University of Melbourne female students at the prestigious co-educational Melbourne Ormond College who accused their college master, Alan Gregory, of indecent assault in October 1991. One of the women's problems was that there had been no sexual harassment policy or procedure at Ormond College. The women had been trying to resolve the matter informally with the college council and the master since November 1991 (Trioli, 1996, p. 17). In March 1992 the council stated that it had "full confidence in the master and in his performance of duties at the college" (Trioli, 1996, p. 18). Unhappy with the outcome, the two women took their complaint to the police. In May police laid two charges of indecent assault, but the master was later cleared of both in September 1993. In May 1993 Gregory stepped down from the job, prompting Garner's book, which went on to become a best-seller, selling about 70,000 copies in a year (Trioli, 1996, p. 14).

Garner questioned the role of sexual harassment discourse, as the young women had deployed it, and asked where to draw the line between 'clear-cut' examples of harassment and the 'gray areas of innocent flirtations.' She lamented that today's young feminists had become puritanical and punitive about harassment. Feminist academic Jenna Mead (1997), who had supported the young women at Ormond College and was one of many vocal public opponents of

Garner's stance, edited a collection of essays in response to Garner's 'trivialisation' of sexual harassment. Melbourne journalist Virginia Trioli (1996) also weighed into the debate critical of *The First Stone*, wanting to repackage young feminists and feminism as alive and well. Trioli and Mead both note that the political pot had been boiling in the United States around what young feminist scholar Katie Roiphe (1993) termed 'victim feminism'—an obsession with rape, abuse, and harassment out of proportion to 'reality' and to a woman's inherent ability to deal with it. They claimed that it was only a matter of time until this take on feminism reached Australia. Garner's book created or tapped into a similar skepticism. It created a panic and resentment over sexual politics, but it also did much more than that. As Trioli (1996, p. 14) suggests, the Garner book "fired and defined a national debate about feminism, sexual harassment, women and personal power that was unprecedented in its range and passion." National commentators, broadcasters, and journalists, academics, social analysts and community leaders took positions on the debate.

The meaning of sexual harassment in Australia was implicitly changed by the Garner book and the six months of extraordinary media attention it spawned in 1995—a significant passage of time, given a medium known for its short attention span, according to Mead (1997). The debate about what constitutes sexual harassment also enabled a significant reconfiguration of feminism in Australia. From the mid-1970s women, and the media, had used a discourse of sexual harassment, but Garner's book allowed an amplification of an existing discourse about feminism. A new chorus of conservative voices had stood up against what they saw as the gagging effect of 'political correctness.' This conservative discourse suggested that the subjects imagined in and enabled by feminist discourse and government legislation were women who use the term against men to destroy their careers; women who complain and take sexual harassment claims to court when they could and should work the problem out themselves; and that therefore sexual harassment is the resort of the weak, the humourless, and the bureaucratic, women who have been empowered by feminism but now have gone too far; and that women who claim sexual harassment are manipulative. More than 10 years after the publication of the Garner book and the ensuing media attention, and the same period of conservative government in Australia, a vitriolic and antifeminist discourse has become entrenched in popular discourse.

The media considers sexual harassment as newsworthy, but it is now raising the question of gender neutrality. The following article is an example that highlights this point, although it doesn't have the same prominence as the Aldridge case, Enfield judgment, or the Garner controversy. I don't claim it is representative, but see it as illustrative of some current media discourses on sexual harassment. In 2004, *The Age* newspaper published an article that heralded the 'facts' that men and women experienced equivalent 'low level' harassment in the workplace, questioning why the focus was always on women. Reporter John Mangan (2004, pp. 4–5) finds that "new research is challenging the assumption that women are mostly the victims of sexual harassment." Mangan notes three scholarly studies (what he terms a 'rash of research') that support his position, although he does not give exact references. It appears that Mangan is referring, firstly, to a paper in the *American Sociological Review* by Christopher Uggen and Amy Blackstone (2004); an Australian Psychological Society conference paper by University of New England researchers Roberta Martin and Don Hine (2004); and a paper in the *Journal of Social Psychology* by Australian researchers from Deakin University, Marita McCabe and Lisa Hardman (2005). Mangan fails, however, to note the American researchers' further comments that "adult women remain the most frequent targets of classic sexual harassment markers, such as unwanted touching and invasion of personal space" (Uggen & Blackstone, 2004, p. 64). Mangan provides neither a serious analysis of the cultural and social structures that privilege male power and masculinism (which Uggen and Blackstone do, and to a lesser extent McCabe and Hardman), nor any engagement with the overall content and limitations of the research. This is the case, even though McCabe and Hardman (2005) and Martin and Hine (2004) acknowledge that the limitations of their research are small sample sizes and non-random sampling.

The 'Jokey Blokey'—Sexual Humour and Power

I will now move on to discuss how my interviewees talked about sexual harassment. Jokes are an often used method of invoking power. Very little of the literature on organisational culture explores the meaning behind sexual humour in the workplace. Feminist research on organisations more often describes sexual humour and provides an analysis. In relation to the occupations of computing and engineering, Sue Lewis (2000) includes humour in the "ways of according status and prestige, strategies for ordering and differentiating members from non-members, which all contribute to a distinctly masculine culture." Michael Mulkay argues that humour, and especially sexual humour, is used to preserve existing organisational structures:

> It is yet another 'paradox of the humorous mode' that, although semantically humor involves confrontation with a subversion of a dominant pattern, it is used most effectively for serious purposes mainly in structured situations where it works to maintain that pattern. (Mulkay, 1988, p. 177)

Feminist scholar Mary Crawford, writing about how people talk about sexuality in everyday interaction and how people use humour in everyday life to negotiate sexual meanings and understandings, also acknowledges that sexual humour "maintains a sexist social order" (2000, p. 220). Crawford, however, contends that humour may "subvert the social order and create new realities" (2000, p. 224).

So how do my interviewees talk about and theorise (sexual) humour? The idea that joke telling in the newsroom is a gender-neutral activity is given expression by Simon, a 27-year-old regional reporter:

> Simon: All in all, there's certainly no—things get very bawdy out there, very . . .
>
> LN: In what way?
>
> Simon: Just a little bit of cheeky ribaldry. Sometimes I find it goes a bit far but it's good in the sense that if someone does—like, yeah, especially the stuff that you get through, like news, people comment and make jokes and some of it's very offensive. It's sort of just a way of dealing with it or just showing that it doesn't really affect you. We're just all macho types but even if it does get a bit out of hand there's always—people are very good here at just saying, 'Oi, no.' There's really no malice or any genuine nastiness about it. People just get carried away. You take it to one level and then you have to take it to another, and another, and eventually, you know—I've been guilty of it myself and our news editor at the moment he's thrilled by saying, I guess, you know, offensive things just to get the reaction. He'll go, 'Oooh, [name], God,' and he just laughs his head off. But I don't think anyone could safely, confidently say they're being harassed.
>
> LN: What sort of offensive things would he say?
>
> Simon: Geez, I don't know. Like, real, 'Are You Being Served?' sort of stuff—real bloody 'Mrs Slocombe's pussy' sort of silliness. A lot of it is just old, just like he's been talking to Ugly Dave Grey at lunch and you think, 'Oh,' but, yeah, it's just part of the fun. You all laugh about it and everyone seems to get in on it.[4]

It almost seems as if Simon works in a genderless newsroom. Yet, just before we started discussing jokes in the newsroom Simon had been very specific about gender, noting how his female editor would call on gender to blame men for not taking her seriously.

---

[4]*Are You Being Served?* was a popular British comedy set in a London department store. It aired in the UK between 1972 and 1985. The series spun off into an Australian version, which was shown in 1980–1981. Mrs Slocombe is a female character in the show. Ugly Dave Grey is a British-born Australian comedian who made regular appearances on the popular Australian television game show *Blankety Blanks*. It was broadcast from 1977 to 1979. Grey was renowned for his bawdy jokes and 'Dick did' repartee with the show's host.

. . . I think if they [men] show indifference or don't respond in the way she plans, she says 'It's because I'm a woman and they can't handle a woman editor.' I think 'Well, have you ever considered the idea that perhaps they didn't think much of what you're presenting?'

Simon uses gender-neutral terms such as 'us,' 'we,' 'people,' and 'you all' to describe how and when jokes are used and indeed 'needed' in the newsroom. Yet both of the 'people' he specifies as telling the jokes are male—the news editor and himself. The comment that *'we're just all macho types'* clearly identifies a particular masculine subject position around joke telling in this newsroom. If it is indeed men telling the majority of jokes, then does that mean that women are the intended audience or the butt of the humour? His comment: *'I don't think anyone could safely, confidently say they're being harassed'* is clearly aimed at women who might be offended to the point of experiencing it as harassment. It could be argued that Simon and his male colleagues fear not being able to relieve their stress through sexual humour because women will find it offensive, or worse, make complaints of harassment. The power that sexual humour bestows on men, in this supposed gender-neutral newsroom environment where everyone is in on the jokes, is evident when Simon notes his male news editor's sexualised response that he is *'thrilled by saying, I guess, you know, offensive things just to get the reaction.'* The reaction, for him to be so thrilled, must be from women or those men on the outside who do not engage in sexual humour as a method of establishing the social order and may respond with shock or offense, or who willingly provide the audience and are necessary to his pleasure. Simon also calls upon a gender-neutral discourse of needing release from professional pressures (possibly even upsetting news). For Simon, joke telling is a normal part of newsroom culture that provides a release valve for stress experienced by (male) journalists.

Penelope Brunner and Melinda Costello assert that supposedly innocent jokes expose underlying attitudes toward power relationships in the organisation.

> Although these attitudes may not manifest through conversations with organization members, humor provides an acceptable way for men to express these beliefs. This type of brief interaction, recurring repeatedly throughout a normal workday, may indicate and perpetuate assumptions that men make about women's roles in the workplace. (Brunner & Costello, 2002, n.p.)

William Kahn (1989) demonstrates how humour in organisations sends a message about power relationships. Kahn (1989, p. 145) tells the following story: when a male employee mumbles a one-line witticism, this forces a female consultant to reconsider the gender relationships in their workplace. A female secretary who delivers some papers to the bank's managers accidentally unplugs the slide projector with her foot. A male supervisor's quick comment about 'a woman's touch' provokes laughter from the men in the meeting. Initially the consultant perceives the men in the bank as liberal and nonsexist but with some investigation she finds that the joke signals "issues about resistance to women's control and authority" (Kahn, 1989, p. 47). The explicit and subtle sexual humour observed by Kahn provides insights into existing power structures and gender relationships.

In this next excerpt Susan, a senior metropolitan reporter, finds that joke telling wins support in high places, and as such is a tool to negotiate power. Even though male and female journalists are discussed as all taking part in a joking newsroom repartee, Susan depicts the situation in news conferences as a competition for the editor's favoured response:

> Susan: I remember thinking when I was sitting around the news conferences, there was the 'jokey blokey' and the girls trying to keep up. Terrific women, when I spoke to them on their own, great journalists, but still when they got into that situation—the gold fish bowl—it was 'oh my goodness the big fish are here and they are all being loud and boisterous and I better try,' it was very difficult.
>
> LN: So they would take on the same characteristics as the guys in the news conference?
>
> Susan: Some would, yes, trying to be equally as sort of jovial, jokey, loud, oh, another joke to throw into the pile and laugh very loudly, and the editor cracked a joke, and I thought 'oh dear, we are all trying so hard,' you know, to pick me out, am I the funniest today. The guys loved that game. I think they just do it spontaneously.

It appears that these women know the rewards of 'being one of the boys.' Christopher McLean et al. (1997), in their exploration of engineering culture, find that 'being one of the boys' is one of a set of established occupational subject positions that their female interviewees occupy. A sign of the fluidity of our subjectivity, 'being one of the boys' is a position that allows for acceptance into the rare and privileged position beside men in authority. Perhaps this excerpt also demonstrates the ideas of feminist standpoint theorists that those forced into an acute awareness of their marginal status (women), "develop insights into the mental habits and behaviors of the dominant class as well as a sensitivity to the problems of being located in a secondary class" (Steiner, 1998, p. 157). Although Susan is not specific about whether it is sexual humour, she experiences the jokes as exclusive and about competitiveness ('the girls trying to keep up'). The men set the scene, do so 'spontaneously' (although in this way she naturalises male behaviour, while claiming that women put it on), and a man is judge; the women are clearly behind the 8-ball. The women's behaviour cannot be read as subversive even though they are taking on and becoming part of the masculine discourse. It could only be read as subversive if the women were equally engaged in and leading the joke telling in a way that challenged that culture, or by refusing to take part in the joke telling—neither of which is the case here. Rather than subvert the social order, the women here are mimicking the social order as a coping mechanism.

> Susan: I go into a news conference situation and all the jokes are being shared. I am very much aware that I am a woman, and I am very much aware that I am not a heterosexual woman, and I think to myself we have come a long way, but at the end of the day it's still the boys being the loudest, it's the boys trying to talk over the top of each other, it's the girls tittering quietly in the background and laughing at all the jokes, because they make sure they laugh at the appropriate times, and it's all that sort of stuff which still goes on. There's an unspoken game that goes on about how to get along in your career. You don't be a big ballsy babe walking through the newsroom.

The newsroom for a feminist and lesbian like Susan is an alienating place where men are 'the boys trying to talk over the top of each other,' and she doesn't fit in. In her observations in the interview, she has taken on the final subject position that McLean et al. (1997) highlight in their research, a feminist subject position, one that offers a point of resistance to a dominant group. In the story she tells, Susan neither obviously approves nor disapproves of the journalists' behaviour, but she is separated from the group dynamic by her lack of engagement. Susan's collapse of many events into this one symbolic story is interesting. For example, what of the contradictory account of the women Susan mentioned in the previous excerpt I've quoted as 'all being loud and boisterous' and then 'tittering quietly in the background'? Perhaps this is evidence that she is recalling women's different approaches, in different newsrooms at different times—and simultaneously observing the overall picture.

Interviewees' experiences of sexual humour in the newsroom do not appear to hold the broad transgressive possibilities that Crawford (2000) suggests. Even though I shortly describe how Jessica and her female colleagues turn the tables on their male colleagues by putting up a semi-nude photograph of an Australian cricketer, this is just one small and isolated instance of 'transgression' that I encountered during the interviews with female journalists.

How 'Sexual Harassment' Is Used by the Interviewees

Sexual harassment has corporate meaning, and men talk about it in newsroom banter, but in my interviews, however, only self-identified feminist women used the term to describe incidents of it in the newsroom.

In my newsroom experiences it is not uncommon for male journalists to discuss sexual harassment, using the term in a joking and dismissive manner. Comments from male journalists to other male and some female journalists, like, 'don't touch me or I'll complain of harassment,' are common currency in a discourse that while partly unconcerned about the seriousness of sexual harassment, acknowledges that it exists and that there are repercussions from complaints. Janet, who identified as a feminist, used the term *'sexually harassed'* to give an overall assessment of why female journalists at one regional newspaper were leaving at a greater rate than men; Christine mentions *'a sexual discrimination complaint'* that a former female colleague lodged against the editor; and Susan tentatively suggests that *'I guess you would call it harassment'* to describe a sexually explicit comment made about her by her editor in front of younger colleagues. For the younger female journalists I interviewed 'sexual harassment' as a term has no currency, although they are constantly the recipients of sexually harassing behaviour. Whereas two younger women (Jessica and Sally) discussed sexually harassing behaviour in the newsroom, neither labelled it as such. Ruth, a 20-year-old cadet, was unaware of what the term 'feminism' meant, and issues around sexual harassment were never discussed in the interview.

One of the two men who mentioned harassment was a regional editor, in the industry for 30 years. He spoke of it via a discourse of policy procedure or 'management speak.' We had been discussing unions. Todd replied to my question about whether his newspaper had an equal employment opportunity committee:

> Todd: *We have a clear sexual harassment policy, and that's in our induction manual. We have a 3-day induction program for all new staff. The union's almost non-existent here. We don't encourage or discourage it—it is entirely up to people. We'll take the money out of their pay if they want to do that, but the union has become less relevant, really.*
>
> LN: *Is that an indication that the workplace here is very happy and satisfied?*
>
> Todd: *Oh, gee, I wouldn't be as bold as to say that, but it's probably more about value for money. What's the union offering them? Our award,[5] for instance, has run out about two or three years ago and at the start of each financial year I just call the staff in and say we are giving them a three percent pay rise. Last year, I think I gave them six weeks' paid maternity leave as well. The first year we did that, they said 'oh well, what about negotiations,' and [I said] we don't have negotiations, we have just given it to you, you don't have to give us anything in return.*

---

[5]A document detailing a set of minimum wage and work conditions negotiated between an employer and an employee group such as the industry union MEAA.

The newspapers at which the majority of interviewees worked at the time of interview all have an established sexual harassment policy under News Limited, John Fairfax Holdings, Rural Press, or Australian Provincial Newspapers.[6] However, it is clear from Todd's comments that this regional newspaper has dismissed the union-negotiated and company-agreed award, under which claims of harassment could be lodged within the organisation. Even though there is a sexual harassment policy written into the induction program, and state and/or federal anti-discrimination laws, and the industrial court, the lack of any union support indicates that workers in this company are on their own. Unions are not necessarily the first point of call for sexual harassment complaints, but the support of the union in work-related conflict is helpful in negotiations with employers. Todd's initial reaction to talk of EEO goes straight to 'sexual harassment,' and that in turn stops the conversation. Having a policy, then, closes down that subject in the interview. But what's happening in the interview when Todd slips so seamlessly back to unions when I've asked about EEO and he mentions sexual harassment? EEO is many things; he could have talked about equal pay, for example. His language—'policy,' 'manual,' 'induction program'—are all management words and procedures and he uses these to contain 'sexual harassment' into a matter of policy. It's evident that Todd is more comfortable displacing sexual harassment back into the more comfortable subject of the union—a union that he has rejected and, he claims, so has his staff. Perhaps a discourse of 'rejected,' 'irrelevant' unionism stands in for a similarly rejected feminist discourse of EEO and sexual harassment. There is no 'value for money' in unionism, and similarly it could be that there is no 'value' placed on sexual harassment claims. Todd's benevolent manager persona ('giving them six weeks paid maternity leave') is an interesting shift in the discussion from unions. He claims that his employees have free will ('you don't have to give us anything in return' (for the pay raise)—except don't ask about negotiations.

How useful, then, is the feminist discourse on sexual harassment of women in journalism for advancing women's careers? Even for feminists it seems difficult to use the term to describe the behaviour of the harasser. In this email from Susan, in which I had asked for more information about her experiences of harassment detailed in our face-to-face interview, sexual harassment is used as a legal framework:

> Susan: A select group of editorial and non-editorial people were invited on a
> bus trip to a corporate box at the MCG for a game of night footy. It was a

---

[6]This information is garnered from my own work experience at News Limited and from questions I directed to MEAA staff (who were not interviewees), Fairfax Limited, and questions to interviewees from APN. Rural Press company secretary Helen Thom confirmed via email that it had a sexual harassment policy, but was unsure what year it had been established (email conversation, April 17, 2006).

night of much drinking and eating, but nothing prepared me for the two hands which planted themselves on my bum as I leaned into the bar fridge for a bottle of wine. I turned around to find the general manager ogling at me as his hands squeezed my ass. The next day, he called me into his office and, red-faced and extremely sheepish, he offered an apology for his behaviour, saying he didn't know what had come over him. I suspect the thought of a sexual harassment claim had a pretty sobering effect. (email conversation, March 4, 2004)

It is only when Susan refers to being called into the general manager's office the next day that she uses the term in relation to the legal framework that might frighten him. She therefore accepts the view that 'sexual harassment' is a punitive discourse ('*I suspect the thought of a sexual harassment claim had a pretty sobering effect*'). Susan accepts the general manager's apology, even though she says:

Susan: To be completely honest I was initially shocked by what happened and embarrassed. I was worried that my colleagues would have seen it and that my professionalism would be called into question. (email conversation, March 4, 2004)

She has trouble remembering the details of the incident, appears embarrassed, and is dismissive of its importance, placing the harassment at a time in her life when she didn't know how to handle, or expect, such behaviour—and perhaps, too, this is why Susan suggests that *her* professionalism will be called into question rather than his. Susan responds to my questions by reasserting her acceptance of her powerless position.

Susan: You have to remember that I was young and new [two months into her first job] and he was the general manager. I am hardly going to turn around and tell him to 'fuck off.' I think I turned round and said something like 'Jesus, [name]!' and he might have said something like 'oh, you are irresistible' or something like that. (email conversation March 4, 2004)

Women's discussion of a newsroom culture in which sexual harassment often occurs presents interesting linkages with the term. For example, Susan was discussing her decision whether or not to expose her lesbian sexuality in the newsroom, when she recalled her first experience of sexual harassment. Jessica didn't label her experience of working in a newsroom where pictures of semi-naked women were a common feature as harassment. Janet spoke of seeing the harassment of female co-workers during her career, but not of her own experiences that were later revealed. Questions about feminism sometimes raised narratives about sexually harassing behaviour. For example, when I asked Sally if there were any women in the newsroom who would identify as feminist, she replied:

Sally: I think probably one, she's a general reporter, she's pretty full on, she gets pretty emotional, even if a half picture of half an abdomen or something that's not covered, she starts to get really upset about things.

LN: Would she find it a struggle in the newsroom; she's probably the only feminist there. Is that a struggle for her?

Sally: Well people are saying oh, [name]'s on a rampage again. One of the pictures that she got upset over was a going-away drinks poster, it was like a dominatrix thing. [The poster pictured] this chick with a guy on his hands and knees on the ground, and she had the collar on and everything. They put the face of the guy who was leaving work on to the face of the guy in the poster on all fours. She saw that in the morning and just went absolutely mental.

Part of this excerpt is more thoroughly deconstructed in Chapter Eight. Here, however, I only want to draw attention to the acceptance, or normalisation, of sexually harassing behaviour as part of newsroom culture that is embodied in her response. Similarly, Ruth, a regional cadet I asked to discuss what the term feminism meant to her, claimed she had no idea, yet she was still able to articulate that:

Ruth: It doesn't really worry me. It's just the way the world is.

That world, for Sally and Ruth, is one that accepts sexual harassment and gender inequality.

Janet identifies as a feminist and uses a feminist framework around sexually harassing behaviour. Janet explains two incidents of sexually harassing behaviour, although she is more comfortable explaining how it happened to other women than to herself. Firstly, she explains that women were leaving one newspaper where she had worked because they were being sexually harassed.

Janet: The women [at the newspaper] were leaving, I think, at a higher rate; you know, there was a greater turnover of women.

LN: Why was that?

Janet: Because it was a terrible place for young women to work.

LN: In what way?

Janet: Most women were sexually harassed.

LN: Is that your experience throughout the industry or at a particular newspaper?

Janet: That was my experience at [a particular regional newspaper]. It was not my experience at other newspapers, especially at [a metropolitan newspaper] where there were strong women in key editorial positions. It was a happier place for women to work. I think actually it's about who's above and I think it is about culture to an extent.

LN: So what you are saying is that people in senior management can stop that culture, or stop that element of sexual harassment or the poor treatment of women, but that if it is accepted by editors and general managers than it could infiltrate down the ranks?

Janet: I think so. It is something about it being condoned. I don't know, because it's such a private thing too. I mean, I don't know of anyone who actually officially complained at [newspaper name]. But it wasn't hard to miss at some social occasions. You know the time of year at Christmas parties you'd see a senior editorial bloke with his tongue in a 21-year-old cadet's ear at the Christmas party. It's sending a pretty strong message that it's part of sexual behaviour. That's ignoring the power factors of office relationships.

LN: So young women weren't able to complain. Why didn't they complain?

Janet: I don't think they were able to complain. They made it pretty clear at the Christmas party how they saw young women.

Later in the interview Janet describes her own experience of harassment on her first day in journalism as a type of "rite of passage" (de Bruin, 2004, p. 9), yet without using the term to describe the behaviour.

Janet: It's my experience from day one at [newspaper] you're taken up to the subs desk, introduced to the subs, 'this is Janet, Mr so and so, this is the new sub' and he said 'hi Janet, do you want a fuck.' The seasonal variation of that at Christmas is, 'come and sit on Santa's face.'

A key issue that has surrounded debates around sexual harassment has been the tendency to see the problem as purely one of sexual deviance. Feminist writers such as Jenny Morgan (1995), Bacchi (1998), and Bacchi and Jose (1994) claim that by doing so, sexual harassment is pathologised in ways that reduce the possibility that the deeper problems of sexual inequality, sexism, and gender will be identified and dealt with. As well, seeing sexual harassment as sexual deviance tends to detract from the wider forms of harassment such as innuendo, jokes, and persistent sexual comments, which highlight issues of occupational culture (see for example, Eveline, 1998). Brunner and Costello suggest that:

While societal norms and discrimination laws target the obvious discrimination practices in organisations, subtle methods of prejudice, such as sexual humour, retain and support an organisation's historical structure and are often overlooked. (2002, n.p.)

Making a Complaint and Moral Obligation

Susan, who experienced overt sexual harassment by a general manager in the first few months of her career (see above), and now speaking as a senior metropolitan journalist, recalls that harassment of her (again) and other female staff by one editor happened mostly in social situations and stemmed from the perpetrator's drinking problem.

> Susan: It [the harassment] happened when we socialised in journalistic situations, Christmas parties and that sort of stuff. Looking back, the experience was really dreadful.

She says that when the editor was drunk he would engage in sexual harassment of young female staff. This, she says, 'entailed unwanted touching, kissing, pushing against walls and general groping.' There was an undercurrent of the harassment during work but it was exacerbated by his drinking at after work or lunchtime social occasions.

> Susan: Things would start to be said and they would be more overt, and obvious and loud, and I would be increasingly uncomfortable.

So when the harassment was less obvious it was accepted, by others and Susan, as part of newsroom culture, but when it became more overt she took the only legal action available to her—the grievance procedure. Later in this section I will detail the incident that in part prompted her resolve to rally the other female journalists who were being harassed and to make a complaint. After the complaint process, the editor's daily 'banter' of sexual overtones stopped, as did the editor's presence at social functions, which was not well received by some other journalists who often used those occasions to gain access to, and favours from, the editor. The absence of the editor was seen as the fault of the women who had complained, and the 'victims' of the harassment thus became the problem. Therefore, the culture was seen as the norm—a culture that facilitated male networking and advancement.

Susan talks about having to make the complaint as a moral and feminist obligation and 'just as a staff member,' and in so doing equivocates about whether it's gender politics or a gender-neutral issue:

> Susan: I thought, 'I have an obligation. I have a moral obligation as much as anything, a feminist obligation,' but also just as a staff member, you know, this is just getting way out of control. So I actually took action and I went through the formal channels of the sexual harassment . . . which was the most dreadful experience.

In discussing making the complaint as a 'moral' and 'feminist obligation,' Susan enacts a subjectivity that has already been constituted through sexual harass-ment and then has to act from that position ethically, an ethical dilemma that men are not presented with. This position also distances her from being a victim. Both Susan's 'moral' and 'feminist' frameworks are understood here through a rational and public context: there was an (unemotional) 'problem' that needed to be brought under control and it had to be contained via a very public control mechanism. Susan's experience of the grievance procedure as 'dreadful' reinforces Bacchi's (1998, p. 76) position that grievance procedures (not a term Susan used) are limited because of the imbalances in institutional power—for example, the way in which they constitute the recipient of the behaviour as the attacker and the sexual harasser as the attacked. As we have seen, above, that is exactly the case here, the victims of the harassment were seen as the 'problem.' Yet, Susan says of the process that it 'broke my heart,' because she respected the editor professionally.

> Susan: He said 'I didn't know, if you'd said to me . . . ,' and I said, 'no, no, no, no, no, if I'd said to you it would never have changed, because that was the cycle. I had to do what I did, even though it broke my heart because I respected you so much.' And to this day we are very close.

Here Susan attempts to separate sexual harassment into the private (feminine and emotional, nonrational) realm, and in so doing this elevates the perpetrator's status as the professional (rational) man, above all else. Her romanticising of her relationship with him is relegated to the private, as well, by stating she has a 'very close' and (earlier in the interview) a 'love-hate relationship' with him that continues to this day, even though they no longer work together.

Laura Ring's (1994) reworking of Carol Gilligan's (1986) theory of the ethic of care is useful here in understanding women's embodied responses to sexual harassment. Available conventional discourses of femininity often provide women with positions of submission or compliance, thereby disabling their effective resistance to sexual harassment (Ring, 1994, p. 136).[7] One such set of discourses is the ethic of care.

> As a 'female' moral realm, a discourse of care makes available to women a righteous and powerful subject positioning; the gender-appropriate power that care confers is one which comes with the ability to satisfy the needs of others (and therefore to withhold that satisfaction). (Ring, 1994, p. 137)

---

[7]Sharon Marcus (1992) makes the same point about rape.

This is where Ring departs from Gilligan's theory. Gilligan suggests that when women master the ethic of care, this will include caring for their own lives. Ring argues that a discourse of care "denotes responsibility for the growth and protection of others' egos, demands warmth, nurturance, and caring often precisely to the point of self sacrifice" (Ring, 1994, p. 137). Although Susan has not been submissive in terms of her compliance with sexual harassment, she has, however, taken up a more compliant, protective, and caring role with the perpetrator after the event. I think that this defends against the possibility she might see herself as a 'big ballsy babe,' which would not do her career, or possibly her sense of self, any good at all. Susan is doing five times the work. She is a journalist; she is an object; she is a moral and political subject; she is dealing with the acting out of norms and so she is an outsider; and caring for those she's 'hurt' by her actions, she is a carer. Six months after our interview Susan had left the industry in which she had spent 18 years. Her 'sacrifice' was to leave a profession she has 'loved,' but could no longer survive in. The effect of working in a culture that generally condones sexual harassment is a central reason, although by no means the only one, why she has rethought her career priorities:

> Susan: I guess this [after telling the stories of sexual harassment] is why I have these thoughts, like 'what are my priorities in my life?' because I have given so much to this job in terms of time, sacrifices. I suddenly start thinking 'hang on a minute, what really has changed here, and where am I really going with this, and do I necessarily want to be part of all that?' 'Is that the hierarchy I'm aiming for'?

"Men's power in the extra-organisational world, in the family, the state and civil society, enters the workplace with them and gives even the most junior man a degree of *sexual* authority relative to even senior women" (Cockburn, 1991, p. 143, emphasis in original). Even though Susan's positioning, and dismissal, of the harassment as historical (10 years ago)[8] and in an era when she said it was even more accepted as part of newsroom culture, she does draw on a recent example of harassment at a moment's notice—one that had occurred the weekend before our interview:

> Susan: Someone told me at the weekend a story about someone getting them in for an interview. This person is extremely highly placed, putting their foot on the

---

[8]Trice and Beyer (1993, p. 6) refer to the influence of history in current workplace behaviour when they note that close examination of occupational cultures will "usually uncover residues of cultural ideas and practices that originated at earlier points in its history ... even though these historical residues are buried under current preoccupations ... they can still have powerful effects in guiding current behaviour."

coffee table, and basically sitting back and almost scratching his balls and asking
all about her personal life, and why she wanted this job now. I couldn't believe
what she was telling me, I just thought, 'Oh, here I am sitting in 2004 having
gone through that battle probably 10 years ago, and it's still going on.'

The final sentences of this excerpt where Susan recounts her colleague's experience of sexually harassing behaviour is perhaps related to her own ongoing
ambivalence in coming to terms with the presence of sexual harassment in
the newsroom.

Like Susan, Jessica also experiences the ethical burden of how to deal
with sexually harassing behaviour in the newsroom. In the following excerpt
Jessica details the dilemma of the responsibility falling onto her shoulders, and
that effecting change in newsroom culture is virtually impossible.

Jessica: If you've gone along with it, if you haven't said anything before, then you
are condoning it and then are you just as bad if you make a joke back? Then if
suddenly, you think about it later, and you think that you haven't gone the right
way about dealing with that, it's too late, because you bought into that situation
and then you don't feel like you have got a right to actually take a stand back
and go 'no actually, don't say that or don't speak to me like that.'

Jessica admits that she was so eager to 'fit in' that initially she did not challenge
the overt sexism in the newsroom, and then when she became aware that it
affected the workplace and her opportunities, it was too late to take action.

Young Women, Power and Subjectivity

Earlier in this chapter I provided statistics from the HREOC that showed women
who made claims of sexually harassing behaviour were more likely to be under
the age of 45, relative newcomers to the workplace, and in positions subordinate
to their alleged harassers. Twenty-one-year-old Jessica has an understanding of
embodied female subjectivity and sexual harassment and is aware of the gendered
division of labour within the occupation that creates the 'perfect' environment
for sexually harassing behaviour, even though she never uses the term 'sexual
harassment.' She notes the gendered division between the predominantly male
sub-editors and the predominantly female reporters and observes that this creates the basis for unequal power distribution that, in part, allows or at the least
encourages sexually harassing behaviour in the newsroom.

Jessica: Lots of the subs are older men which I found really intimidating. When
I first started I was terrified of all the subs, I didn't want to go over to any of
them. I'd do night shift and I stayed on my side of the room and they stayed
on theirs. I didn't go over there unless I really had to.

She realised that their power came from their silence.

> *Jessica: They didn't come and talk to you unless they really had to, and then it was 'this is wrong, this is wrong.'*

Jessica clearly articulates an understanding that this power had a quieting effect on her. During the interview I said: *'It's interesting that in one small way that exudes a sense . . .'* and she finished my sentence by saying *'of power.'* At the core of this acknowledgment is an experience of gender inequality. This power of separation and clearly delineated division of hierarchies is also reinforced by lewd jokes or sexual comments (which I have already noted), and often these comments emanate from the news stories and images journalists are working with. In the main, those comments are about women and women's bodies.

> *Jessica: Well they [subs-editors] would be watching TV and like making cracks about the people they would see on TV, or comments about people that we have taken photos of for the paper, and . . .*
>
> *LN: About women or men?*
>
> *Jessica: Yeah, both, to start with I think it was about women, but maybe that's just because I was young and a female and so that was the sort of stuff that I heard.*
>
> *LN: So you don't hear it as much anymore or you are different now? Have you become a bit immune to it or you give it back to them in some way, do you?*
>
> *Jessica: Yeah, probably. I think now I probably start to give it back, or I don't listen, but I am immune to some of it, yeah. You become less sensitive. I think that you have to.*

While there is acknowledgement of power, concomitantly there is a downplaying of the validity of the power dynamic Jessica sees occurring in the newsroom. Her sense of blame about her subordinate role in the newsroom comes to the fore (*'but maybe that's just because I was young and a female'*) perhaps because she knows she is exposing a part of a newsroom culture that defines her role and that of the subs as explicitly gendered—something she tries to avoid.

Perhaps, too, it is not only blame, but a sense of sexual shame. Michael Warner's (1999) analysis of sexual shame and stigma is useful in providing a framework with which to understand many of the participants' experience of gender inequality and sexual harassment. Warner explores how a sense of sexual shame has been exploited by political and religious leaders as a means of reinforcing their *power* over people. For Warner (1999, p. 3) everyone feels shame about sex, but what to do with this shame? "Pin it on someone else." Some people, however, are at greater risk of embarrassment about sex than others, so therefore to shame someone about sex is a political tool, the

Bill Clinton impeachment is used as a case in point. Jessica appears shamed to the point that she does not even use the word 'sexual,' let alone 'sexual harassment' to describe what she experiences. Her phrases *'that sort of stuff,'* and *'making cracks'* and comments about [ungendered] *'people'* and having to stop being *'sensitive'* stand in for and/or let us know, that it is sexual behaviour she is describing.

The other key point Warner (1999) makes is the distinction between shame and stigma. Shame is something attached to particular acts; stigma a condemnation applied to a person because of his or her inherent nature (in particular, because of homosexuality). He argues that although the *stigma* of being gay, for example, is not so great any more, that the *shame* that people who are identified with their sexuality are forced to bear and experience continues.

Jessica's explanation of how she negotiates the power dynamics of the senior men by becoming *'less sensitive'* and *'giving it back'* or ignoring the comments describes common methods of survival for outsiders. This is an important aspect of how young women learn to survive in such a culture. Make too much of female embodiment, speak of and defend it, and you will be relegated to just a female body. Alternatively, quietly accept the sexualised banter and you accept that your biological sex gives you the inferior body of 'other'—just like the pictures the male photographers take of women on 'hot' days:

> Jessica: Often, on the subs desk, sometimes you know if you ever ventured down that way and you went to talk to someone and you know there's the bikini model from three weeks ago up on someone's desk, and you think 'was it taken to put in the paper, or was it taken so you guys can keep them?' which I found a bit inappropriate. I thought that was wrong for them to keep them for their own personal satisfaction. I mean if you want to keep it, keep it at home, but don't take photos for the paper that you personally want to have on a calendar in your shed or something.

Clearly, journalism is not the fairy tale career that Jessica had initially thought possible. There are fearful or possibly slightly sarcastic overtones in her language (*'if you ever ventured down that way'*) that remind me of the normally innocuous nursery rhyme, *Teddy Bear's Picnic*. In that rhyme—"If you go down to the woods today, you're sure of a big surprise"—the surprise is a hopeful one, yet Jessica's trip to the 'woods' is far from a surprise. She knows what is in store. Perhaps as the rhyme continues, if she went in disguise (perhaps as a man) she would have a rather different experience.

Jessica's following quote describes how newsroom culture is internalised and embodied. It's a method she has learned in less than two years in the industry:

> Jessica: You pick up on the way how everyone else acts around people or you watch situations and so when you are in one like that you act a similar way.

There are a lot of unspoken rules of the newsroom. Probably ones you can't even put into words, but just things that happen that everyone accepts.

She understands that the male-dominated subbing desk and the all-male photographic team creates an atmosphere of sexual innuendo, sexual humour, and power. The men tease the younger women and/or make regular comments about personal appearance. However, because it happens so often, this has become less shocking for her—reinforcing a part of 'insiderism' (discussed in a previous chapter) that accepts a newsroom culture that reinforces male hegemony.

Although the majority of these excerpts seem devoid of hope for the future careers of the women I have talked with, I am reluctant to imply that there is no hope. There are small pockets of resistance that demonstrate that female journalists do indeed challenge and confront sexually harassing behaviour. This is how Jessica resisted being confined:

> *Jessica: The only time that everyone saw anything that worked in reverse, was there was a picture of Shane Watson [Australian cricketer] from a nude calendar, holding a strategically placed bat, and all the women in the office had blown them up and stuck them up on the wall, and I think that kind of raised a few eyebrows.*
>
> *LN: Was that in response to some of the men who would keep the page 3 girls that would be in the paper on their desks?*
>
> *Jessica: Yes.*

It may not be the liberal use of a grievance procedure—or an overtly feminist discourse—that is appealing to women in this newsroom, but some have indeed found ways to resist and play with sexuality in a way that is pleasurable for them and perhaps simultaneously reminds sexually harassing male journalists of their oppressive behaviour.

"You're Just a 'Pussy Pumper' "—the Embodied Lesbian and Sexual Harassment

Referring overtly to a woman's 'alternative' sexuality is another method of undermining professionalism. This is discussed by Susan (below), and it is evident that sexual harassment is a male intervention for the assertion of power. It comes as an early warning to a woman not to step out of her 'proper' place. This type of open and concerted attack is, as Cockburn (1991, p. 42) suggests, aimed at diminishing any sense of power a woman in the workplace may be acquiring and "to remind her 'you're only a woman, that's the way I see you. And at that level you're vulnerable to me and any man.' " It's what Patricia

Yancey Martin would term a 'gendering episode' (1996, p. 187), an enactment of
'competitive masculinity' (see Collinson & Hearn, 1994; and Kerfoot & Knights,
1993). Yancey Martin uses the term 'gendering episode' to describe a verbal
attack that she had overheard, during which she observed that gender played
a significant part in the accusations being made by a senior male university
colleague to another male colleague about a senior female colleague. She recalls
the comments as graphic, rude, and hostile. Moreover, gender is the theme she
identifies as central to the interaction; hence a 'gendering episode.'

Susan describes harassment that involved her sexuality being raised as
a method of undermining her senior role in the newsroom. She recalls that
the editor constantly joked about her sexuality ('I actually thought he must have
been some sort of giant homophobe, because he just started to pay me out, you
know, and it was joking, it was always joking'). Then the final cutting comment.
Susan's editor reminded her of her 'proper place' when he chastised her via
her sexuality in front of her younger colleagues. The incident took place at a
work social event where alcohol was being consumed:

> Susan: It's embarrassing to say it, but [the comment] was along the line of 'what
> would you know, you're just a pussy pumper?' It was in front of a group of
> young journos who were my colleagues.

Is Susan embarrassed to tell me because it makes obvious her lesbianism to me,
and if so is she fearful about exposing this to an industry colleague, or revealing
it to a relative stranger? Or was it because her sexuality was positioned outside
the norm and her professionalism devalued by the slight on her sexuality? And
what of the significance she places on this comment being made in front of a
group of younger journalists? This discussion occurred towards the end of our
two-hour face-to-face interview during which Susan's sexuality had already been
made clear. That the editor used a derogative comment to his senior journalist
in front of a group of younger colleagues suggests that issues of power are at
the centre of the comment. The experience of exclusion diminishes the power,
or potential power, of the receiver. This type of crude sexualised comment is
designed to alienate a senior woman in two ways; to reinforce the male editor's
powerful position and the power he has over the younger colleagues in which
he made the comment and thus set him up as having more authority than
Susan; and second, by drawing attention to Susan's (homo)sexuality reinforces
her as embodied not only as 'other'—as a female body in a predominantly male
authority position, but that of a lesbian body—a body presumably that he can
never have, but possibly one that he can fantasise about, and certainly one that
he can make comment on. There is, too, a success in the creation of Susan as a
sexually embarrassed/shamed subject that finds resonance with Warner's (1999)
thesis. The stigma and shame that Warner (1999) explores is experienced by

Susan in the memory of one comment. It was an 'event' more than 10 years previous that she has kept within the confines of one group of female colleagues on whose behalf she made the later claim of harassment against the editor. It seems an experience that could only be understood by those who had shared a similar history. For Susan there was a fine line between being viewed as a trouble-maker in the industry and upholding her journalistic reputation.

Conclusion

What then does this say about the culture of journalism when men rarely mention sexual harassment and women do, even when not asked specifically? Is there a silence about the constitutive affects of sexual harassment in creating 'a journalist' in journalists' occupational culture that the women I speak to break? (Although having said this, I am wary about the trope of 'breaking the silence.') Michel Foucault (1979), for example, is interested in the way sexuality has come to be seen as a fixed aspect of identity—as something that tells us the truth about who we are. He warns us that confession, and any claim to 'reveal the truth,' has productive effects—instating the speaker in the discourse of truth that is spoken. For example, women may be avoiding becoming 'victims of sexual harassment' by avoiding talk about sexual harassment, especially when they have few discursive resources to draw on that will not position them as victims. As I have noted, there is banter about sexual harassment that occurs in the newsroom, and written policy about it. For example, News Limited recently updated its Standards of Business Conduct brochure (News Corporation, 2004, p. 9) to note the 'special problems of sexual harassment.' The interview material, however, suggests that sexual harassment can be discussed in some contexts, but not in others (for example, do not complain about it).

Sexually harassing behaviour as a (repeated) practice creates gendered journalists: in its male initiated challenge/assault; in how it makes women feel; in how they respond; and in how they are understood by others. I have discussed how harassment is used by some interviewees in exclusionary terms, but it also has productive effects in the constitution of men and women journalists. Weiss's (1999) notion of 'embodiment as intercorporeality' is important in understanding the constitutive effects of sexual harassment. If, as Weiss (1999) suggests, we can only come to know and understand our bodies through encounters with others, then as the female interviewees make clear, their encounters are constant reminders of how their bodies do not 'fit' and/or where and how they do fit in this occupation. These encounters, however, happen between already culturally mediated bodies constituted through a range of gendered discourses that distribute humour, judgment, shamability, care, and compliance unevenly. When female journalists enter the industry, sexually harassing behaviour is just one of the many ways in which they are excluded, marginalised, and in some cases become outsiders. When male journalists enter the industry, engaging in sexually harassing behaviour of women is one of the many ways in which some occupy the privileged position of an insider. But women do survive and indeed succeed even in the face of it. Butler's (1997) equally important assertion that gender is "put on, invariably under constraint, daily and incessantly, with anxiety and pleasure" (1997, p. 415) is a reminder of the invariable pressure that male and female journalists find themselves under, especially in regard to available subject positions in the workplace. Three of the available subject positions for those who are the objects of sexually harassing behaviour are to accept the liberal narrative of sexual harassment and to use the grievance procedure, to deny that it exists, or to resist (or challenge) the behaviour and risk becoming an outsider. I'm not suggesting that sexuality doesn't belong in the workplace, as Rosemary Pringle (1988) makes clear in her study of secretaries. But which kind of sexuality comes to dominate? As I have argued here, the privileged discourse is often male-dominated heterosexuality. It will take a quantitative leap at many levels for women to be *subjects* of sexuality rather than *objects* of sexuality in the newsroom.

It is important to note that in probing questions of gender inequity, I do not want to suggest that all men are sexual harassers and that women are only the victims. As Ring (1994, p. 134) rightly points out, such an argument "casts women as passive, devoid of agency, and posits gender relations as an immovable, unchanging bind." It is sufficient to note that much has been written about women's compliance and participation in the very systems that oppress them.

In this chapter I have reflected on how sexually harassing behaviour is remembered and told in interviews, how feminist discourses, government legislation, and company policies about 'sexual harassment' have great costs, or at best, limited benefits for female journalists, because the term itself has been captured by liberalism and antifeminism to mean things that minimise and mock its original challenging potential. This is not to say that legislation is not useful, because it is, at the very least, a 'rational' reminder that sexual harassment is unacceptable and unlawful. My analysis of the interviews has shown that sexually harassing behaviour is a defining part of the occupational culture of journalism. But the use of the term 'sexual harassment,' or its lack of use, also tells us other things about the place of feminism and/or feminist-inspired government legislation in journalism's occupational culture.

My research indicates that women are less inclined to take up the discourse of sexual harassment because it will be used against them. In this way, feminism and sexual harassment become linked. Female journalists in my interviews are fearful of the repercussions of the term sexual harassment because of its link to feminism and the socially constructed negative discourse that emerged

from the public debate sparked by the Garner case (although none specifically mention Garner). Far from the euphoria of the mid-70s when naming
'sexual harassment' promised women freedom from it, it now taints them and
ties them to devalued subject positions. If women identify and name sexual
harassment, they fear they will be labelled as whinging feminists, or victims,
or unable to accept 'normal' gender relations. 'Sexual harassment,' then, is a
discursive object that feminists identify, but which the majority of women in
newsrooms—especially younger women—do not. What then is the usefulness
of feminist discourse in newsrooms, when women (as well as men, which we
might expect) refuse to take up one of feminism's key discursive resources for
analysis and action in the workplace?

Intersubjective relations that could be called 'sexual harassment' in
some discursive contexts get embodied journalistically as other things. Some
of the themes that arise in the interview excerpts regarding sexually harassing
behaviour include: denial; projecting complaints of sexual harassment on to
a feminist other in the newsroom; the ethicalisation of making a complaint;
exclusion—sexually harassing behaviour reflects on the recipients, not the perpetrator; shame—'learning to live with it'; the liberal narrative (for example,
Susan believes in progress, Jessica believes in rationality); a public/private divide
that works for men, but not for women; leaving the industry.

In some interviews, particularly with younger women (Jessica, for example),
there is an acceptance that sexually harassing behaviour is part of the workplace
that they need to *learn* how to negotiate. Sexual harassment is thus normalised,
rather than viewed as an indication of "criminal, antisocial pathology" (Ring,
1994, pp. 131–132).

Irrespective of the difficulties, women are determined to be 'journalists.'
Maybe the reason that female journalists don't find feminist discourses of 'sexual
harassment' helpful is because of the contradiction between all the available subject
positions for those subjected to sexually harassing behaviour and 'journalist.' So
denying sexually harassing behaviour and avoiding the use of the term 'sexual
harassment' might be what is required to be a journalist—for a woman. Simon
says that '*no one could safely confidently say there are being harassed.*' He is right.
Women cannot 'safely' complain, and certainly not with confidence.

The interviewees use, and we need to theorise, more complex strategies
to survive. Hopefully these strategies may, in the future, promote a more robust
challenge to gendered power relations, but in the meantime, women's use of
available discursive reasoning must be commended for its survival-promoting
capacity. In some cases women should also be questioned about their complicity
with and therefore reproduction of oppressive normative gender relations.

Chapter Five

Global Industry Change and Its Gendered Implications in the Newsroom

Our profession has changed dramatically. The boundaries have changed—things we are prepared to do now in Australia as journalists. I mean I look at the Code of Ethics and I think that's a joke. Love the concept, doesn't happen, wish it did, but it doesn't. We bend rules all the time because at the end of the day if the competitor's got what you haven't got, that's what matters. (Susan)

The world media industry had undergone dramatic changes during the past 30 years, the period commonly described by the term 'globalisation.' In that time, at a structural level, new technologies have emerged that change the way that 'news' is produced, delivered, consumed, and understood. Desktop computers, the Internet, mobile phones, satellite television, and video recorders have shaped a new era of journalism (Carter & Steiner, 2004, p. 4) and consequently a new era for newspaper journalists. The increased speed in which news is found and then transmitted to television screens has impacted on newspaper content and also on the output of newspaper journalists. News gathering and producing practices have intensified. As Susan's excerpt indicates, there is an increased pressure to have the same news as the competitor, but because so much news can reach television audiences before it can reach newspaper readers, there is also pressure on newspaper journalists to source different angles to major news stories, provide a more in-depth analysis of the news stories shown on television the night before, or find 'exclusive' news to sustain reader interest. The interviews conducted for this research indicate that newspaper reporters are under increased workplace pressure and are increasingly cynical about their profession. There are a number of reasons for this, not the least being shrinking resources and, in particular, the declining number of journalists employed in the industry, which is part of changing global news practices. In the nonstop news cycle reporters have less time to investigate, and this encourages a reliance on official sources (often government media spokespeople) that can provide the information quickly. The downside is that journalists then have to spend more time (or not) wading through the 'spin.'

Anecdotal evidence, the interviews I've conducted, newspaper reports, and statistics from public reports from a range of newspaper organisations lodged with the Equal Opportunity for Women in the Workplace Agency[1] (EOWA) point to the acute reduction in permanent newspaper staff in Australia.[2] For example, it was reported in 2005 (Day & Lehmann, 2005, p. 15) that John Fairfax Holdings Ltd, which publishes The Sydney Morning Herald and The Age, had called for up to 65 voluntary editorial redundancies that would help save the company up to $10 million a year.[3] In August 2008, Fairfax Media (which changed its name from John Fairfax Holdings in January 2007) announced that it would cut 550 jobs in Australia and New Zealand. It was reported that the company CEO David Kirk said that about 180 journalists were likely to be made redundant (www.news.com.au/business/story/0,27753,24242979-462,00. html). Redundancies in the Australian media are not limited to newspapers. In November 2005 the Nine Television Network was reported to have called for voluntary redundancies before it was necessary to undertake forced redundancies (Meade, 2005a, p. 3). The EOWA reports also indicate an overall reduction of staff working for newspapers, including journalists.[4] In 1998 Davies Bros Ltd, a News Limited subsidiary that publishes the metropolitan daily The Mercury in Hobart, employed 432 staff. That number decreased slowly until 2004, when it had 398 staff (Davies Bros Ltd, 2003, p. 2; 2004, p. 2). It appears that its journalistic workforce has remained steady during that time, but it is not possible to accurately confirm this because the staff categories the company uses in its reports have changed during this period. By 2006 staff numbers had risen to 410 (Davies Bros, 2006, p. 2). It is not possible to analyse its journalistic workforce because it no longer uses a category that clearly defines its editorial staff in its report. In West Australia, West Australian Newspapers Ltd, which publishes the West Australian in Perth, saw its total workforce fall by 97 between 2000 and

---

[1]The reports, which list total workforce numbers including editorial, production, advertising, and ancillary staff, can be found at www.eowa.gov.au (accessed September 2, 2005).

[2]Casual employment as a journalist remains steady, according to the EOWA reports accessed.

[3]This is while the outgoing CEO, Fred Hilmer, received a retirement package of $4.5m on his departure in November 2005 (Catalano & Porter, 2005, p. B1).

[4]I draw upon these four newspapers because they are the most specific in their report detail and the most accessible in terms of finding the names of the business, which are not listed under newspaper titles. For example, the News Ltd owned The Mercury, and its subsidiary newspapers in Tasmania are listed as 'Davies Bros Ltd,' and this name would only be known to those who work in the industry in the state. NSW and Victoria, for example, have variously owned newspaper groups and are listed under names that do not make clear it is a media group, which makes finding specific newspaper reports, among thousands of other businesses, extremely difficult.

2001 (West Australian Newspapers, 2002, p. 2). Its 2004 report is staggering in its staff reduction, noting that the overall staff numbers had dropped by 216 (total 1,567) in one year, even though two new companies were added to the group, which included an extra 111 staff. Its journalistic workforce shrank by 49 between 2002 and 2004—or around 12 percent (from 373 to 329) (West Australian Newspapers, 2004, p. 2). In its 2005 report its journalistic workforce remained stable at 328, even though its overall workforce numbers had risen to 1,672 (a new company had joined the group, which accounts for an extra 34 positions) (West Australian Newspapers, 2006, p. 2). At Queensland Newspapers (a News Limited subsidiary that publishes *The Courier-Mail* in Brisbane) total staff numbers have slowly decreased. In 2001 it reported a total staff of 1,400; in 2002, 1,300; and in 2003, 1,293. By 2006 the total workforce had been reduced to 1,139. Its editorial staff numbers decreased by 78 between 2001 and 2006—or 17.7 percent (from 439 to 361). (Queensland Newspapers Pty Ltd, 2001, p. 1; 2003. p. 1; 2006, p. 1). At the *Northern Territory News* in Darwin total workforce numbers dropped from 275 in 2001 to 246 in 2004 (Nationwide News Ltd, NT Division, 2002, p. 1; 2004, p. 1). Its editorial workforce has dropped from 54 in 2002, to 50 in 2006. This is the case even though its overall workplace numbers had risen in 2006 to 264 (Nationwide News Ltd, NT Division, 2006, p. 2).

Alongside this overall reduction in the total number of journalists working for newspaper organisations in Australia, women have entered the industry in unprecedented numbers. Women's entry into the profession has been one of the most significant changes in the industry, and this has been extensively discussed in the Introduction. The increase of women working in the media has been labelled the 'feminisation of the media' (Limor & Lavie, 2002). Yet this term also refers to a changed ideology or philosophy of what is presented as news. Many have noted, and some lamented, the increased use of 'soft' news stories (entertainment, human interest, and lifestyle) as opposed to 'hard' news stories such as politics and business, and its concomitant negative effects on democracy. This global shift in media content has been variously linked to corporate concentration, conglomeration, and hypercommercialism (for example, McChesney, 1999, p. 15), processes that are inextricably a part of the globalisation process.

The majority of news media scholars assert that among the most influential impacts on global news media practices and what I am interested in here—its impact on journalists and newsroom practices—is the concentration of media ownership (for example see Byerly, 1998; McChesney, 2001; McChesney & Scott, 2003; Manne, 2005a, 2005b; Quesada Tiongson, 1999; Rantanen, 2005). The shrinking ownership of media outlets worldwide into the hands of even fewer (white, Western) men, and specifically, the increasing monopoly of newspaper ownership in Australia, where News Limited owns 70 percent of the mainstream print media (Manne, 2005b, p. 2), not only puts issues about news content into a new context, but impacts on the career prospects of its workers, reducing the variety of job opportunities and making it difficult in Australia for those who do not fit the News Limited philosophy. The concentration of ownership and technological advances have aided in reducing the number of newspaper journalists, which has added to the intensification of work practices, a process that has occurred across the labour force in general. As Australian sociologist Timothy Marjoribanks (2000, p. 8) argues in his assessment of technological changes in the media, "the local workplace is a crucial area of investigation when the impact of globalisation on workplace reorganisation is being considered."

Recent academic critiques of the concentration of media ownership have considered the phenomenon largely through a gender-neutral lens (Byerly, 2004b, p. 245), making it difficult to see how both female journalists and female readers and male journalists and male readers may have experienced the situation differently. The situation is the same in the literature on changing media technologies. Marjoribanks' (2000) book, an exploration of technological changes and workplace reorganisation in newspapers owned by News Corporation, is a pertinent example of this failure to see gender as crucial to research about changing media technologies. With the development and use of new technologies, issues around gender access and participation need to be considered (Carter & Steiner, 2004).

The concept of 'globalisation' and its inherent connection with the media industry has enjoyed renewed currency in scholarly debate in the past decade. I say renewed because globalisation is far from a new concept in academic scholarship. Marshall McLuhan was one of the earliest globalisation theorists with his idiom 'the medium is the message' linked to his idea of the 'global village' (McLuhan & Fiore, 1967). British media and globalisation scholar Terhi Rantanen (2005), who has a long relationship with this area of study, suggests that since McLuhan's linkage between globalisation and media was established, there has been much acknowledgement of the words, but few have taken up the study. Fewer still have concerned themselves with how gender is implicated in the globalisation of media.

I argue that gender is a deeply entrenched but seemingly invisible aspect of the global changes in journalism. This chapter is concerned with how the changing nature and structure of the media industry, through globalisation, impacts on the newsroom and specifically, the gendered nature of the newsroom. To do this, I explore how the industry is changing on a global level. I ask what are the implications of the growing phenomena of media conglomerates that place media ownership into the hands of just a powerful few? How does this concentration of media ownership play out with the global expansion of one of the most influential distributors of news, News Corporation, especially as it relates to its stranglehold on Australian newspapers? What are the debates, themes, and propositions that arise from global changes? In particular, I want to know how the media and globalisation literature understands the gendered nature of change in the media? What are the gendering effects of this global march? Who benefits from media globalisation among those working in the industry? What specifically is the effect of globalisation on Australian newsrooms? The following two chapters are linked to this discussion. In Chapter Six I turn to the interviews I have conducted to explore personal narratives of change and resistance and then in Chapter Seven I consider global change through three important Australian legal cases that reveal a contested media culture in a much more public context.

Backgrounding Globalisation and Media Research

Rantanen (2005, p. 1) posits that globalisation and media have been connected via three separate fields of study: communications studies, media and cultural studies, and globalisation studies, all of which have been narrowed by an Anglo-American concentration of researchers. Communications studies as a discipline began in the United States after World War II, and communication studies theorists have preferred the term 'international communication' rather than 'global media.' The war highlighted the important role that media and communications played as a consequence of rapidly developing electronic communications (McQuail, 2000; Mowlana, 1997; Rantanen, 2005). Rantanen (2005) plots the course of the study of global media and finds that initially, international communication studies understood the media as shaping people's behaviour and attitudes through propaganda, but then, as a subfield of communications studies, it became primarily interested in institutions. For Rantanen (2005, pp. 2–3), this meant that 'people' (or audiences) were left out of research that engaged with how emerging globalisation of media and communications played a pivotal role in consumer's experience.

British media studies have similarly concentrated mainly on the role of media institutions in the process of globalisation, again emphasising communications structures rather than individual experience. Rantanen (2005) claims that unlike media studies, cultural studies concentrated on the broader issues of culture instead of media. She refers to Australian journalism and globalisation scholar Jan Servaes and Dutch globalisation and communication scholar Rico Lie, who observe that "cultural studies cannot be seen as either media or audience-centred, but instead tends to consider the whole process of communication as a cultural process" (Servaes & Lie, 2000, p. 314).

Studies on 'globalisation' emerged in the early 1990s, mainly in sociology and geography (see for example Giddens, 1990; and Robertson, 1990). According to Rantanen (2005), it was not media and communications scholars who started or actively contributed to the debate. Consequently, she claims that the role of media and communications in globalisation theories remains vague and unspecified, and 'media studies' "missed the 'big picture' of globalisation and have been contributing little to theoretical discussions on globalisation" (Rantanen, 2005, p. 4). Feminist media scholars and feminist organisations with an interest in media have only recently begun to explore the idea of globalisation, and in so doing make gender a central concern; for example, Carolyn Byerly (1998, 2004b) and Isis International's[5] Mari Luz Quesada Tiongson (1999).

As is evident, a singular definition of globalisation has been impossible. The term 'globalisation' generally refers to the global economy that has come about since the early 1980s (Byerly, 1998). As Byerly explains it:

> The process has meant a decrease in the importance of national borders, the integration of economies into a single capitalist world-system, a single division of labour, the location of production sites for labour-intensive processes in the developing nations, the privatisation of many publicly held functions and enterprises, and a concentration of ownership among transnational corporations. (1998, p. 4)

Underlying this perspective is the notion that globalisation manifests mainly though economic institutions such as banks and consumer markets, but globalisation "has also deeply involved and affected communication systems on many levels" (Byerly, 1998, p. 4). At the same time, globalisation has been made possible by these very communications systems. Most theorists agree that there is no globalisation without media and communications, as many of the definitions of globalisation acknowledge, at least indirectly (Rantanen, 2005, p. 4).

Well-known British sociologist Anthony Giddens (1990) defines globalisation "as the intensification of world-wide social relations, which link distant localities in such a way that local happenings are shaped by events occurring many miles away and vice versa" (1990, p. 64). Another influential theorist of the same era, John Thompson (1995), suggests that "globalisation . . . refers to the growing interconnectedness of different parts of the world, a process which gives rise to complex forms of interactions and interdependency" (1995, p. 149). Both these approaches define globalisation without specifying the consequences of it as homogenisation or heterogenisation. The question of consequences remains open, although Martin Albrow's (1990) definition implies homogenisation: "Globalisation refers to all the processes by which the peoples of the world are incorporated into a single world society, global society" (1990, p. 45).

---

[5] Isis International was formed in 1974 and is a feminist nongovernment information and communication organisation. Quesada Tiongson writes for the organisation's Asia Pacific group in Manila (www.isiswomen.org)

Rantanen (2005), reflecting on these various positions, argues that they fail to adequately and specifically acknowledge that globalisation is a mediated process—one that takes place increasingly through media and communications. She posits that "globalisation is a process in which worldwide economic, political, cultural and social relations have become increasingly mediated across time and space" (2005, p. 8). As a result of globalisation there are shifts in the nature of social relationships. But does this mean that close, intimate (genuine) relationships are being replaced by new, mass-mediated (not as real) experiences? For Rantanen, the starting point for an exploration of globalisation is the acknowledgement of media and communications in the process. It's not the only contributor to globalisation, "but it would be too simple to think that media just connect (as mobile phone companies advertise); rather they mediate, which is a much more complex process that involves individuals and their activities and practices" (Rantanen, 2005, p. 11).

Australian scholar Barbara Creed has an optimistic view about the effects of the globalisation of various media, especially the virtual media of the late twentieth and early twenty-first centuries (the Internet, email, websites, virtual reality, cable and satellite television). Focussing on audience reception, Creed (2003) argues that these new media forms are distinct from older formats such as television, film, radio, newspapers, and popular fiction because they eliminate the distance, or the gap, between the user and the medium. From this shift has emerged a new way of thinking about the self "through the metaphor of the global self" (Creed, 2003, p. 3). Like the various new media she studies in her collection of essays, the global self is fluid, hybrid, mobile, and interactive. "The global self morphs across boundaries into unknown spaces" (Creed, 2003, p. 3). Creed does not suggest that the boundaries have actually collapsed, but rather that:

> The traditional media, while seeking to undermine boundaries, are simultaneously always in the process of drawing new ones, new philosophical and moral borders beyond which one should not push or penetrate just yet. The virtual media, however, offer the possibility of traversing boundaries altogether. (Creed, 2003, p. 4)

This new global self is in interaction with the media and, in its quest to explore unknown territory and make new discoveries, there is a blurring of the boundaries between public and private, reality and fantasy. The mass media, Creed argues, has eroded the boundaries that traditionally separate the private and public spheres, the public arena becoming more feminised via these changes. Historically the public sphere has been defined as a male domain where the worlds of business, politics, law, and commerce take place, separate from the private, domestic sphere of home, family, sexuality, women, and children. Creed suggests that before the advent of television in the 1950s, the media did not report on personal matters such as family, relationships, health, housework, divorce, abuse, and addiction—"the very topics which have become central to contemporary media—from the evening news to TV sitcoms" (Creed, 2003, p. 5). The media has thus aided in creating a more feminised public arena. Consequently the key question for Creed is not what the media *do* *to* the individual, but what the individual *does with* the media (Creed, 2003, p. 8). So the global self is not a passive recipient of the mass media, but rather an active participant in encounters with it. "There is not one 'true' or fixed interpretation or point of view, but many interpretations" (Creed, 2003, p. 8). For Creed, the new media is able to easily communicate around the world, and the new global self is able to experience life from the viewpoint of others. Creed makes this point even though she describes the media's reporting of world crises, for example, as neither neutral nor impartial: "The media are participants, pathfinders whose own perceptions of an event . . . are susceptible to bias and distortion" (2003, p. 10). If we were to wholly take up Creed's position on the effects of globalisation on the media, then it follows that we would have to maintain the notion that the new global self would rise above notions of distortion or bias and be able to interact with, or at the least understand and accept, the bias. In this way Creed's understanding of the 'global self' begs the question about the global selves who not only consume the media but also who *produce* the media.

The ongoing processes of globalisation have long been argued around the opposing paradigms of the homogenisation or heterogenisation of outcomes. Oliver Boyd-Barrett (1977), for example, has been influential in the field since the mid-1970s and he has presented the cultural imperialism perspective on a globalised media. He observes that the media are possibly the most influential single component of cultural imperialism (1977, pp. 118–119)—a pre-'globalisation' theory. American media scholar and media commentator Robert W. McChesney (2001) also argues that global media systems are dominated by Western, particularly American, perspectives because of media concentration and the current neoliberal climate, which will be discussed later in the chapter. In this approach the global media has a homogenising effect on cultures, but the faults of this theory were soon highlighted by many media and cultural studies scholars (Rantanen, 2005, p. 78). Boyd-Barrett (1998) switched his imperialism theory in 1998, acknowledging that his original thesis was wrong on several points and, most importantly, that there needed to be an account of the multidimensional aspect of media activity. These included that the perspective did not take account of the question of audience; it identified the United States as the single centre of a process of media-centric capitalist influence and assumed that these programs had "an inevitable and self-sufficient ideological effect upon their helpless audiences on the periphery" (Rantanen, 2005,

p. 79). Later, 1990s theorists of culture, media, and globalisation saw outcomes other than homogenisation as globalisation's main consequence. They started using concepts such as 'heterogenisation,' 'hybridisation,' and 'fuzziness' (the basis of Creed's perspective). For example, Jan Nederveen Pieterse (1995, p. 49) and William Rowe and Vivian Schelling (1991, p. 231) understood globalisation as hybridisation. Significantly, they saw audiences as active and able to resist the power of the global media.

The heterogenisation school of thought has also been criticised. Rantanen (2005, p. 94) notes that the criticism has been mainly directed at the power it gives to audiences, its neglect of the economic resources and power of global media companies, neglect of the fact that the biggest media companies are located in the United States (most recently News Corporation's move to the US reinforces this point), and its neglect of inequality of access of members of the audience to media and communication. McChesney (2001) has been a vocal critic of the heterogenisation approach, making the point that 'convergence' and 'consolidation' are the order of the day in media ownership. "Specific media industries are becoming more and more concentrated, and the dominant players in each media industry increasingly are subsidiaries of huge global media conglomerates" (McChesney, 2001, p. 3). He maintains the homogenising thesis that the global media system plays an explicit role in generating a "passive, depoliticised populace that prefers personal consumption to social understanding and activity, a mass more likely to take orders than make waves" (McChesney, 1999, p. 113). He notes that in the past 30 years media and communications have become a much more significant sector for business activity (McChesney, 1999).

The traditional response that the commercial media system has provided to account for the lack of competition "has been the idea that its journalism would be subject to the control of trained professional journalists who would be neutral and non partisan" (McChesney, 2001, p. 11). But McChesney (2001, p. 11) maintains this point has always been a flawed construct, "because power remains in the hands of the owners, and what little professional prerogative existed to go against the political and commercial interests of owners has diminished in the past decade." This point about writing a newspaper's (or owner's) news agenda is discussed by interviewees and analysed throughout various chapters in the book. McChesney's argument is persuasive, but as Rantanen (2005) suggests, we need to understand that the effects of globalisation in relation to media audience and media ownership are both homogenisation and heterogenisation and that neither is mutually exclusive as consequences of globalisation.

Rantanen's definition is the one that I take up here because it neither claims a homogenising or heterogenising effect. Her position asserts neither that global media companies are all-powerful evil empires that only harm national cultures (an oppressive bogeyman that dumbs down cultures perspective), nor does it seek to present the audience with as much power as the media corporations. These discussions about media and globalisation don't explore the media workforce; rather the focus is on consumers, not producers, of media. Therefore I expand on that definition to acknowledge that the globalisation of media has different, multifarious, and complex effects and outcomes for the *producers*. There is no specific research on what globalisation means for the media producers, but we can find useful information in the general literature that backgrounds some of my later discussions in Chapters Six and Seven.

The Global Media Worldview—Concentration of Ownership

Media concentration is not a new concept, either globally or in the United States, where four of the five huge multinational media corporations are based today (Time Warner, Disney, Viacom [formerly CBS], and News Corporation). Sean Siochru and Bruce Girard (2002, p. 29) note that in the late nineteenth century the global market for news was controlled by a media cartel established by three European news agencies that had agreed in writing which markets each would control. In the United States, chain ownership of newspapers started by 1900, and according to Benjamin Compaine and Douglas Gomery (2000, p. 7, 46) cross-media ownership was common by the 1940s. However, government regulations about media ownership in the United States prevented monopoly ownership until the 1980s when, characteristic of globalisation, an era of deregulation created a period of "rapid concentration of ownership in US-based business and industries of all kinds" (Byerly, 2004b, p. 247). In his seminal book *The Media Monopoly*, published in 1983, Ben Bagdikian chronicled how some 50 media conglomerates dominated the entire U.S. mass media—including newspapers, television, radio, books, recorded music, films, and magazines. The revised 1997 edition notes that the dominant firms numbered just 10 (cited in McChesney, 1999, p. 19). In the 2004 edition, Bagdikian finds that there are just five huge corporations: Time Warner, Disney, News Corporation, Bertelsmann (Germany), and Viacom.

Today, News Corporation is the largest and most dominant force in the newspaper world, publishing 176 newspapers in Australia, the United Kingdom, Fiji, Papua New Guinea, and the United States. Newspapers have been the centre of the development and globalisation of News Corporation (Marjoribanks, 2000, p. 95). In August 2007 News Corporation owner Rupert Murdoch crowned almost 50 years of empire building when he bought the American media company Dow Jones for almost $A5.6 billion. Its stable includes the influential *Wall Street Journal* (www.news.bbc.co.uk/1/hi/business/6923474.stm). In the late 1950s Murdoch's empire began with the purchase of Adelaide's afternoon newspaper, *The News* (Marjoribanks, 2000). The company later expanded into Perth, Sydney, and Brisbane and then nationally through the broadsheet *The Australian*. In 1986, it became the dominant newspaper company in Australia when it purchased the newspapers of the rival Herald and Weekly Times group. Internationally, News Corporation became influential when it bought the British tabloid *News of the World* and then *The Sun* in the 1960s. It then entered the U.S. market and continues today to make inroads into other countries (Marjoribanks, 2000). Before buying the Dow Jones News Corporation, News Corporation employed about 15,000 people worldwide in its printing of more than 40 million papers a week (www.newscorp.com/operations/newspapers.html). It also owns Australian television interests, FOXTEL and Fox Sports Australia, and the U.S.–based Fox Broadcasting Company, British Sky Broadcasting, book publishers HarperCollins, and film studio 20th Century Fox.

In 2005 News Corporation expanded its global cross-media ownership, buying the Internet group, Intermix Media Inc. (Murray, 2005, p. 25) and later the growing online property business realestate.com.au (www.ketupa.net/murdoch.htm).

Some of News Corporation's major newspaper mastheads include: in the United States, the *Wall Street Journal*, and the *New York Post*; and in the United Kingdom, *The Times*. In Australia, the list includes *The Australian* and metropolitan dailies in every capital city of every state (except Western Australia, where it owns weekly metropolitan *The Sunday Times*.) Its suburban catalogue includes a total of 78 titles nationally.

From 2000 to 2005 News Corporation's annual revenue from its massive stable of newspapers worldwide and other media ownership had almost quadrupled. In 2005 it had amassed US$55 billion in assets, and annual revenue had grown to US$24 billion. By 2007 its total assets had risen to US$62 billion and annual revenue to US$28 billion (www.newscorp.com.investor). By April 2004, some 75 percent of revenue was attributable to operations in the United States (www.ketupa.net/murdoch.htm),[6] so it was no surprise, then, that News Corporation announced plans to shift its corporate headquarters from Australia to the United States.

It's a common conclusion that News Corporation is influential and powerful, if only arrived at simply by adding the number of newspaper titles it owns. Yet it is not only a question of numbers: Rupert Murdoch and his top managers also clearly determine editorial content in his major metropolitan news publications. Australian academic and influential media commentator Robert Manne (2005c) establishes this point when he finds that *The Mercury*

---

[6]The Ketupa website is part of an Australian Internet research, analysis, and strategies consultancy business, Caslon Analytics (www.caslon.com.au). Ketupa.net provides a resource that provides statistics and research about media industries and the information economy.

newspaper, which in 2002 initially took a negative stance on the then possible U.S. invasion of Iraq, switched its position to one of support after receiving one letter from 'head office' (Manne, 2005c, p. 76). Australian scholar David McKnight (2003) also furthers this point in his study of Murdoch's flagship, *The Australian*. He argues that the political views of Murdoch strongly determine the outlook and ideological stance of the newspaper (McKnight, 2003, p. 356). This occurs through Murdoch espousing certain political views publicly and making those views known to his editors and senior staff (McKnight, 2003, p. 356). Quoted by the BBC News website in 2007, former editor of the News Corporation–owned British newspaper the *Sunday Times*, Andrew Neil, said that Murdoch selected like-minded editors who "broadly share" his worldview. "But when there is something he [Murdoch] feels strongly about or when some of his business interests are at stake, he leaves you in no doubt what he wants you to do" (www.news.bbc.co.uk). McKnight finds that through his stable of newspapers, and specifically *The Australian*, Murdoch "helped forge a neo-liberal consensus" (2003, p. 347) from the late 1970s, both within conservative political circles and within the Australian public. In terms of political power, it is also recognised that the support of Murdoch-owned newspapers has been crucial to the success of a range of political leaders worldwide. Marjoribanks (2000, p. 96) maintains this is evident in the British tabloid, *The Sun's*, support of Prime Minister Margaret Thatcher in Britain from the late 1970s until 1990, and the *New York Post's* endorsement of Ed Koch, the mayor of New York City between 1977 and 1989. Manne (2005c) also clearly demonstrates that Murdoch-owned newspapers in Australia support a John Howard–led Liberal Government. Murdoch's hands-on approach is evident in an early 1990s interview in which he comments on the challenge of striking a balance between allowing editors to operate independently and taking responsibility himself (Coleridge, 1993, cited in Marjoribanks, 2000, p. 97). Murdoch claims that he allows executives at the local level to deal with day-to-day problems, although he will intervene in a 'crisis situation.' An example of a 'crisis situation,' then, as my earlier discussion indicates, must be when some editors choose not to follow the Federal Government's line on the Iraq war.

Fairfax Media is News Corporation's main rival in Australia in terms of newspaper ownership, but its titles are mainly confined to the Australian states of NSW and Victoria, and, internationally, New Zealand, and include a majority of less-influential community newspapers (48 titles in Australia). Key mastheads include *The Sydney Morning Herald, The Age,* and *The Australian Financial Review*. In 2003 Fairfax acquired most of the publishing interests of New Zealand's Independent Newspapers Ltd. This added 84 newspaper and magazine titles to Fairfax's operations (www.fairfaxnz.co.nz/ publications/index. html). In 2005 it extended its ownership in New Zealand with a $10 million acquisition of three more mastheads in the Rodney district north of Auckland. It also bought the dating website RSVP.com. In 2006 Fairfax purchased the New Zealand auctions and classified advertising website Trade Me for A$625 million. In 2007 its merger with Rural Press Limited added, among others, the *Canberra Times* and rural masthead *The Land* to its stable. It also announced a joint $1.35 billion acquisition of Southern Cross Broadcasting (www.ketupa. net). Although Fairfax has branched into internet and broadcasting media it has far less cross-media ownership, and therefore global news setting power, than News Corporation

Australian Provincial Newspapers (APN) is another major newspaper owner in the country. It is Australasia's largest operator in regional newspapers, (23 daily and about 100 non-daily regional newspapers in Australian and New Zealand) and sustains a presence in specialist and educational publishing radio broadcasting and outdoor advertising, with interests in pay television and digital media. APN's largest shareholder is Dublin-based Independent News & Media PLC (INM). APN and INM encompass more than 200 newspaper and magazine titles (www.ketupa.net/apn.htm and www.apn.com.au/aboutus.asp).

It is not possible to conclude if there is the same level of owner interference in newspaper content at Fairfax and APN as there is at News Limited. Much has been written, both in popular and scholarly publications, about Rupert Murdoch, his family, his business, and his influence, but little is known or written about other CEOs' influence. In 2005 after Fairfax's new chief executive, former All Blacks rugby union captain David Kirk, took up his post there were newspaper stories published about his appointment. They, however, were mostly focussed on his planned axing of 60 to 70 editorial staff at the company's major newspapers *The Age* and the *Sydney Morning Herald*. Interestingly, Kirk was quoted by *The Australian* (Meade, 2005b, p. 18) as saying, "a lot of factors determine the quality of newspapers. The number of journalists is not one of them."

Although it is not possible to definitively argue that different owners or boards of newspaper organisations impact on the newsroom culture and gender structure of the organisation, I do speculate about this in my analysis of the interviews. As has been noted in this book, there is difficulty not only in obtaining statistics on men's and women's participation in the mass media (see for example Christmas, 1997; Dougary, 1994; and Gallagher, 1995), but as the EOWA reports demonstrate, the statistics that are provided by media companies are ad hoc, making gendered or international comparisons, or clearly detailing vertical segregation, very difficult. It could, however, be stated that numerical gender differences exist between male and female journalists employed in metropolitan and regional newspapers. Anecdotally, it is known within the industry in Australia that regional newspapers are where less senior and less experienced journalists are often predominantly located.[7] Regional newspaper journalists are also paid at a significantly lower rate than their metropolitan peers. In terms of gender breakdown, EOWA reports demonstrate that the proportion of female journalists compared to male journalists working in regional Australian newspapers is higher than in metropolitan newspapers. For example, the major regional newspaper group in South Australia, Messenger Newspapers, shows that 62 percent of its journalists are women (Messenger Press Pty Ltd, 2005, p. 3); at Queensland group Quest Community Newspapers 45 percent of its journalists are women (Quest Community Newspapers, 2005, p. 2). The Leader Newspaper group in Victoria does not have a category for 'journalists,' but shows the total percentage of women working in senior management and management is 47 percent and 44 percent respectively (Leader Associated Newspapers Pty Ltd, 2004, p. 2).

Neoliberal Industrial Style and Organisation

News Limited has been at the forefront in offering Australian Workplace Agreements (AWAs) to its senior staff. The MEAA notes (2004, p. 10) that News Limited has made extensive use of AWAs—individual contracts that are formalised and registered under federal legislation in place since 1997, and that are regulated and promoted by the recently created Howard initiative, the Office of the Employment Advocate (OEA).[8] These agreements complement a neoliberal ideology. The agreements are allegedly about individuals and management privately negotiating higher than award pay rates. The agreements, however, commonly include that requests for overtime be part of the overall pay package and restrictions on involvement in strike action. The OEA lists the type of AWAs employees may be offered and highlights the benefits of negotiated annual leave provisions, annualised salaries, family friendly working arrangements/hours, and training that takes into account the introduction of "a

---

[7]Delano (2003, pp. 278–279) clearly establishes in his analysis of research conducted in Britain that women are proportionately underrepresented in 'high prestige' national daily newspapers. The highest female proportion was located in 'low prestige' independent television and radio, and Sunday newspapers. Regional newspaper categories are not included in his research.

[8]In November 2007 a Labor Federal Government was elected and has since disbanded the office. In March 2008 the government banned new AWAs when the *Workplace Relations Act 1996* was amended by the *Workplace Relations Amendment (Transition to Forward with Fairness) Act 2008*. The Act provides for a new no-disadvantage test and was a central plank of the Labor government's election campaign. I have retained the information in this section relevant to the previous government because it demonstrates how neoliberal ideas were perpetuated in the workplace at the time. This is not to suggest that those ideas do not still surface, but rather that it is too early to analyse.

career structure and a rostering arrangement which will give employees diversified work experience and on-the-job training" (OEA, n.p). The government's push to simplify pay arrangements in a bid to water down the use of unions in pay negotiations is evident in its positively glowing assessment of AWAs. Its philosophy is underpinned by this sentiment:

> An AWA may be used to replace complicated award pay arrangements for ordinary hours of work, shift work, overtime and penalty rates into a regular rate of pay which applies throughout the year. Annualised salaries benefit the business by reducing the need for administrative work in calculating employee's entitlements each pay period. They may also benefit employees by allowing them to receive a regular and predictable rate of pay regardless of the shifts and overtime they may work from week to week. (OEA, n.p.)

Some of the options available to employees who take up AWAs include allowing a cash-out of part of their annual leave, and cashing out annual leave loading at an increased rate of pay. These set of provisions are based on a philosophy and workplace culture that accepts and expects increased intensification of work practices.

The Federal Government argues that its workplace relations reforms are aimed at creating a single national industrial relations system, simplifying workplace agreement-making processes and balancing unfair dismissal laws (Dodson, Banham, & O'Malley, 2005, p. 1). Under the changes, workers can choose to be covered by an award or an AWA. Here again we encounter the neoliberal philosophy of individual choice. The reforms note that employment contracts and agreements have to meet only four basic minimum standards: on annual leave; personal leave; parental leave; and working hours. However, in 2007 public and union concern drove more changes to AWAs. The federal government introduced a Fairness Test that would, "guarantee that protected award conditions such as penalty rates and public holidays pay are not traded off without fair compensation" (OEA, n.p). Still, the powers of the Australian Industrial Relations Commission remain curbed under the reforms. There are now tougher penalties for unlawful strikes and industrial action, and new rules restricting the right of union officials to enter workplaces (Robinson, 2005, p. 3). During 2005, the International Federation of Journalists (IFJ), the world's largest journalists' group, protested the Australian Government's industrial relations reforms that were enshrined in law in December 2005.

The IFJ's concern was focussed on the proliferation of individual agreements within media organisations. It argued that AWAs would "reduce morale within the media industry and compromise the atmosphere of professionalism on which independent journalism thrives" (IFJ, n.p). The IFJ argued that the planned rules would push more workers on to individual contracts, and workers who did not wish to sign such contracts would be intimidated through fear of dismissal. AWAs had to include comparable pay and conditions to the union-negotiated agreements.

Many have argued that organisations with a prevalence of workers on AWAs are a more compliant workforce, 'compliant' because the workers have no union support and it is up to individuals to negotiate pay rises and address workplace concerns and conditions with employers. Australian researchers David Peetz and Georgina Murray (2005) examine how neoliberal economic ideas associated with work, promoting anti-unionisation and individualisation manifest at the micro level of practice and resistance in the firm. They maintain that there has been a growing use of 'individualisation' strategies by some large employers in the past two decades. These 'individualisation' or 'anti-unionisation' strategies aim to reduce the influence of unions so that they are not recognised for bargaining purposes. The use of such strategies has been particularly evident in Australia, New Zealand, and the United Kingdom (Brown et al., 1998; Dannin, 1997; Gilson & Wagar, 1996; McCallum, 1996; Morehead et al., 1997; Oxenbridge, 1999; Waring, 1999; Wooden, 2000).

Work Intensification in the Australian Media

Industrial changes, technological changes, and media concentration all lead to an intensification of work practices in the industry. It is difficult, however, to ascertain the intensification of work practices in journalism because there has been no specific academic research that I am aware of that addresses this issue. An increasing number of journalists and former journalists do provide anecdotal evidence in books and essays about this intensification. A former journalist and now part-owner of alternative Australian Internet news website Crikey.com.au, Eric Beecher (2005, p. 9) argues that in the past 10 years there has been an increasing and constant pressure on editorial departments to create efficiencies and do more with less. Although Beecher's essay centrally laments the loss of so-called 'serious journalism,' which stands in for the 'feminisation of news' and is arguably another effect of globalisation—he makes the point that work intensification is brought about by massive changes at many levels in the media industry. Beecher asserts that changes in media ownership, commercialisation, and technology are some of trends that have a cumulative effect on the media landscape in Australia. "As the commercial vice tightens on well-funded, high-grade journalism, media owners are responding with measures designed to maintain their profitability" (Beecher, 2005, p. 9). The result, he argues, is fewer editorial resources, lower budgets, fewer reporters and editors, fewer foreign bureaus, and more syndicated content—in all, an intensification of journalism practices. Similarly, in an interview with freelance journalist and author Margaret Simons, Australian Broadcasting Commission (ABC) veteran reporter Kerry O'Brien notes a compromise in news coverage and a decline in quality due to a lack of resources. Simons notes that the ABC-TV current affairs program *The 7.30 Report,* formerly produced separately in each of Australia's states and territories, has lost a third of its editorial staff since it turned national in 1996 (Simons, 2005, p. 124). Little, however, is discussed about the ensuing pressure on those journalists left at the coal face. Australian media researcher John Henningham (1998, p. 98) reports on a telephone survey of more than 1000 news journalists (newspaper, TV and radio) in 1992 and 1994 in all regions of Australia and found that two thirds described the level of stress they experienced at work as high or very high and that nearly 70 per cent believed that stress levels were increasing—and that was more than 10 years ago. Although Henningham's research does not detail the gender differences in relation to stress, he does consider some aspects of the gendering effects of the occupation. He found that men were more satisfied with their jobs than women and suggested that this may be the case because "most women journalists believe that a gender bias exists in Australian newsrooms" (Henningham, 1998, p. 98). In answer to the question 'Do you think it is more difficult for capable women journalists to get ahead in their careers (in comparison to capable men journalists)?' 72 percent of women said 'yes.' Male perceptions were vastly different, with only 39 percent answering 'yes' to the question. He also argues that because women, as a core group, are relative newcomers to the industry this is why they are far less likely to occupy executive or managerial positions (Henningham 1998, p. 95). He does not link the surveyed women's concerns of gender bias in the newsroom to the reason why just "3 per cent of women occupy the position of newspaper editor or deputy editor" (1998, p. 95).

Intensification in journalism work practices also occurs due to company policies. For example, from December 2000, News Corporation adopted a freeze on hiring staff (noted in Queensland Newspapers Pty Ltd, 2003, p. 3) that lasted for about two years. Under the policy, if a staff member resigned, no one was hired to replace that worker. Also, in its 2005 report West Australian Newspapers Ltd (2006, p. 2) noted that many vacancies were not filled, rather the "tasks were reorganised."

The Gendering Effects of Work Intensification

The widespread emergence of work intensification in general has been illustrated in large-scale government surveys (see ABS, 1998; Morehead et al., 1997), and academic researchers have also begun to study and problematise work intensification. Barbara Pocock (2003) suggests that not only has there been an increase in hours worked in Australian workplaces but that there has been an accompanying increased intensity. As early as 1995 an Australian Workplace Industrial Relations Survey found that 59 percent of employees said that their work effort had increased during the past 12 months, 50 percent said that stress was higher, and 46 percent said the pace of work was faster (Morehead et al., 1997, p. 274, in Pocock, 2003). Increasing evidence of intensification is found in studies across a range of industries. A pertinent example is nursing, where workers have challenged increased workloads and dramatically reduced staff levels (Allen, O'Donnell, & Peetz, 1999; Considine & Buchanan, 2000). Teachers and finance sector workers have also experienced similar workplace issues (Probert, Ewer, & Whiting, 2000). Intensification takes different forms in different industries. Pocock notes, for example, that teachers' class sizes are larger, paramedics have a greater proportion of more acute cases in their workload, and: "Public sector workers describe work design that minimises staff 'until the system screams.' People in these work situations are 'managed' to high levels of stress, and they in turn 'manage' by working harder and working long hours" (Pocock, 2003, p. 23).

This intensification of work creates a 'work/life collision,' the title of Pocock's book, which is "a moving vehicle of change in work patterns and in family structures, meeting a solid wall of relatively unchanged labour market institutions, culture and practice" (Pocock, 2003, p. 2). It is an economy of care that underpins an economy of production and consumption. "Conventional categories of labour and economic analysis, which treat paid work as separate from home, life and the care that essentially underpins work, is hopelessly inadequate to the task of understanding the whole" (Pocock, 2003, p. 15).

Governments are implicated in this 'collision.' Journalist and well-known feminist author Anne Summers cites conservative Australian government policies[9] as working to put women back in the home—and in this sense she addresses concerns about the gendered nature of government policy and how they impact on women in work. "Since the late 1990s the government has made ruthless use of childcare, employment, family assistance and taxation policy to steer women with children out of the workforce and into full-time motherhood" (Summers, 2003, p. 8).

Both Summers (2003) and Pocock (2003) discuss the link between declining fertility rates and a labour market culture that still naturalises and legitimises the ideal worker as male. Summers (2003, p. 8) argues that the push to reverse the falling fertility rates makes it difficult for women to have jobs and have children. Furthermore, Pocock suggests that the rigidity of work patterns, domestic workloads, and social and cultural beliefs contribute to the falling birth rate.

---

[9]Summers is referring here to the 11-year reign of the John Howard-led conservative Liberal government. The Liberal government was defeated in November 2007 making way for Kevin Rudd's Labor Party.

If women believe that they must have their working lives on track before they have children, or see that the current terms of parenting will overload them, they delay birth and reduce the desired size of their family. (2003, p. 5)[10]

According to Pocock this uneven development lies in the Australian work/care regime and its gendered system, with the male breadwinner at the centre of the paid workforce and carers at home—and sometimes paid allowances to be there.

A male-dominated employing class, eager to minimise labour costs, governments willing to subsidise motherhood by means of allowances to mothers-at-home but opposed to recognition of them as workers, and a union movement dominated by men and their preoccupations, all contributed to an industrial regime that saw a three month break after ten years' work (long service leave) and annual leave bonuses, as more important than a paid break for workers who have just had a baby. (Pocock, 2003, p. 212)[11]

And even the remnants of government instruments that were set up to ameliorate women's disadvantage are getting less effective. The notion of equality is a central tenet in a Liberal feminist position on women in paid work. Margaret Thornton (2001), in critiquing the simple notion of equality, argues that the neoliberal political climate has changed the meaning of equality. Legislation in place to 'protect' women from inequality—Affirmative Action (AA) and EEO—has been weakened by "minimalist interpretations currently in vogue in official discourses" (Thornton, 2001, p. 78), and this maximises profit and business ease.

Associated with work intensification, are concerns that unions are less influential in the workplace. There is a newsroom—and public—myth that union membership in the Australian media is falling. Yet the Media, Entertainment and Arts Alliance's 2003–04 annual report details that union membership in its 'media' section has progressively risen from 7,480 in 2002 to 7,558 in 2003 and 7,971 in 2004 (MEAA, 2004, p. 17). The Alliance's 2005–06 report shows that 'media' section membership continues to rise. At the end of June 2006 it

---

[10]Australia led the world on the eight-hour day in the mid-1800s and pioneered long service leave; however, two-thirds of Australian women still await paid maternity leave more than 80 years after the ILO adopted its first maternity leave convention (Pocock, 2003, p. 212).

[11]On September 29, 2008, the Productivity Commission recommended the Labor federal government pay new mothers and fathers 18 weeks' parental leave. It has recommended that the government adopt a taxpayer-funded leave scheme which would pay the primary care giver at the minimum wage rate, currently $544 a week. (www.news.theage.com.au/national/commission-proposes-18-week-parent-leave-20080929-4ptp.html)

had 8,420 financial members (MEAA, 2006, p. 18). Although these figures do not provide details on gender makeup (or News Limited/Fairfax membership) fewer women, than men, are union members. Although this is most likely because there are fewer women than men in the industry and because women are more likely to be in part-time and casual positions, Margaret Gallagher (1981, p. 94) notes that women journalists worldwide have had a poor record of active union membership. In Britain in the mid-1990s, women lagged well behind men in joining the National Union of Journalists. In 1994, 83 percent of NUJ members from national newspapers were men (Delano, 2003, p. 280). News Corporation–owned newspapers are the least unionised in Australia. In a 1996 survey of Australian journalists, the MEAA found that respondents from Fairfax newspapers, as opposed to News Limited newspapers, were more likely to be union members (MEAA and IFJ, 1996, p. 42). The fact that there is a public myth that union membership in all occupations is falling is linked, I suggest, to neoliberal strategies and philosophies that work to undermine union cohesion.

Technology and Changes in Journalistic Practices

I want to suggest in the following section that changed journalism practices have different outcomes for male and female journalists. Technology, its use, or implications for the industry, was not mentioned by the interviewees; however, I had not set questions around this theme. Yet, because interviewees don't use the words or phrases 'globalisation,' 'media consolidation,' or 'technological change' doesn't mean that their lives, their work as journalists, their reflections on and experience of change in the industry are not products of, and comments on, globalisation. For example, the interviewees' discussions of the feminisation of news can tell us a lot about the gendered impact of globalisation.

In print news journalism, changes in technology, for example, have affected male and female journalists differently as a result of where men and women are located in the editorial department. Yet, journalism studies in Australia have so far failed to seriously consider and analyse how gender is implicated in these changes. Marjoribanks (2000), for example, does not mention gender in his book about the introduction of technologies in the newspaper industry, which specifically examines technological innovation and workplace restructuring carried out by News Corporation in its newspaper holdings in Australia, Britain, and the United States. Given that feminist scholars have long critiqued the profoundly gendered character of technology, it is remiss that gender is not considered one of the powerful forces shaping technology.

Statistics are almost impossible to gain about the gendered breakdown of the sub-editing sections in Australian newspapers, as I've already stated; however, it is common industry knowledge that technology-heavy role of sub-editing is a male-dominated area. (Photography is another male-dominated editorial task that requires high-level technical skills not only in digital photography, but also in computer skills that enable photographers to download and manipulate images). All interviewees agree that sub-editing is a job dominated by senior male journalists and that the general reporting roles are most often the domain of female journalists.[12] For example, Sally describes the sub-editing desk at the metropolitan newspaper where she has worked for 10 years:

> Sally: We have got two bosses. We have the chief-of-staff and then we've got our editor. The chief-of-staff hires women, and our editor hires men. There's only two girls on the subs desk now, so we are getting pushed out. Every time a chick leaves she gets replaced with a man. I don't know if that's deliberate, but it's a little unnerving after a while.

This anecdotal evidence is supported by the journalists' union. Reporter Sally Jackson found that *The West Australian* daily newspaper employed 45 male sub-editors in the most senior grades (over Grade 8)[13] and two women (Jackson, 2003a, p. 3). My own count at *The Mercury* and *Sunday Tasmanian* newspapers in Hobart shows that in 2002 it employed 31 full-time male sub-editors compared to three full-time female sub-editors. Sub-editing is where the most senior journalists are usually located and where story choices, layout, and headline decisions are made. It is an area in which massive technological changes have affected production processes. What then can we understand about technology and gender in the newsroom?

Twenty years ago sub-editors worked with 'hard copy' from reporters (carbon-copied typed pages). Subs penned a complex series of learned marks indicating changes, deletions, or rewrites. Typesetters would type the hard copies into the system, and compositors would receive the text on sticky paper and make up 'dummy' pages for a check-sub to approve. This system has given way to the introduction of full editorial pagination, which was identified as the "biggest advance in newspaper production since hot metal gave way to the first typesetters" (Mitchell, 1997, p. 2). Electronic pagination allows for an entire news page, comprising text, graphics, pictures, and advertisements to be created on a computer screen ("Language . . .," 1996, p. 2, cited in Marjoribanks, 2000, p. 139).

Technology plays a major part in the intensification of sub-editing practice. Today subs are required to be fast and accurate not only with reading and correcting copy but to have the computer skills to lay out and design pages. The

---

[12]Specific rounds such as politics, sports, and police reporting, however, are acknowledged as 'male.'

[13]See Appendix 2 for list of journalist grading levels.

most senior subs are those who can both design and lay out pages and copy sub. As a result of the technological changes in the past 20–25 years—(the *Adelaide Advertiser* was the last Australian [metropolitan][14] News Corporation newspaper to introduce full pagination in 1997 [Marjoribanks, 2000, p. 139])—staff have been retrained and there have been critical issues over job demarcation, pay rates, and employment levels.

Technology, however, also recreates or intensifies gendered structural and cultural distinctions. Early feminist research on technology highlighted this with research on the gendered implications of the introduction of word processors into the office (Wajcman, 1991), and later research about computers and women's access to the Internet (Spender, 1995). In journalism the gendered structural distinctions are evident in the role of sub-editing, which is highly valued and generally more highly paid than reporting jobs. Sub-editors' job description has dramatically changed over the years due to technological changes. All subs are trained in copy subbing on computers, and each newspaper has various software systems in place that need to be learnt. Fewer subs are trained as layout and design subs, due, in part, to the difficulty and time it takes to learn and remember the skills. It is also because there are fewer jobs for layout subs and, as such, the jobs are more highly prized, as it involves a degree of autonomy and decision making not available to copy subs. Layout subs, for example, often decide if a story gets published and always where stories are placed on a page, including if a story will lead a page and how much space is allocated for the story, and often what headline is attributed to it. They also often decide what picture will accompany a story—which involves learning how to access international, national, and local pictorial files. They have the final say on the overall look and content of the page. Subs use more sophisticated technology and have more decision making control than reporters, yet subs are also more removed from the people the news is about. They do not meet the people the story has been written about. At metropolitan daily newspapers, the major decisions about what story will lead a page and pictures, however, are always based on a twice-daily editorial conference with section editors (predominately male), in which the editor confirms preferences from the available story list and makes suggestions for story ideas that should be followed up.

On the other hand, reporters' job descriptions, in terms of technological knowledge and skill in relation to sub-editors, have changed little. Reporters use the computer as little more than an advanced typewriter, except that now each has access to the Internet in order to search for information about a story they may be writing or researching. Often the Internet is a fast and convenient way to provide background information to a story, check facts

---

[14]The South Australian-based Messenger Newspapers was among News Limited's last group to introduce full pagination in 2006.

or spellings of names and places, and check other news sources for breaking stories. Newspaper reporters often check radio websites or alternative Internet media for news. Another example of reporters' Internet use may include accessing government departments, which often list press releases on a website, almost making the newspaper office fax redundant. Reporters also use digital technology to record interviews.

Sub-editors are also privileged by their access to information. Subs have fewer restrictions than reporters on accessing computer files established by the newspaper's editorial management. For example, at *The Mercury* sub-editors have access to most editorial files including a group reporters file, picture files, emailed media release files, and stories filed in advance for future sections, not only for the newspaper they are working on but for associated company publications. The reporters have access to the group reporters file and their own personal file in which they can store their upcoming stories.

The technological changes to production have coincided with the period of women's increased entry into the profession. As women have entered and been accorded a place, that place has been downgraded. This is a common observation across occupations and is noted, for example, by Rosemary Pringle in her study of the medical profession (1998, p. 4). The technological changes in journalism sit on top of an existing occupational hierarchy and add new layers and gendered meaning. Male journalists, who dominate numerically in sub-editing positions, have benefited from technological changes. Female reporters dish up the dinner (the copy) and the subs decide if it's good enough to consume.

Changing News Content: The Feminisation of the News?

Monika Djerf-Pierre and Monica Lofgren-Nilsson (2001) posit that in most Western countries the increasing number of women in journalism has run parallel to significant changes in how news is defined. Tabloidisation, feminisation, infotainment, commercialisation, and popularisation are concepts frequently used to describe the style of news journalism. In my experience, when these terms are used by journalists they are rarely in a positive frame. This process of feminisation is generally considered a 'dumbing down' of the industry, based on a privileging of hard news as being rooted in a masculine ethic of what news really is. Djerf-Pierre and Lofgren-Nilsson (2001, p. 1), whose study focusses on television news production in Sweden, suggest that the changes in news content, specifically the increase in human interest, 'soft'-style news, is frequently described in gendered terms. They suggest that 'female journalism' is associated with personal engagement, empathy for the subject, and a wish to cater to the audience, whereas 'male journalism' is more concerned with distancing, neutrality, and being the impartial observer and being detached from the audience. Liesbet van Zoonen (1998b, p. 35) also argues that news and journalism is becoming more 'feminine' because of the proliferation of human interest topics and angles, despite the ongoing minority position of women in journalism. But rather than just simply ask the age-old question about whether an increase in female journalists would change the type of news produced, she turns the argument around to show "how changes in the news genre allow for more female journalists to enter the profession" (1998b, p. 35).

Female journalists, in Djerf-Pierre and Lofgren-Nilsson's study, attempt to distance themselves from 'soft' news stories. So how do journalists, male and female, experience this? They don't want to be associated with their female-ness, and why would they? Australian television journalist Virginia Haussegger (2005) in her autobiographical account of some of the traps of being a female journalist makes it very clear that she wanted to stay well clear of 'colour' or soft stories. She had made complaints to her senior editor:

> The men on the program were being assigned all the best stories—the overseas trips and the war jobs—while the women were stuck with the 'colour' stories. I was told to shut up and pull my head in. So off I went on yet another soft story, only to return hours later to find a present in my office. It was a very large, long, thick black rubber penis, sitting upright on my desk. (Haussegger, 2005, p. 49)

How would she handle such a situation? Victim or victor, she asks herself. She walked in to her boss's office with the penis on her head and says "Well, look at this, I've got one too! So now do I get the overseas assignment?" She got the overseas assignment—to Hawaii to cover the Supermodel of the World competition (2005, p. 49). As an aside, the fact that Haussegger's senior editor had ready access to such an object at such short notice suggests that he had one in his office for just such an occasion.

One of the female interviewees describes why and how softer stories are constantly allocated to women in her newsroom. As well, she makes transparent apparent discrepancies in workloads at her newspaper:

> *Christine: We have all male editors and they like relating to their women as women, not relating to them as workers, right. So that instantly sets up discrepancies where you find that the boys in the newsroom get the better jobs, police reporting and politics, and the girls go out and interview Noni Hazlehurst [presenter of a popular lifestyle television show] when she comes to town about the TV show.*
>
> *LN: So those political stories are considered better news and therefore those people get promotions more quickly and easily?*
>
> *Christine: Well, they are seen as more challenging areas of journalism. The girls can write ten stories a day about the soft stuff, but the men can just work on*

*one or two stories in the hard news areas because they're more challenging, a
bit more difficult, they give those jobs to the boys.*

Mark, 55, has been in the industry for 38 years and is one of two interviewees who longs for yesteryear and tells a nostalgic story about when news was
'serious' (read 'not feminised') and *he* was taken seriously. Now the newspapers
are filled with lifestyle stories and frivolous content that works to reassign his
ideas to a back page.

> *Mark: It's about advertising. If you were to ask me what has changed in the time
> that I have been in newspapers . . . we have changed newspapers from being an
> organ to provide you with information, to newspapers that actually provide you
> that information, but packaged around in such a way that it's either entertainment
> and lifestyle or whatever it has to be. That's what attracts the advertisers because
> they think they can actually sell things to people. So, say they're a [metropolitan]
> paper like [newspaper name] which has a circulation which can only be described
> as miniscule in the scheme of things, it survives quite profitably, whereas if we
> were doing it the same was as we were 25 years ago, it would have gone out
> of business. So, I mean, there are plusses and minuses.*

> *LN: Is it frustrating to you?*

> *Mark: Very much so, because basically and indeed for many, many years I used
> to do op eds [opinion editorials] which allowed me to get ideas. You can't do them
> now because there's not that requirement to have a couple of large pages filled
> by somebody's ideas, because we're actually doing lifestyles, so the serious issues
> aren't there. And indeed this particular gig that I'm doing now, I've reserved
> part of the paper that nobody wants, which is on a Saturday, which is at the
> back of the classified ads, to write about resources and energy. Nobody wants
> to do that because it's not an area of great impact. But people who read me
> know that's where they are going to find me, you see.*

Mark's perspective is an interesting account of the feminisation of news. Mark
does not suggest that the feminisation of news is inherently bad, but rather his
concern is underpinned by his loss of masculine authority and the emasculating
effects of the move to a lifestyle focus on news. Mark's concern concludes with
an account of how he (the man of ideas) still has his followers—who read
'*me*'—not, for example, 'what I write' or 'my ideas.' This is indicative of his
personal investment in the notion of the 'man of ideas journalist.'

Jessica, a young regional reporter, is frustrated by being located around
'soft' news stories. She doesn't suggest gendered inequality when she is asked
to do menial reporting tasks, but clearly she finds it belittling:

> *LN: What's the most frustrating thing about being a journalist?*

> *Jessica: The Mickey Mouse jobs you have to do.*

LN: And how do you describe those jobs?

Jessica: On Saturday for example, I had to go out on a boat up the [name of river] with six St. Kilda [Australian Football League] players, who were just filling in some time. Do you know what I mean? They weren't there to do that, they were here for something else, but because obviously someone had rung up and gone 'oh, look you know, there's a great chance for some pics, you want to bring a reporter along, go on this boat?.'

But is the news genre changing because of the increasing number of women in the industry, or is the industry more aware of market forces then ever before because of the changing and increasing avenues available to people to access news? Media ownership and cross-pollination—or 'convergence'—affect news content. Convergence is becoming a global trend as media companies continue to expand their holdings beyond their original core products (Singer, 2004). 'Convergence' in its current media context refers to some combination of technologies, products, staff, and geography among the previously distinct areas of print, television, and online media (Singer, 2004). Journalists no longer work for a newspaper, or a television station, rather they work for an information company. The crossover of media interests by media owners changes news content (and journalistic practice) and, I suggest, adds to the trend of more 'feminised infotainment' news. This is evident in Rupert Murdoch–owned newspapers. News Corporation owns Twentieth Century Fox Film Studio, and films from the studio are heavily promoted in the News Ltd stable of newspapers. News Limited now has an increasing interest and reason to promote softer, entertainment-type stories, because its owner is directly and indirectly demanding cross-coverage.

As I have shown in the introduction, there are more women working in the newspaper industry than ever before, and there has been a strong case put that the news is increasingly 'feminised' and that women are prominent in opening up these channels. Soft news stories may be increasingly published and sought by newspapers editors and owners, but this form of 'news' certainly isn't valued as highly as 'hard' new stories. This is evidenced in journalistic awards. In 2005 News Limited established its own yearly awards ceremony, allocating a total of $65,000[15] (category winners win $5,000 each and the overall winner $15,000) to reward outstanding company journalists from newspapers, magazines, and news websites from Australia and the South Pacific (News Limited Corporate Affairs, 2005, p. 1). So important were the awards that Rupert Murdoch attended the inaugural ceremony in Adelaide. Of the 12 awards allocated to journalists, 11 went to individual male journalists, and a team of four (which included two women) won the online journalists of the year. No individual

---

[15]Rising to $100,000 in 2006.

female News Limited journalist who worked in those specified media owned by Rupert Murdoch (70 percent of the Australian print media) was recognised for outstanding journalism in any category. Two of those categories included 'feature journalist of the year' and 'young journalist of the year,' areas where women traditionally feature prominently in newspapers and magazines. Of the 14 individual category winners in the 2007 News Limited awards, just one was a woman—the prestigious 'Sir Keith Murdoch award for journalism.' The 'feature writer of the year' and 'young journalist of the year' categories were again won by men (www.newsawards.com.au/07-winners.html). The news may be more 'feminised' than ever before, but 'soft' news still doesn't bring the financial rewards or peer accolades that 'hard' news does.

The following excerpt from Stuart reinforces the point that 'hard' news is more valued than 'soft' (it also is about 'being a journalist').

> Stuart: There is that pressure to get the news. You don't feel like a journalist until you've had a couple of front pages under your belt.
>
> LN: Although the human interest ones seem to mean a lot to you.
>
> Stuart: Yeah, they do, which always makes me question about what I am doing, because there's either news or, because you can be in the media without having to be in the news, and I think, sometimes I question how good a journalist I can be if I'm still mainly focussed on human interest rather than news, which is all part of adaptation I think.

Conclusion

Global news practices have changed in the past 30 years. More women work in the news media then ever before, there has been a dramatic and increasing concentration of media ownership, and technological advances have changed the way that news is produced, practiced, and consumed. There are a decreasing number of journalists employed by media organisations, and they work with fewer resources than ever before. This intensification of work practices in the media is a process that has occurred across the labour force in general. In Australia, News Limited's stranglehold on newspapers—owning 70 percent of the mainstream press—not only places issues about news content into a new context, but reduces job opportunities if complaints are made about news production practices or gendered pay inequality, and at the same time makes for a more compliant workforce. This more compliant workforce is, in part, created by a neoliberal climate: a neoliberal climate that is underpinned by an increased drive for profits creates employees who work more intensively. This is evidenced by sweeping industrial relations reforms in Australia in late 2005 whereby the Federal Government has, among other things, encouraged workplace agreements (AWAs) that effectively disempower unions and place the focus on individual bargaining rather than a collective workforce. The new Federal Government, elected in late 2007, plans to make some changes to those policies, but at the time of writing, these have not been enshrined in law.

In this chapter I have also been concerned with how this work intensity, brought on by the effects of globalisation, has affected journalists. I explored the gendering effects of the industry's changing technology, suggesting that changed journalism practices have different outcomes for male and female journalists. For example, in print news journalism, changes in technology have affected where men and women are located in the editorial department. Women are more likely to be en masse in the reporting side of the industry whereas men are more likely to be in the technology-heavy editing side of the profession. These editing roles are more highly valued and generally more highly paid than reporting jobs, and promotional opportunities are well known to come from the editing side of the profession than the reporting. This means, then, that women have less opportunity to rise to decision-making positions than men.

Another aspect of global change with a gendered dimension is the proliferation of human interest–style stories. This 'tabloidisation' or 'feminisination of the news' has occurred alongside women's increased participation in the industry. Female journalists, however, work to distance themselves from 'soft' news stories. Even though there are more colour stories in newspapers then ever before, the rewards are still not as great as producing the newspaper's 'hard news' stories. Lip service is paid by newspaper owners about the value of 'soft' stories, because when it comes to promotions and kudos the hard news is still where it is at. I showed evidence of the privileging of 'hard news' in the News Ltd in-house awards; even though the company leads the way in the tabloidisation of news, hard news writers still win the awards.

Chapter Six

Gendered Confidence/ Cynicism and the Effects of Neo-liberalism

Personal narratives of change and resistance in the industry have been a focus of this research, and here I extend the analysis of technology and the feminisation of the news debates to explore narratives of confidence and cynicism in the industry and how neoliberal discourses affect newsroom culture. How do the journalists I interview experience and speak of changes in the newsroom? In what way is being a journalist different now to when they entered the industry? In effect, how have journalists changed as a result of journalism's changes? What does it mean to become a journalist in the current context? How do journalists experience the dimensions of journalism that are specifically the result of the last 30 years of change? What are their memories and visions of personal change that arise from an intensified workplace? The interviews contain rich narratives with which to explore how participants remember and make sense of the industry changes.

One dimension of industry change that emerged from the interviews I conducted concerned the benefits of being a journalist. Discourses of cynicism about the industry or the interviewee's role in it were clearly evident. Nevertheless, discourses of power and access to influential people permeated some discussions about the benefits of being in the industry. This was a gendered difference. Some senior male journalists acknowledge an increased confidence via access to powerful men in politics. For example, Todd is a regional newspaper editor who has worked in the industry for 30 years—roughly the period of 'globalisation.' I asked him if journalism had changed him:

> Todd: Probably [it's changed me] a bit. I'm certainly a lot more confident than I would have been then [at the beginning of his career], but that's probably part of age. I've become more opinionated and brasher—that might also be age.

> LN: So you are more confident and more opinionated, that's the way that journalism has changed you?

Todd: Yeah, I think so, and that's partly because as editor I get to mix with key power players in the state and I know that if I wanted to—I don't do this, it would be awfully rare if I did—I could ring up the premier's office and ask to speak to him and I know he would either take the call or ring me back, and that's because I'm the editor of the paper, not because of me. So I do understand that there is that access to power that goes with the position.

Todd tends to naturalise his privilege to be brash and opinionated through a narrative of age, downplaying the power of his role as editor, suggesting he wouldn't take advantage of the privilege that position may provide. Yet, certainly it was his access to 'key power players' in the state government that led him to leave the industry just a few months after our interview and take up a very senior advisory role within government.

Nicolas, a senior metropolitan news editor who has been in the industry for 18 years, also makes the point that his position opens powerful political doors:

Nicolas: Oh yeah, I'm not shy anymore, but a job like I do, for instance if I meet [state deputy premier] or the [state premier] I can introduce myself as being a representative of the company, and he'll take you that a bit more seriously than if you were Joe Blow, in the street, not that Joe Blow in the street should be disrespected. I don't think [I've changed], but it just gives you that little bit of extra, you know, yeah. Do you have any more tough questions for me?

Both Todd and Nicolas present clearly gendered positions in these excerpts. For Nicolas being a *'representative of the company'* demonstrates a hierarchy of benchmark men being taken seriously by other men. He doesn't compare himself to a woman, and perhaps this is evidence also of the increasing corporatisation of the media. The other interesting aspect of this excerpt is Nicolas's query as to whether I had *'any more tough questions'* for him. This excerpt is near to the end of the interview and, perhaps he was suggesting an end to it; yet it could be that Nicolas was uncomfortable with this line of questioning because it required a personal response. Throughout the interview he was more at ease explaining how the industry worked than answering questions that asked for a personal response. This is probably not surprising, given the ideology that a journalist must remain 'objective' in all situations, and any connection to the personal must remain outside the workplace—for men at least.

Pat is a regional editor, and like Todd has worked in the industry for most of her working life. Pat's period of employment in the industry totals 39 years, also spanning the period of globalisation. So how has the industry changed her?

Pat: I think I'm a lot humbler. I know that sounds funny because people will probably see me as arrogant but I think I'm a lot—humbler. In saying that, occasionally you can feel a little bit of arrogance creeping in and you have to be very conscious of it: very, very conscious to push that aside.

Unlike Todd, who is proud of becoming more opinionated and brasher, Pat discusses change not in terms of what the job has offered her (contacts with influential people) but how she keeps in check emotions that may not be consonant with those befitting a female editor. Arrogance is behaviour to be eschewed. Moreover it may be, in Pat's opinion, that the arrogant persona of 'editor' does not fit so comfortably with a female editor.

Nicola is a 44-year-old senior metropolitan journalist who has a different response to Todd and Nicolas about how the industry has changed her:

Nicola: A little bit, yes. I think I'd probably be far less in awe of people in authority—probably more cynical. There are a lot of fakers. Until you get into this profession you don't really realise about all sorts of people, from politicians to celebrities, to celebrity cooks, to academics. You find out they're just human too. Yes, I think I'd be a little bit more cynical. I think it's probably given me a much better grasp of the world.

Unlike Todd and Nicolas, Nicola does not find power and influence through access to influential political or celebrity figures, but finds out that they are all like 'us,' human. Access to these people doesn't increase her personal or professional confidence; rather, being a journalist has demonstrated to her that they are neither special nor different. There is an overall reticence in this excerpt, one of a cynicism, and she mentions that word twice.

Simon acknowledges his increased confidence via a masculine discourse, something akin to the profession of policing or spying:

Simon: I think it's [journalism] made me much more confident. I think it has enabled—I've always been a very scattered thinker. I think the pressure of having to get things to coalesce into a story helps straighten one's mind out a bit. My interrogation skills—yeah, like I said, I'm far more direct and confident in gleaning information on things that I needed off people. You learn a few manipulative skills as well which are . . .

LN: Sorry, which skills?

Simon: You know, you learn how to manipulate people a bit, just ways of getting them to say things, or getting them to reveal things that they normally wouldn't.

Simon's idea that the pressure of working as a journalist helps 'straighten one's mind out' is an interesting example of contextualising his 'scattered' (read feminine) mind into the public and rational male realm. His use of the word 'manipulative' to describe his method of encouraging people to give information more freely is couched in terms of the feminine, although masculinised by his initial word '*interrogation*,' an action more in line with occupations such as policing, the military and spying. Simon's excerpt certainly provides an alternative approach to the value of meeting people. Simon focusses on accessing the information he needs by whatever means; it's a job, not an interactive process with the source of the story.

Susan says that her increased confidence has helped her outside the newsroom (public sphere) and locates the increased confidence in the social realm. Perhaps, however, she finds dealing with influential people in social situations more comfortable because of the increased confidence that her role as a journalist gives her. So her identity as a journalist makes her feel more confident.

> Susan: In a positive way I have become a lot more self-confident in dealing with social situations outside of the newsroom. Like I would walk up to [state premier] and not be remotely fazed. That has been a good thing. It's made me much more confident in dealing with the big wide world out there, you sort of get more brazen. It's also changed me to the extent that I have become a lot more compassionate towards people, and so much more aware of other people's worlds and that's the joy of this job.

Here Susan reiterates Todd and Nicolas, who all describe increased confidence via a reference to access to the premier.[1] Access to the premier is apparently a cliché in the discourse of journalism. It certainly is a repeated signifier of the power of the journalist. The changes, however, that Susan describes are always in relation to other people: becoming '*aware of other people's worlds*,' and '*more confident in dealing with the big wide world*.' It's a joy not evident in any of the interviews with male reporters.

The '*joy*' of the job for Susan was in the interaction with other people and is similar to how Jodie, a 45-year-old freelance journalist, describes her career in journalism.

> Jodie: I think it's given me—next to having my daughter—the most fantastic thing I could ever do in my life. I can't believe, I'm constantly amazed, at human nature, how fantastic it is. How strong. I'm constantly amazed at how lucky I am that I got a foot in the door in this wondrous career that you can take anywhere with you. The entrée into people's homes and hearts. Most people don't get that.

Jodie is singularly the most upbeat about the industry, poignant for the fact that she hasn't worked in a newsroom situation for 20 years. Jodie's comment about

---

[1]Australia's six states are each governed by a state government. The state government is led by a premier. The country's federal government is led by a prime minister.

the 'wondrous' industry that gives access not to influential politicians, but to 'people's homes and hearts,' is more in line with an autonomy that freelancing has provided her while also compensating for a lack of power, prestige, and job security that full-time work with an organisation offers.

Janet, like Susan, locates her increased confidence in the realm of the social.

> Janet: I suppose it made me less shy. I think that you can sort of work undercover (inaudible). I was a shy woman and journalism encouraged a lot of confidence and social graces. The fact that having a notebook and being a journalist got me access to a whole range of people and places that I felt more comfortable with and I really appreciated and enjoyed that. You know what I'm trying to say? That if you were going somewhere as a journalist you go with some kind of authority as well, that I would never ever have got without being a journo. Sometimes it's about education, you can go to university and find yourself a profession and build on that profession, get started and get promotions. But this [journalism] is instant, broad, fairly general and meaningless kind of thing but still quite . . . it's power. Yes, I think so; it's an access that is otherwise denied. You can marry into it—a kind of broad social acceptance, or work your way into it in certain professions, but I think one of the most obvious professions is journalism.

Her role as a journalist has allowed her access not to influential people who may have helped her career progress but rather opened up doors to people she believed she would never have otherwise had interaction with. Journalism has afforded her access to influential people in a social situation, rather than, as for Todd and Nicolas, access to influential public figures. It's clear that the outcome of being a journalist is about access to a power that Janet did not have in the private realm.

Both male and female journalists interviewed acknowledge that the profession has changed. Female journalists, however, are more likely to express this change in terms of a *professional* dilemma, but a *personal* success. On the one hand journalism has offered increased personal confidence (Susan, Janet); 'social graces' (Janet); an 'entree into people's homes and hearts' (Jodie); while also being 'humbled' (Pat); and becoming 'more compassionate towards people' (Susan)—but this appears to not fit with the professional values they are forced to embrace and display. Most find increased pressure to work long hours, many have decreased idealism and increased cynicism about their profession, and Jessica, in the job for less than two years, finds journalism 'soul-destroying.' She expresses disdain for 'dragging information' out of people, whereas male reporters are more likely, like Simon (above), to enjoy the challenge of 'manipulation' and 'interrogation' and getting people to say things they wouldn't normally. On the other hand, later in the interview Simon did acknowledge feeling jaded.

Cynicism in the Industry

Many of my interviewees discussed feelings of being 'jaded,' 'burnt out,' and 'worn out' by their jobs and/or had an overall feeling of cynicism about the industry and their role in it. Some attributed this to various aspects of the industry such as ethical dilemmas, and, for women, gender discrimination played a large part in why they felt cynical. After 10 years in the industry, 36-year-old Christine suggests women who don't play the traditional feminine gender game are disadvantaged.

> LN: *What happens to women like you then, who are putting in the hard work, who have the qualifications?*
>
> Christine: *I think we become disillusioned and leave the industry. Go and do other things, you know, go and work for the [name] Aboriginal Corporation as their media assistant, or go and work for the government, or you go and work for Greenpeace. I think that eventually they wear you out.*

Ethical dilemmas have brought about Simon's feelings of being jaded. He's worked in the industry for six years on a regional newspaper. These feelings arose after management told him not to write negative stories about advertisers:

> Simon: *I guess I'm pretty jaded about the whole thing now. It's [the notion of 'truth' and objectivity in journalism] just crap and we just look at it and go, 'Well, you know, I am but one man and it's not going to change at any time soon.' How many times can you bang on about it? There are some things that I stew about it. I really shouldn't.*

As Simon so rightly points out, he '*shouldn't*' '*stew*' over things he thinks he can't change because in the neoliberal world his main concern should be individual advancement though opportunity and choice. If he 'stews' over things he could be seen by the company as a liability. Simon's 'choice' then is restricted to one path, that of leaving.

When I asked Susan how journalism had changed her she said that the industry had made her more cynical and she felt burnt out.

> Susan: *In a not so good way it's [journalism] made me probably very cynical. I'm not able to take things on face value. I'm a little bit burnt out, it's changed me, and it's taken a lot of energy out of me.*

Cynicism is another effect of global industry change, especially for female journalists, of various ages and industry experience. Christine acknowledges being idealistic at the start of her career, only to find that constant challenges to her moral values undermined her belief in the profession.

Christine: I'm less idealistic, I'm more realistic about what you can actually change. I don't think I can change the world anymore. I think I can just make small gains, so I used to think I could make a huge impact and make a big difference, but no, not anymore.

Like Christine, Jessica's initial idealism for the industry has been eroded by actual experience. Her ideals, or assumptions, have been compromised after just two years in the world of journalism:

Jessica: I became a bit cynical [on the political round]. Everyone says you get hard and cynical but I did. I didn't see good news, I found that everything was about dragging information out of people who didn't want to give it up, and if that's all you do, it's very soul destroying. It's not happy, you don't want to go to work just to try and get things out of people who don't want to tell you anything.

Jessica: I think you can get really just worn down, you just find it so hard, you get overworked, you work some really long days and you work some really nasty shifts, and then you get some stupid jobs to do and you wonder if it is helping. Like some days I write some stories and I think 'but how has that helped anyone?' I think every story ideally has got something in it that people can take away.

Jessica's response to doing the political round and *'dragging information out of people'* and describing that process as *'soul-destroying'* is in direct contrast to Simon's earlier description of how he manipulates and interrogates people to access information that people don't want to provide. Jessica has a more feminine discourse of journalism as *'helping'* people. I wondered at the time of the interview whether she would toughen up, leave, or continue to be divided? Less than a year later, Jessica had left newspapers and was travelling overseas. Jessica's excerpt sums up the pressures of work intensification, and arguably it is a gendered response—although this is not to say that men would not share it.

For example, Stuart, who has been a cadet for a year at a regional newspaper, wants to have good relationships with those people his stories are about. He is the only male interviewee to express such concern. In so doing Stuart acknowledges that being a journalist has meant learning how to *'play the game'* and that was not consonant with the initial innocence he brought to the job:

Stuart: When I came in there wasn't a lot of—there were young people—but I definitely came in as the youngest. First year out of college, and I think I brought, yeah a little bit of naivety almost, or an innocence, to the industry and the office. It took a lot of learning, you know, how to play the game, and how to deal with the bureaucracy of small councils and that kind of thing. I don't know if I've brought a different perspective, but I've definitely had to adapt my perspective, and I would hope that I have retained something of bringing in all my skills, people skills as well. I think it is important not just having to write, but also having good relationships with the people you are writing with or about.

A few months after the interview with Stuart, he was posted by his newspaper to another city where for 18 months he was a political reporter. In 2006 he returned to the newspaper's home base to write features stories for the weekend edition. His final sentence in an email he sent me at this time, read:

Stuart: My eyes are open a bit wider to the big bad world of newspapers and I have developed a healthy cynicism towards most aspects of life as a result. (email conversation January 16, 2006)

A year after this email I learned that Stuart had taken on a new reporting position on a Sunday paper where he is able to write more human interest stories—a role that sits more comfortably with his idea of journalism.

In summary, these excerpts from the interviews identify changing perspectives on journalism—both personal and professional impacts—that can be read against a background of global industry change (for example, the increased entry of women into the workforce, simultaneously with the concentration of media ownership). I find that cynicism is experienced by both male and female interviewees, but that the female interviewees and younger male and female interviewees are more likely to express these feelings to me.

Neoliberal Discourses at Work

The senior and experienced journalists interviewed were all aware of the intensification of work production and the increased stress this caused. Some female journalists attributed this to having to work longer hours to be considered as serious about the job as a male journalist, but overall it seems the intensification of work is an accepted, if challenging, change to the industry and work in general.

Sally was a full-time sub-editor when she took maternity leave, prior to the birth of her baby. During the week she worked as a sub-editor and at the weekend she undertook the check subbing duties (proof reading of pages). When Sally returned from maternity leave three months later, the check subbing position was offered on a part-time basis. She took the job and for the next three months did a full-time job for part-time wages. After those three months, she took up the check subbing job full-time.

Sally: Before I went on maternity leave I was the check sub [full-time on weekends and a sub-editor during the week]. When I came back from maternity leave I'd heard talk about them changing the check sub shift from four to midnight to normal hours like 2.30pm to ten, so I said if they were going to do that, I would be happy to have a go, if they were happy with that, and so I just walked back into the check sub job full time. Started out [for three months] about five nights a week, five hours a night, so for 25 hours a week that's part-time, so doing a whole paper in five hours which was a bit tough, but it was good, because I had a lot of problems, I didn't have problems, but it was getting to me not having any adult conversation.

LN: So, instead of doing the amount of work you needed to do in the eight-hour shift, you were doing it, condensing it into five, because of your child care responsibilities?

Sally: Yep.

LN: That must have been really hard for you?

Sally: It was hard, but it was good, like to be back into it, and to not be at home with a child every hour.

LN: Were they paying you a full-time rate?

Sally: Yes, I was being paid my normal hourly [rate], yeah, just for 25 hours instead of 38. [Sally was not on casual rates, she was being paid the normal hourly rate of a J4 full-time journalist]

LN: But you were getting 38 hours worth of work done, in 25?

Sally: Yep, which is what you do anyway practically, you usually do about 60 hours in 38.

In this excerpt, Sally, a single mother, provides a very individualised account of her work situation. She individualises the 'problems' that led to her taking up a job that allowed her contact with other adults and a freedom from the constant responsibilities of caring for her two-year-old son, then corrects herself using a conciliatory discourse. 'It was a bit tough,' she says of doing eight hours work in five, but that she was 'happy to have a go' if her employer was happy. Sally takes this on as a personal challenge, not an exploitative situation. It's a position that occludes a discourse of exploitation, while also leaving her in control, a last-ditch stance against how much she's at the mercy of the employer. Sally does not have a discourse around gender inequality through which to understand, or frame, her situation. She considers herself the one with the problems, although she corrects herself on this, citing a need for more adult stimulation in her life, a need she considers attainable through work. During this discussion in the interview, she seems grateful that 'they' (management) allow her to hold a senior position even though she isn't able to work full time. In fact she presents as almost proud that she could do 'a whole paper' in five hours. It seems that Sally's childcare responsibilities set her apart from her mostly male colleagues and define her as explicitly gendered via her mothering. In exploring workers' self management practices through their narratives of work, Walkerdine (2004, p. 9) suggests that younger workers have a "psychological discourse" through which to understand work as "being created and related to their personalities and capacities." This is also how Sally views herself: a person with her own problems. Walkerdine suggests that a young woman, for example, can be in an exploitative work situation, but understand it through current neoliberal values in which the subject is free, autonomous, choosing, and flexible. Walkerdine (2004) uses the example of a young woman worker who doesn't complain about being phoned at 6.30 am to work a shift, because she understands it as helping her boss. Her boss is a woman in need, rather than an exploitative boss, even though the young woman works for long hours at low wages in poor conditions (Walkerdine, 2004, p. 5). There are, of course, gender-specific ways that these values are played out. Walkerdine posits that the young woman's narrative of being helpful to her boss's neediness is what allows her to stay in the job, "because in reversing the relation of exploitation she marshals helpfulness (femininity) not anger" (Walkerdine, 2004, p. 10). In my example, Sally demonstrates gratefulness towards the (male) bosses that allow her to finish an eight-hour job in five hours so she can attend to her childcare responsibilities. Although this job and its specifications that were created especially for her, and also suit the employer, put her under much more intense work patterns than her colleagues, Sally clearly experiences it as helpful to her circumstances. Sally explains this through suggesting that *she* was the one with the problems, not that her employer needed a qualified worker with her specific skills.

> Sally: *Without even thinking, without even realising I'm making that conscious decision [to put family before career] it happens because one day you go 'oh, work's really busy today,' and my kid's sick and you go, 'oh, I'm staying home with my kid.'*

It is interesting to note that Sally's change to a focus on family, rather than career, is understood as an individual choice, rather than as one aided by employment structures that do not support work/life balance. In this way, current neoliberal values get played out in her account of the decision and discussion of her choices. Perhaps these neoliberal discourses are highlighted, too, in her changed perspective on career advancement. Now her child comes before her job. Sally's excerpt also tells us about the dilemmas surrounding mothering for female journalists. The 'ideal mother' struggles with her need for personal time out, adult stimulation and employment, and her child's need for her care. Sally wants and needs the adult interaction and financial security offered by the job, even if it means she is exploited by her employers. Sally had been discussing promotional opportunities with me and how, in general, she has managed to secure regular pay rises. Now that she has a child, she appears more reluctant to ask for promotion.

> Sally: I think I'm worth more than what I get now, but also with my young son, it's hard to work nights, and if I wanted to go back to day shift, I would have to go back to reporting. There still isn't a guarantee of a five or six o'clock knock off, because if something happens, well, it's tough titties, you're out there, do your story. I'm a bit hesitant to think about going back to reporting just because I don't want that, like I can't be that flexible because of babysitters.

It's the negotiation around work and childcare that makes Sally realise the 'perfect' worker is flexible—something she thinks she is not, but has definitely been. Again it becomes Sally's personal issues ('with my young son' and 'because of babysitters') rather than a workplace that is not flexible.

In comparison to Sally's story of, arguably, objective exploitation told through a discourse of individualistic choice, opportunity, and compromises, some male journalists whom I interviewed seemed locked into a discourse of female advantage in the industry. During the interviews, two senior male journalists argued that women were advantaged in gaining employment in the industry because they 'presented' more professionally and were more articulate than young men during job interviews. Although it is true that young women are increasing their participation in the lower ranks, motherhood and caring responsibilities later become a problem for some, as Sally's excerpt indicates. Paul weighs in on the 'advantaged women' debate:

> Paul: I actually think at [metropolitan newspaper] they are keen to be seen to be proactive and if you're a . . . I think it's more advantageous to be a young woman with a bit of spark and ability, than to be a young bloke with a bit of spark and ability. I think they are keener to promote the women quicker.

> LN: Why is that?

> Paul: To redress the balance at the top end, because there's a lot of criticism that there's a glass ceiling for women, you know, not [enough women] in the senior editorial positions. Maybe that could be a valid criticism. So they are keen to be seen doing some affirmative action kind of stuff.

> LN: Does that work though?

> Paul: I don't think so. I just think it should be merit based. It goes both ways, just because someone is a bloke, doesn't mean you should get the job, neither does it mean because we have this agenda of wanting to be seen to be doing the right thing, and to be politically correct, we promote someone into a job that they're not capable of because they're the right sex.

Here Paul demonstrates a familiarity with the concepts of gender inequality, using liberal feminist language to describe women's disadvantage ('*glass ceiling*,' '*affirmative action*'). But Paul also uses a corporate, manager-speak type of narrative, where women are reframed as the advantaged '*right sex*,' and men become the disadvantaged, if unmentioned, gender. Paul doesn't gender men in the same way as women and in this excerpt 'men' are never 'men,' rather the more familiar '*bloke*,' and this seems to me to be a key term that signifies 'insider.' Far from being disadvantaged, when I contacted Paul two years after our initial interview, he had been promoted by his newspaper another 2.5 gradings, and at 28 years of age is a J7 with a margin, which is a very senior grading in the industry. He has moved from political reporting to working with a special investigations team.[2]

Mark subscribes to a similar story of gender bias towards women. He argues that women's advantage should be addressed as a matter of corporate necessity:

> Mark: *We consciously had to reassess the balance some time ago when we were hiring cadets, because we were hiring nine or ten women and two or three blokes—which is just silly, for obvious reasons. At the end of the day you ended up with this great hiatus after five or six years where you had somebody out of the workforce who you spent a lot of time training, who wasn't there and may never come back to you.*

Both Paul and Mark use the neoliberal discourses of opposing 'special rights' for women, which is commonly how a feminist position is viewed: that feminists want special treatment. Like Paul, Mark also subscribes to the familiar language division between '*women*' and '*blokes*.' There are a number of other important points to explore in Mark's comment. Firstly what is 'obvious' about needing a reassessment of hiring practices because more women then men were being hired? The discourse of hiring on merit, with gender not being considered, is specifically noted in almost every News Limited EOWA report about hiring practices in newspaper organisations. For example, both *The Advertiser* (Advertiser Newspapers Pty Ltd, 2003, 2006, pp. 3, 4) and *The Mercury* (Davies Bros Ltd Ltd, 2003, p. 6) state that their recruitment and selection policy "is directed entirely toward the recruitment and retention of the best available applicant or employee for the task based on merit, without reference to gender or other discriminatory characteristics. Capacity to perform the task is the sole criteria underlying any recruitment activities." If this equity discourse is to be accepted as real cultural change, when is a reassessment needed on the grounds of gender? When Mark responds to questions about gender issues during our interview, he

---

[2]Email conversation, January 16, 2006.

is prone to talk about women as 'somebody' or another similarly gender-neutral term. 'Somebody' consequently becomes nobody in terms of a language and discourse about women. This lack of specificity about gender creates the illusion that everyone is equal in the newsroom; that there is a job to be done and that genderless journalists perform that job in a vacuum from gender politics. Yet clearly Mark is making comment on women who take maternity leave or leave the industry to become full-time mothers. Mark speaks to the common popular discourse that it is a waste of scarce resources to train women, because inevitably they leave and have children and don't return to work. Men are thus, in his view, a better investment and more reliable workers than women. Yet the same problematisation of so few men being given early career jobs is not considered in the same way as the problem of there being so few mid-career women in the higher ranks in his media organisation (News Limited), or the media industry in general. The analysis is simply one of biology: women have babies and are therefore not reliable or long term workers. Mark's discourse certainly explains Sally's.

An alternative account of the same belief is provided in Haussegger's (2005) recent book. Haussegger has written one of the few books by a working female journalist that offers some insight into a newsroom culture that defines female journalists not by their skill, position, or seniority, but as 'mother' or 'nonmother.' Haussegger (2005) describes the various subject positions that she takes up in order to be considered a 'serious' journalist. At one stage of her career, her boss 'toasted' her with the dedication "to the many babies yet to be born" (2005, pp. 48–49). When Haussegger explained that she had no interest in having children, she was relegated to her inferior biology: "My boss jumped to his feet and started jabbing his finger in my direction: 'That's unnatural!' he yelled, for the benefit of the whole bar. 'You're bloody unnatural!' " The next time a male boss tested the waters on her baby plans "I knew to be a little more 'feminine' in my empathy." She knew she had to get the answer 'right' in this job interview. Haussegger was faced with this from the male interviewer: " 'The problem is,' the well known executive huffed, 'we get these smart sheilas in here and they keep going off and having kids.' " Haussegger saw this as a test of her position and "this time I artfully made an equally flippant attempt at mocking maternity, enough to secure the job, but not enough to appear 'bloody unnatural' " (Haussegger, 2005, p. 49). In another account, Haussegger details how she acted as a go-between for a female colleague who wanted information on job security if she were to take time off from her current position in the industry to have a child.

> She was terrified that anyone at the network, even the HR manager, would get a whiff of the fact that she was considering pregnancy, as they might start lining up her replacement and her career would begin the ugly and

humiliating downward spiral we've all witnessed other women endure. (Haussegger, 2005, p. 294)

Conclusion

From the interviews conducted I have found that the intensification of work practices, ethical constraints, and gender bias have aided in creating a cynicism among many of the journalists, from cadets to senior section editors. Nevertheless, the majority of interviewees said that a career in journalism has increased their personal and/or professional confidence. There are, however, gendered differences in this experience. Male interviewees often describe their professional confidence as increased because they have more access to people of influence, such as politicians. Female interviewees are more likely to explain their increased confidence as primarily benefiting their social worlds. For example, they are 'humbled' by their role in journalism, privileged by having access to 'people's homes and hearts,' and are more 'compassionate' towards people because of their experience in journalism

I have argued that although women with children find it increasingly difficult to perform/manage the tasks that are expected of 'journalists,' many have made the industry work for them. Sally's example of being prepared to do 38 hours' work in 25 hours and be paid for 25 (and be underpaid by not being paid casual rates) is a result of global industry changes that affect female journalists differently than male journalists. Sally speaks through a neoliberal subjectivity in describing the gendered implications of work intensification. Her situation is an example of how male and female journalists experience globalisation very differently. Male journalists interviewed, however, seem locked into a discourse of female advantage in the industry. Two senior male journalists argue that women are advantaged in gaining employment because they present better than young men. One suggested that men were more reliable workers. His interpretation resonates with a common popular discourse that it is a waste of scarce resources to train women because they leave work to have babies. Another insisted that women were advantaged in journalism because of political correctness, rather than merit.

Moreover, the interviewees discussions of confidence gained or cynicism experienced tells us about the gendered impact of globalisation and the (very gendered) subject positions available in a period characterised by globalisation. These stories illuminate how some journalists live the massive changes and intensification to their industry, and how they accept and/or challenge the effects of neoliberalism. Finally, I want to make the point that the majority of the experiences of cynicism and confidence expressed by the interviewees in this chapter are specific to print news journalism. It may also be the case in other media industries. Journalists are at the cutting edge of global communication technology changes, adapting their skills for an ever-changing industry that requires more intensity and more output in less time with fewer resources. They interact with news sources and situations that are often traumatic and stressful—and then they have to report it to deadline. This is, however, not to say that some experiences such as those outlined here of female journalists with children are not shared in other industries.

Chapter Seven

Signs of Resistance?

There are other aspects of global change that reveal a contested media culture in a much more public context. This chapter is concerned with analysing those interviewees who identify their place in journalism in a critical way, or who experience discomfort in who they have to be, or who long for a different way of being a journalist. All of the excerpts demonstrate forms of resistance that occur in various ways and are discussed via a framework of the 'ethical' journalist and the 'corporate' journalist. This analysis is backgrounded with a brief discussion of the industry union's Code of Ethics and the inherent assumption in its wording that the journalist is an objective, neutral, rational, liberal subject. Moreover, it fails to acknowledge the other restrictions on individual journalists in acting morally. I pose the question here: are ethics a form of resistance to neoliberal changes in the workplace?

I then extend this notion of resistance to analyse three important Australian legal cases. These cases, reported in the print news media in 2000, 2003, and 2004, involve three senior Australian female journalists who all claim discrimination on the basis of their gender. In presenting these cases I ask: are ethics gendered? All the cases involve a claim of pay disparity with male colleagues. When *The Australian* reported in August 2000 that Tania Ewing from the Fairfax-owned *The Age* had lodged a claim with the Industrial Relations Commission (IRC) about pay inequality it was, according to my research, the first time that gender bias in Australian newsrooms entered public discourse. This is not to say that other female journalists have not taken legal action against Australian media organisations—they have—but rather to make the point that it is the first time that the news media itself published stories about the legal claims. Less than three years later, Kerry Coyle, from the independently owned *The West Australian*, took her complaint of pay inequality to the Human Rights and Equal Opportunity Commission (HREOC). It has, however, been the case of *The Age* property editor Aileen Keenan that has received the most sustained media attention. In August 2004 she lodged a claim of pay discrimination in the Victorian Civil and Administrative Tribunal (VCAT). This case went further then the previous two and named, and to some extent problematised, the 'blokey,' 'boys' club' culture of newsrooms that worked to exclude women.

The MEAA's (Journalism branch) Code of Ethics was drawn up in 1944 by the then Australian Journalists Association (AJA) and was based on the ideals of members displaying honesty, fairness, independence, and respect for the rights of others. The code has changed several times since its inception and was last updated in 1995 when two extra clauses were included that made specific reference to privacy (Warren, 1995, n.p). This in itself is an interesting development in the context of the breakdown of public/private boundaries elsewhere, and in fact is probably the reason behind a point on privacy being included. The MEAA's 12-point Code of Ethics (Journalists) (see Appendix 1) includes points about honesty, accuracy, and fairness in reporting; disclosure about conflicts of interest and about payments made for stories; presenting accurate pictures; plagiarism; attributing sources; correction of errors; and respecting private grief.

The code is legally binding on union members, but the MEAA maintains that all journalists, whether union members or not, acknowledge and believe they are 'bound' by the code (Warren, 1995, n.p). This, however, is questionable. Denis Muller, a former Fairfax journalist and now researcher at Melbourne University, says that journalists are ignorant of accountability mechanisms in their industry. Although Muller did not specifically ask journalists about their understanding of and commitment to the Code of Ethics, he did probe their knowledge of external accountability mechanisms, including the MEAA ethics panel, the Australian Press Council,[1] and the Australian Broadcasting Authority.[2] About 51 percent of journalists felt unable to offer an opinion. They answered that they didn't really know enough. "So we have a situation in which the journalists themselves, or many of them, feel quite ignorant about the accountability mechanisms that are meant to exist for their own profession" (Muller, 2005, n.p.). However, one mechanism of accountability that journalists admire, although some begrudgingly, is the ABC Television program, *Media Watch*. The weekly 15-minute program, hosted by a journalist, challenges,

---

[1] The Australian Press Council, established in 1976, is the self-regulatory body of the print media. Its two main aims are to help preserve the traditional freedom of the press within Australia and ensure that the free press acts responsibly and ethically (www.presscouncil.org.au). Anyone can make a complaint concerning the press. The council is funded by the newspaper and magazine industries, and its authority, problematically, rests on the willingness of publishers and editors to respect the council's views, to adhere voluntarily to ethical standards, and to admit mistakes publicly.

[2] In July 2005 The Australian Broadcasting Authority (ABA) merged with the Australian Communications Authority (ACA). The newly formed Australian Communications and Media Authority (ACMA) is responsible for the regulation of broadcasting, radiocommunications, telecommunications, and online content. ACMA's 'responsibilities' include "promoting self-regulation and competition, while protecting consumers and other users; and fostering an environment in which electronic media respect community standards" (www.acma.gov.au).

questions, and investigates journalism practices in Australia. It works as an industry watchdog and is a respected accountability mechanism.[3] Muller (2005) suggests that the program is the most severe deterrent to unethical journalism because it is humiliating to be publicly castigated by peers. Journalists' respect for the program is not surprising given that the MEAA is hamstrung by its lack of legal power over industry ethics. It is only journalist members of the MEAA who are legally bound by the Code of Ethics. The federal secretary of MEAA, Chris Warren, says:

> Any person can currently lay a complaint alleging that a journalist has breached the Code of Ethics. That's heard by a committee of five working journalists selected at large from among the journalists in each particular state. And there are appeal structures up to the national level. If the breach is found to be proved, then the journalist can be rebuked or censured, fined up to $1000, or expelled from membership of the Alliance. (Warren, 1995, n.p.)

The problem for the MEAA and its Code of Ethics is that owners, management, and editors are not beholden to the code because they are generally not members of the MEAA. Another weakness is that even MEAA members who breach the code face only a punitive (and rarely imposed) fine of $1,000—which is a token gesture at best. The code, then, is in effect, ineffectual and at best a cursory acknowledgment of ethical dilemmas.

In the terms of the Code of Ethics individual journalists go about their daily work without the demands or pressures of editors, newspaper styles, or competitors. Yet in Susan's excerpt noted at the beginning of Chapter Five, she laments *'bending the rules'* because of the increased pressure to have the same story as the competitor. The ethical journalist, then, becomes subsumed into the corporation, a competitor in the market place, and the ethical journalist ceases to have a place to exist.

Ethics in journalism is a continuing academic debate. Australian media theorists Elspeth Probyn and Catharine Lumby explain that the often fractured relationship between codes of ethics and journalists has always been evident. "As anyone who's worked in the media can attest, codes of ethics and journalistic ideals have always had a tenuous relationship with the messy realities of professional practice" (2003, p. 1). Journalists simply do not, or cannot, abide by the code because it fails to take account of the realities and complexities of popular media practice (Probyn & Lumby, 2003, p. 1). As Anne Dunn (2003, p. 146) asserts, ethical thinking and behaviour do not reside in codes. In her

---

[3]Although, in recent years many editors and producers of major newspapers, TV, and radio programs have been much more public and vitriolic about what they see as the watchdog's attack on their craft. The program regularly shows replies to the program's queries and requests for responses.

very liberal defence of ethics, Dunn argues that ethics come down to decisions made by individuals who have to balance self-interest and other pragmatic considerations with wider ideals. Surprisingly, Lumby and Probyn, who have in the past made gender a central component of their work, don't provide a gendered analysis of ethics, or hint that gender should be a consideration in this debate. Their hesitation about acknowledging the gender politics of journalists' ethics is, of course, embedded in the code itself. The code, especially points 2 and 4, about not placing unnecessary emphasis on personal characteristics and not allowing personal interests or beliefs to undermine fairness or independence, provide almost a mandate to consider all journalists as disembodied liberal subjects. This notion of ethics completely occludes the ethics of the constitution of gender in the newsroom. It assumes the journalist is an objective, neutral, rational, liberal, subject.

Well-known Australian broadcast journalist Ellen Fanning argues that most professionals (journalists) adhere to an "internal moral code or some basic, if tattered, rules" (2004, p. 35). Fanning's article, published in the industry magazine *The Walkley Magazine*, is headlined on the cover as "The Ethical Line." I wish to discuss the article at length because it elaborates clearly the liberal position on ethics in journalism. Fanning uses the article to defend journalism from its cynics and highlight stories of individual journalists acting morally or demonstrating distress over what moral choices they should make. She suggests that ethics in journalism is not just about making the right decision, but more about what American journalism professor Jay Black says: "Ethics entails making tough decisions—not the obvious choices between right and wrong but the tough choices between not-quite-completely-rights even choosing the lesser of two wrongs. To make such choices . . . is a demanding intellectual and philosophical and profoundly pragmatic process" (Black, quoted in Fanning 2004, p. 35). There is no acknowledgement of the other restrictions on individual journalists in acting morally, or even an analysis of what acting 'morally' means. The increased pressure to get stories, the intensification of the workplace, the ramifications of media concentration, and the control of the owners are not raised by Fanning as issues affecting ethics or ethical decision making. With the increasing pace of editorial decision making I question whether any journalist has the time to undertake any deep 'philosophical' process. Is this a last-ditch stand against the impacts of globalisation? Is Fanning trying to keep the moral professional subject intact? Fanning's article serves only to expose the dilemma and 'agonising' that selected journalists say they have experienced in some decisions about whether to publish certain facts or pictures. For example, Fanning uses the case of photo editor Greg Newington agonising about his decision to publish, on the front page of a major metropolitan newspaper, a disturbing picture of a man jumping to his death from the World Trade Centre after the terrorist attacks of September 2001 in the United States. He decided to publish. Part of Fanning's analysis is that: "Whether they made the right decision or not, they were motivated in large by the tricky business of telling the truth" (2004, p. 35). But what Fanning fails to make clear here (aside from the questionable notion that objective 'truth' is identifiable and a concept that all subjects in an 'event' can agree upon), is that the decision-making process goes beyond the individual. Fanning defends the notion of an ethical journalist, without acknowledging the broader context of journalism practices and structures. The whole point seems to be missed. The discussion is one thing; at least there is recognition that there are indeed ethical dilemmas in journalism. But the journalist subject who is having the discussion is already constituted through neoliberal/globalising discourses that make 'ethics' in the traditional sense seem redundant.

Although Fanning is at pains to demonstrate an ethical consideration or moral goodness in individual journalists, a worldwide study of journalists found that the only practice that journalists seem to universally agree upon is not revealing news sources who have been promised confidentiality (Weaver, 1998, p. 479). Weaver, in summarising the research, indicates that there were large differences in opinions as to whether it might be justified to pay for information, pose as someone else, to badger or harass news sources, to use documents without permission, or to take a job in order to gain inside information.

Weaver's assessment resonates with Susan's dilemma and observations of her changing industry.

Susan: Our profession has changed dramatically. The boundaries have changed—things we are prepared to do now in Australia as journalists. I mean I look at the Code of Ethics and I think that's a joke. Love the concept, doesn't happen, wish it did, but it doesn't. We bend rules all the time because at the end of the day if the competitor's got what you haven't got, that's what matters.

Susan doesn't think that 'bending rules' is acceptable, but to some extent it is inevitable. I asked Susan if she had to bend the rules to get stories and she replied:

Susan: Absolutely. I try not to bend them too much and there's certain things I just would not do, like lie overtly, or, pretend I wasn't who I was, and all those sorts of things, but there are expectations there now. . . . I find the privacy thing particularly interesting, that there's this, what used to be the boundaries for privacy and personal grief, and I don't know where those boundaries are anymore. I mean it's a hard industry anyway, because it's dominated by blokes, all the editors are blokes.

Susan's comment about shifting boundaries is an often noted quality of globalisation. The breaking down of boundaries is seen as a positive aspect, yet in this example it provides a new and complex set of dilemmas in the practice of journalism. Susan knows the industry's ethics charter and is bound by it, yet the pressure to get stories that involve invading another's privacy is challenging to her.

Point 11 of the Code of Ethics is "Respect Private Grief and Personal Privacy. Journalists Have the Right to Resist Compulsion to Intrude." As it is written, this is an ambivalent point and open to interpretation. What one person considers 'respect,' others, like Susan, may not. For example, Paul, a young metropolitan reporter, describes the benefits of a career in journalism:

> Paul: I suppose, by virtue of what company or newspaper organisation you work for—in a funny way you have the right to intrude on, well, you don't have the right, but you are able to intrude on a private person's life and ask of their time, and usually they'll hear you out.

Jessica articulates the ethical dilemma found in Point 11 of the code in this next excerpt. Like Susan, she has a similar concern about invasions of privacy, yet even while acknowledging an understanding of the principle she maintains she has little choice in the decision to abide by the code if the editor demands the story. There was just one occasion when she refused to chase a story she was asked to pursue because it involved what she considered to be a breach of privacy and ethics. Another journalist pursued the story instead.

> Jessica: There was only once when I refused to chase a story: that's when they wanted me to go and doorknock around John Smith* who was in the navy and was lost overboard. He was a Smalltown* guy originally, and they wanted me to go and door knock his old [former] neighbours, and get them to say what a great kid he was. I said 'there is no way I'm going to do that.' It was on a Sunday; I said 'no.' That's the last thing I would do. What happened was there was someone else willing to go. They went and did it and came back and went 'God I feel so bad, I made the old man next door cry.' We ran a picture of their house on the front page, obviously the house where he lived, and they didn't invite us to the funeral. I think they rang up and said 'if you show up there's no way we're speaking to you.' We did ourselves a real disservice I think by intruding on that.

> LN: So the reason you refused to do it was because it was an intrusion on their privacy?

> Jessica: I didn't think there was a need for that. We were still getting information. If we rang the Defence Force media, they go and ask the family. You know we could ring up and say 'look can you tell us where he went to school' and they'd go and ask the family and they'd come back and tell us. It's different if they're not, if you are not getting anything,

LN: But there was a push for the emotive side of it wasn't there, that the Defence Force couldn't offer you that kind of thing?

Jessica: Yeah. I remember being told so many times, what is it? You can resist the compulsion to intrude. I know it's one of the, the guidelines, one of the . . . [pause]

LN: The Code of Ethics?

Jessica: Yeah, the Code of Ethics, yeah, and that's one that stuck with me.

*pseudonyms have been used in this excerpt to provide anonymity to the journalist and the family in this discussion

Evidence of the Code of Ethics being enforced, or even given cursory consideration, by senior editors is hard to find. Jessica's individual resistance to invading privacy based on her interpretation of the Code of Ethics even though she cannot recall its title without prompting is devalued by another journalist being asked, and agreeing, to do the task that she would not. It's not just news facts that can be provided by another source (in this case the Defence Force) that the media wants; it's the emotion (another example of the feminisation of the news). This excerpt reflects my earlier point about the constant pressure on journalists to find different news angles on a story from those of their competitors. The regional newspaper in the town where the deceased sailor grew up had the opportunity to access an emotive angle at a local level even though he actually died elsewhere. The fresh, local angle, however, must be sourced from someone who remembers the sailor and is prepared to talk to the media about him. It's an angle that a metropolitan newspaper, being removed from this context, may not get or even want. Hence, knocking on doors and causing 'the old man next door to cry' becomes linked to status in the regional newsroom. The new and emotive angle was created. Jessica failed to attain this status, but someone else succeeded, even though this reporter appears somewhat uneasy about his actions. Furthermore, Jessica's description of the event lacks fleshed-out figures. Who asked Jessica to doorknock the neigbourhood? Who eventually obliged? Who is 'we' and who is 'they'? Jessica doesn't describe a scene peopled by individuals (a liberal view)—and she has avoided staking a claim as an ethical individual, or a scene peopled by subjects shaped through power relations—she's avoided seeing herself as an exploited junior reporter. Rather, she identifies with the corporation ('*we did ourselves a real disservice . . . we were still getting information . . . if we rang the Defence Force*'), even though she had resisted that corporation by her once-only refusal to act upon a request. In the end, Jessica's refusal was an individual act of resistance that had little, or no, effect on the published story or the corporation. It seems, also, not to be much of a personal victory because the way in which she tells the story is what does her out of a personal victory. If she had told this story differently it could have been a great personal victory, morally or institutionally. It appears that there is so little support for ethics, let alone resisting management's instructions, at her workplace that the only subject position that is easily available to her is that of identifying with the newspaper, and given her discomfort and her resistance, the conclusion to her story is a feeling that she's flailing around, clinging to the life raft of the Code of Ethics, even though she cannot readily remember its title.

Of the eight male journalists whom I interviewed, two younger regional journalists made comments about ethics in journalism. Simon discussed ethical dilemmas in terms of management positions on certain stories and how this affected his day-to-day duties, and Max was concerned about journalistic integrity in terms of not being involved in stories if he was known to be close to sources (alluding to point 4 of the Code of Ethics about not allowing personal interests to undermine accuracy, fairness, or independence). Simon also draws on a nostalgic view of what 'news' is: for him it is supposed to be 'hard' and serious:

> Simon: There are things that I've been assigned to do that I thought had no place in a daily hard newspaper.
>
> LN: Like?
>
> Simon: Just usual self-indulgent tripe that management like to slip in about their favourite hobby, for example, or a particular industry that they may have associations with, or stories that I thought are newsworthy and have been crushed, thrown out to the side because we've got to keep sweet with so and so. I was unaware of just how many sacred cows there are in a regional newspaper. I don't know whether that's representative of other places but there are just—it's changing a bit now. We've got a much more robust news editor who just sees things as news or not news which is an absolutely marvellous counterpoint to what has been in the past. I think there are just some things that I've said, 'look, I've been assigned to do it,' and you just look at it and, you know, or been warned off things because they say, 'Oh, no, he advertises with us.'
>
> Simon: Yeah, it's funny when you say ethical dilemmas too, because there's not an ethical dilemma for the people who actually are assigning it. There's just no question, you know? 'We're not the ABC. Get your preciousness out of your, you know, get your precious head out of your arse. This guy spends $500,000 a year with us so we've got to tiptoe around him.' It doesn't matter how much of a scum-sucking son-of-a-bitch he is, and I loathe that. I absolutely loathe it. I hate the fact that we have to kowtow to anyone in that regard.

For Max, ethical decisions have only arisen when his 'objectivity' as a journalist might be questioned:

Max: Often if I was given an assignment where I thought that was going to come up [he knew someone and knowing them may compromise him], I would say 'look I feel that there's not a conflict of interest, but I don't know if I'm going to be able to be as objective as I should be,' and thankfully it's never been too much of a problem. I've always just said 'look I don't think I'm the one to do this story.' And there's never been a problem in giving it to someone else.

There is a gendered dimension to the varying nature of these interviewees' concerns about ethics: Simon dislikes being subordinated by more powerful editorial mangers; Max keeps his hands clean of any connection with conflict of interest concerns; Paul enjoys the aspect of journalism that allows him to intrude; Jessica dislikes intruding and draws on the Code of Ethics to support her point; and Susan dislikes deceiving and is also concerned about privacy. None of the interviewees (and not journalist Ellen Fanning earlier) acknowledge the gendered nature of the professional subject, or the ethical subject, but clearly there are differences. Max and Simon have a very businesslike approach to their ethical concerns: there seems a distinct right and wrong way to address ethical problems. In Simon's case, someone else can be blamed for the dilemma, and in this way he removes himself from a personal or professional ethical quandary. Max manages his ethical concerns about objectivity by drawing on the code to dissolve any concerns. Paul shows no knowledge of the Code of Ethics when he suggests that a benefit of a career in journalism is '*the right to intrude on a private person's life.*' Susan and Jessica, however, understand the ethical aspects of journalism very differently from Max, Simon, and Paul. Both struggle with point 11 of the code, about respecting privacy and resisting the compulsion to intrude. For Susan and Jessica, journalism's professional requirements are not consonant with their personal ethics, and hence there is always a dilemma that they need to negotiate themselves.

To what degree, then, can 'ethics' function as a form of resistance? Although ethical frameworks have a place in journalism, at least as a reminder of journalists' obligations to sources, they are rarely enforced in any way (financially) that would make 'code breakers' reconsider further similar breaches. The Australian Code of Ethics is a toothless tiger, prowling a cage but with no bite. It is still the *Media Watch* program that serves as the strongest reprimand for unethical journalistic behaviour. Negative exposure on that program results in public exposure of ethical breaches.

More Signs of Resistance:
Using Legislative Measures to Pursue Change

The three cases I present in this section provide instances of overt resistance to the gendered culture of journalism. I have moved beyond my interview material in this instance so as to explore change and resistance at another level. The women I discuss have done, and are doing, things that none of my interviewees have. I consider the three cases namely from an analysis of media reports. In one case I initiated email contact to supplement my understanding of the woman's personal experience of the legislative process and to some extent of the newsroom culture that underpinned her decision to make a legal challenge.

The three senior female journalists have mounted legal challenges to the pay disparity between male and female journalists performing similar tasks in Australian newsrooms. The cases involve white, middle-class professional women acting individually against inequality. I do acknowledge that working-class women, women from ethnic backgrounds, and nonwhite women and lesbians struggle to find a sense of place in work environments in which Anglo, white, middle-class, heterosexual women are the norm by which all 'others' are judged. The three cases do, however, expose the masculine newsroom culture. The cases highlight the culture and practices of journalism that hinder the career progression of women. These are attempts at change in an unfavourable climate. The women's actions also, perhaps, have provided positive flow on effects for other women working in the industry.[4]

Female journalists in the United States have lodged legal complaints of discrimination on the basis of their gender since the earlier 1970s, spurred on by an increase of women in the industry and the women's movement and the availability of legal avenues for redress. It is not clear to me, however, if any of the cases were published as 'news.' In the United States in 1971, 27 women filed a joint discrimination complaint against an NBC–owned television station in Washington (Beasley & Gibbons, 1993, p. 26). Maurine Beasley and Sheila Gibbons write that the leader of the complaint went on to be 'very successful' in the industry and helped pave the way for new opportunities for other female journalists. Not all female journalists in the United States involved in sex discrimination complaints, however, found that their situations improved. Beasley and Gibbons (1993, p. 27) note that in some cases journalists who brought complaints were then ostracised, felt the wrath of their male bosses, and discovered that fighting for the rights of others derailed their own careers. However, according to Kay Mills (1988, p. 167) the legal challenges, whatever the outcomes, led to women moving into areas previously denied them. From my reading, it appears that the three Australian cases that I present here are the first individual gender-discrimination cases by female journalists reported by the Australian print media.

---

[4]For example, soon after Aileen Keenan lodged her claim of gender discrimination at *The Age* newspaper, a switchboard operator working at *The Age* lodged a similar claim of being paid less than her male colleagues (Jones, 2004k, p. 30).

The Australian media is more inclined to report *individual* claims of gender discrimination in their own newspapers, by their own journalists,[5] than stories about an endemic problem in their own industry. This secrecy about gender bias in the media is highlighted by senior *The Age* journalist Claire Miller in an interview for *The Walkley Magazine* (see Savage, 2003). Miller is one of the few female working journalists to publicly discuss and challenge gender discrimination in the media. It is telling that she was, at the time, also the federal vice-president of the MEAA. Also telling is that Desiree Savage (2003), who wrote the article in which Miller is quoted, is a freelance journalist. She is much freer to write about the prejudice that keeps women out of positions of power and influence in the newsroom when publishing in a union-based magazine, than if she were to try and sell this article to a newspaper. Savage argues that the media prides itself on scrutinising society and uncovering instances of injustice and bias, yet fails to ask of itself whether it is similarly implicated. Miller is reported as saying:

> We write editorials about the need for better work place practices, we write about the lack of women in corporate life, we write about domestic violence and we write about the representation of women in the media. What we don't write about is women in the media itself. (Miller, cited in Savage 2003, p. 20)

In 1999 Miller wrote an article titled "How Our Media Are Failing Women" that struggled for four months to be published. Miller is quoted as saying:

> [it is seen as] an internal industry matter, and that there was no public interest in running this sort of stuff, about what was happening inside the media. Yet people make a big deal about the lack of women corporate leaders, the lack of senior women lawyers, the lack of senior women in medicine and the lack of women in politics and positions of power. It's like the dirty little secret of journalism. We will not look at ourselves. (Miller, cited in Savage, 2003, p. 20)

A key (male) media player says nothing more needs to be done for female journalists. The chief executive of News Limited, John Hartigan, has been reported as saying "We have seen an explosion of women entering [newspaper] journalism . . . and I would seriously question if women were worse off than men in remuneration" (in Jackson, 2003b, p. 3). The reporter Sally Jackson provides figures from the Australia Bureau of Statistics in the same article, showing that

---

[5]The exception is in the case of Kerry Coyle, whose employer *The West Australian* never reported her case, leaving it to the News Limited–owned *The Australian* to publish the story.

there is a gender disparity in average weekly earnings of journalists in all age groups and that it worsens with age. In a News Limited article, Fairfax editor-in-chief Mark Scott, however, is more forthcoming, suggesting that women's under-representation in the senior ranks *is* a concern. "What we are doing is creating an environment that is less blokey and provides more of an opportunity for women to take senior management and leadership roles" (quoted in Jackson 2003b, p. 3). How this 'environment' is being created in not discussed in the article. Neither is it discussed by the newly appointed editor-in-chief of Fairfax's *The Age,* Andrew Jaspan, who on his appointment was quoted in his own newspaper as saying: "Quite often newspapers are run by men with very much a male-oriented agenda" (Catalano, 2004, p. 22).

Inside the Industry: Women's Challenges to Gender Inequality in Pay And Promotion

The three women's cases that I detail here are just one thread among many that bear on women's position in the journalistic workforce. The repercussions of lodging a complaint are both professional and personal. The media coverage of the Tania Ewing (2000), Kerry Coyle (2003), and Aileen Keenan (2004) cases demonstrate how individual 'gender inequity' has become acceptable media discourse deemed 'serious news.' What these cases do clearly indicate is how women are using public, governmental means to pursue issues of sex discrimination in a neoliberal climate. My assessment of the outcomes of the three finalised cases is that the current legislative mechanisms are not working to the benefit of the complainants.

The three journalists each used different legal frameworks to make their claims of gender inequality. Ewing pursued her case through the Australian Industrial Relations Commission (AIRC)[6] and eventually settled out of court. Coyle initiated her claim through the Human Rights and Equal Opportunities Commission (HREOC)[7] in 2003. She then moved to the Federal Court, and in April 2006 Coyle withdrew her claim (email conversation, April 24, 2006). Keenan lodged her claim through the Victorian Civil and Administrative Tri-

---

[6]The commission can facilitate equal remuneration for work of equal value (AIRC, n.p).

[7]HREOC is an independent statutory organisation that reports to the federal Parliament through the Attorney-General. Established in 1986, it is concerned with the protection of human rights of a broad range of individuals and groups. The commission has responsibilities for inquiring into alleged infringements under five antidiscrimination laws—the *Racial Discrimination Act 1975*, the *Sex Discrimination Act 1984, Disability Discrimination Act 1992* and the *Age Discrimination Act 2004* as well as inquiring into alleged infringements of human rights under the *Human Rights and Equal Opportunity Commission Act 1986* (www.hreoc.gov.au/info-_sheet.html).

bunal (VCAT),[8] which ruled against her in four of the five instances that she had claimed. The company appealed the decision, but it received no further media attention. It is understood the case may have settled out of court.[9]

Ewing had worked for *The Age* newspaper in Melbourne, Victoria, for seven years before she made her complaint to the IRC in 2000. During her tenure with the newspaper she had risen from a general reporter to a specialist reporter covering gambling and casino issues. In 1999 she was promoted to transport and aviation editor. Ewing claimed that she received unequal pay for equal work because in those seven years working for the newspaper her salary was increased only once while her male colleagues received several pay raises. She also claimed that both times after she had taken maternity leave, she returned to work and was offered a less senior role. In the only story published about the case at the time, *The Age*'s rival, *The Australian*, quoted Ewing (in line with Miller's earlier comments) as saying: "What irks me is when my former newspaper and the media in general editorialise about other organisations that treat their women unfairly and yet they treat women within their own organisation just as poorly" (Dodd, 2000, p. 5). It was not until 2003 that it was briefly noted by *The Australian*'s Sally Jackson (2003b, p. 3) that *The Age* had settled out of court and part of that settlement included a 'gag rule' that Ewing not comment on the outcome. Ewing no longer works in the industry.

In 2003, Coyle, a senior sub-editor working at Perth's independently owned *West Australian* newspaper lodged a claim of gender discrimination with the HREOC. As part of the HREOC process, if a complaint is terminated because there is no reasonable prospect of settling the complaint by conciliation, the complainant can have the case heard and determined by the Federal Court (www.hreoc.gov.au/aboutthe commission/functions/_index.html). Coyle, backed by the industry union, the MEAA, began using the Federal Court option in March 2005. In coverage by the only newspaper to report on the case, *The Australian*, she is quoted as saying she was "working alongside men of the same experience and length of service," yet she was graded much lower (Jackson, 2003a, p. 3). *The West Australian* at the time employed 45 male sub-editors in grades 8 and above (the most senior) and just two female sub-editors. Union statistics reported by Jackson showed that the newspaper had 246 graded

---

[8]The VCAT (created in 1998 by amalgamating 15 boards and tribunals) deals with a range of disputes including discrimination claims. VCAT powers range from a slap on the wrist, to asking the respondent to stop committing any further acts of discrimination, through to a direction to pay compensation, but even then the direction can be appealed to the Supreme Court of Victoria, although only on questions of law (which *The Age* ultimately did do). Disputes taken through the VCAT begin with a mediation directions hearing or compulsory conference (VCAT, n.p).

[9]I base this claim on discussions with industry and union sources.

journalists of whom 35 percent were women. Of the women, 80 percent were ranked in the bottom six grades. Of the men, almost 70 percent were ranked in the top six grades (Jackson 2003a, p. 3).

On March 18, 2004 *The Australian* noted that the MEAA had agreed to pay for a barrister for Coyle's case (p. 19). In August 2004 *The Australian* (Yallop, 2004b, p. 3) wrote that Keenan's case was the first legal challenge over alleged pay discrimination on the grounds of gender to be funded by the MEAA. There is some confusion, however, in the media, and indeed Coyle herself is unclear as to whether her claim is the first legal challenge over alleged pay discrimination on the grounds of gender funded by the MEAA. Coyle withdrew her claim in April 2006. She still works full-time for *The West Australian*.

In our email communication[10] Coyle says that her professional confidence has been eroded because: "[I] have had my work whittled down and down, though the company would claim that was due to other factors such as routine changes of workloads etc." On a personal level the stress and longevity of the legal process has affected her health. "My hair is thinning through stress and my weight had crept up through depression, I think" (email conversation, June 14, 2005). The MEAA, although funding Coyle's Federal Court bid by providing lawyers, "failed to see the urgency of processing the case." She noted that at a directions hearing, the judge had to excuse himself because he had previously worked for the newspaper (WAN), but Coyle concluded that: "The federal court is becoming impatient with 'my' delays" (email conversation, June 13, 2005). When I contacted Coyle in April 2006 to ask how the case was progressing she replied that she had withdrawn the claim that month (email conversation, April 24, 2006).

The case received just four mentions in *The Australian*—one small brief one in a wider feature about pay discrimination in the industry (Jackson, 2003b, p. 3), and two specifically about the case itself (Jackson, 2003a, p. 3; 2004, p. 21). The initial story was located in the 'Media' section of *The Australian*, with a picture of Coyle, and warranted an 18-paragraph story (double the space of Ewing's), and written again by Jackson. It is evident that there is an increasing interest and coverage of gender discrimination in the industry, but as previously noted those articles are more likely to cover individual cases of discrimination.

In 2004 a claim of gender discrimination in pay was lodged by another Fairfax journalist, this time *The Age* property editor Aileen Keenan. Keenan's barrister was reported in *The Australian* as suggesting that the newspaper was a "boys' club where a culture of mateship decided how much journalists were

---

[10]Kerry Coyle has given written approval for me to use details from our email communication in this book. She is the only one of the three women involved in the cases with whom I have had email contact.

paid" (Dunlevy, 2004a, p. 7). The barrister was reported as saying that "mateship rather then competence determined the grading of journalists, with the result being that females were generally paid and graded lower than male colleagues." In the VCAT, Keenan claimed that she has been discriminated against on the basis of her sex. Keenan's case proceeded to a hearing, giving her and *The Age* the opportunity to call or give evidence, ask questions of witnesses, and make submissions. *The Age* did indeed call ten witnesses. It was reported on December 23 (Jones, 2004l, p. 13) that the tribunal found that in relation to the five allegations (four workplace discrimination and one victimisation claim) made by Keenan, the newspaper did not breach equal opportunity laws. Just one allegation was upheld with a ruling that *The Age* discriminated when Keenan was not given a work car because she was female. It was reported that *The Age* would appeal against this ruling (Binnie, 2005, p. 12); however, no further reports were published about the case in News Limited or Fairfax-owned newspapers after that date. It is therefore unclear whether the appeal went ahead or if the case settled out of court. Keenan left *The Age* in December 2005[11] and it is understood she no longer works in the industry.

The most extensive coverage of the Keenan case was by rival News Limited Victorian newspaper the *Herald Sun* (16 stories and five with accompanying pictures; see footnotes)[12] and the national News Limited broadsheet *The Australian* (13 extensive articles and seven with pictures; see footnotes).[13] *The Age* covered the case, but only seven small stories were published and no pictures (see footnotes).[14] This case even made the industry gossip columns, where Keenan's professionalism was questioned (for example, Leys, 2004, p. 9; Edmonds, Dunnehy, and Danaher, 2004, p. 22).

One of the fascinating aspects of the representation of the three cases is the increasing space allocation given to the stories, and the use of feminist language to explain the journalists' claims. Keenan's case, in particular, is the first in which media coverage discusses the masculine culture of the newsroom and reports a legal case based on this premise. Nevertheless, exposing this culture is never as simple as telling a story. It is common knowledge within the industry that those who make claims of inequity and then become the

---

[11]The MEAA confirmed that Keenan had left *The Age* in December 2005 and she was no longer a union member (email conversation, August 2, 2007).

[12]Binnie, 2004, 2005; Edmonds, Dennehy, & Danaher, 2004; Jones, 2004a, 2004b, 2004c, 2004d, 2004e, 2004f, 2004g, 2004h, 2004i, 2004j, 2004k, 2004l, p. 13; "Reporter's Work Queried," *Herald Sun*, 2004, p. 22.

[13]Dunlevy, 2004a, 2004b; Jackson, 2004; Kaszubska, 2004; Leys, 2004; Yallop, 2004a, 2004b, 2004c, 2004d, 2004e, 2004f, 2004g; "MEAA foots bill," *The Australian*, 2004, p. 19; "Union backs legal challenge to paper's perceived 'blokey' culture," *The Australian*, 2004, p. 43; "Sex bias claim," *The Australian*, 2005, p. 17.

[14]Munro, 2004; Shtargot, 2004; Ziffer, 2004a, 2004b, 2004c, 2004d, 2004e.

'news' will find securing further work in the industry difficult, if not impossible. Reporter Richard Yallop (2004f, p. 43) acknowledges this point in his summary of the Keenan case. He reports that Keenan's "apparently obsessive determination to pursue the case" was seen by some colleagues "as brave but foolhardy if she ever wanted to get another job in journalism." These comments serve as a threat in themselves, rather than just a point of fact. Yallop then ponders, without crediting a named source, the insidious sexual insinuation that "this made some involved in the legal defence wonder if she [Keenan] was a woman spurned by Catalano in an affair" (2004f, p. 43). Catalano was the previous real estate editor compared to whom Keenan claimed that she was paid less for doing the same job. Catalano had previously been mentioned in the article as having a "confident swagger that led some at The Age to dub him 'the Italian stallion.'" Clearly Catalano has also been sexualised, but arguably not to the same disadvantage as Keenan. The scurrilous assault on Keenan's personal life has no place in the reporting of a legal case but somehow finds its way into Yallop's story. What is Yallop's aim by making these comments? Is he making an unsubtle public castigation to undermine Keenan's professionalism and place her back in the private/sexual/female context? Yallop's claims, based on unnamed sources ('some involved' and 'some colleagues'), works to assist management in devaluing Keenan as a journalist.

Gender politics aside, these stories also offer rival companies the opportunity to publish 'bad news' about how competitors run their companies, and in turn, make the publisher of such stories appear squeaky clean. Rival newspapers are, not surprisingly, more likely to publish stories about claims of discrimination by their competitor's staff. News Limited has not had any publicly documented claims of gender discrimination against it. It would be incorrect, however, to therefore conclude that gender discrimination does not occur in the organisation. That News Limited owns 70 percent of Australia's mainstream print media could in itself be a deterrent to complaints, especially if we take into account the earlier (above) comments of News Limited reporter Richard Yallop. The interviews, some from participants who work for News Limited, and statistics on the gendered workforce clearly point to inequalities. These cases, particularly Coyle's, also serve to reinforce the interview material. Coyle's lack of confidence and an overall malaise about the industry resonates with many of the female interviewees' lived experience in the newsroom.

Ewing, Coyle, and Keenan have challenged workplace inequality by stepping outside the confines of the 'matey' newsroom and pursuing claims through court. But this process, for these women, seems so limited and so costly. Although more young women are entering the industry than ever before the senior, mature women (Coyle is the only journalist of the three whom I know considers herself a feminist, although this is not to say that Ewing and Keenan are not) making legal challenges to sex inequality cannot, it seems, beat a discriminatory culture and practice. The current neoliberal framework and backlash against feminism at a social and cultural level is a disempowering place from which to begin any legal challenge vis-à-vis gender. When women do make it to court, statutory bodies with liberal frameworks keep women complainants in check. As Thornton (2001, p. 96) argues: "EEO alone is incapable of delivering just outcomes for women, least of all conferring authority on women." This is the case because of the ascendency of neoliberalism, which suggests that individual good outweighs common good, "which means that systemic discrimination is conveniently ignored" (Thornton, 2001, p. 96). Although they are in court, the culture of payback is working against them. The coverage of Keenan's case by Yallop is an example of a male journalist working against her challenge to the masculine work culture that positions female journalists as less financially worthy than their male counterparts.

Three senior female journalists make legal complaints of inequity. Of the handful of journalists who cover the stories, one is a feminist journalist from *The Australian*—Jackson, who has a history of researching and writing about the concerns of female journalists and supports her work with statistics. One is an influential male reporter—Yallop, who also reports for *The Australian* and relies on gossip, unacknowledged sources, hearsay, and sexual innuendo to undermine Keenan's case.

The very up-beat commentaries of the U.S. women who make complaints (whom I mentioned at the start of this section) don't seem to hold sway in today's newsrooms in Australia. Of the three female journalists who made legal complaints and subsequently had their cases published in the Australian media between 2000 and 2006, one is still working full-time for the newspaper against whom she made her claim (Coyle). All have experienced a number of professional and personal hurdles, including depression from the drawn-out legal process (Coyle), media scrutiny of her personal life (Keenan), a slow withdrawal in the allocation of significant news stories (Coyle), and a gag on ever talking about the events that led to her legal claims (Ewing).

Conclusion

The resultant intensification of work practices, media concentration, and the technological changes to journalism in all forms provides a background for issues such as ethics in journalism to be raised by some interviewees. The pressure for journalists to secure the same story as their competitors, but then to go one step further and uncover other aspects of a story that the competitor does not have, blurs the boundaries of ethics. Again there are gendered differences in how journalists describe ethical dilemmas. Both Susan, an experienced journalist, and Jessica, a cadet journalist, struggle with ethical dilemmas that ultimately become an individual consideration rather than an organisational one. Jessica dislikes intrusive reporting practices and Susan dislikes deceiving. Both are aspects that relate to the Code of Ethics, and both women tussle with the issues and experience them as ethical dilemmas that they alone must somehow surmount while staying true to themselves and their professional obligations. Paul, however, sees it as his right as a journalist to be able to intrude on people's private lives. Max and Simon manage ethical considerations by removing themselves from any dilemmas. Simon's ethical dilemma is the fault of management, and therefore management needs to deal with it, and Max keeps clear of ethical discussions by passing them off before they become a problem.

The effects of globalisation in the Australian print media turn up a complex terrain of change across individual, social, union, government, and industry dimensions. To explore that complexity, I have concluded this chapter by considering global change through a window of three important Australian legal cases. Those cases were reported in the Australian print news media in 2000, 2003, and 2004 and involved three senior Australian female journalists who all claimed pay discrimination on the basis of their gender. Their 'failures' have been both personal and professional. What their legal challenges do demonstrate is how women use public, governmental, and legislative means to pursue issues of sex discrimination in a neoliberal climate. That it has to occur demonstrates that even after more than 20 years of EEO legislation and an increasing number of women entering the lower journalism ranks, there is still a 'blokey culture' in the media, exacerbated by the globalisation of the media, which works against female journalists. But what are the choices for women in a neoliberal climate? Valerie Walkerdine (2004, p. 8) discusses the effects of neoliberalism and the notion of choice for workers, and particularly how it relates to women. "The production of subjects within neo-liberalism as free, autonomous, choosing, flexible, always has failure built into it" (Walkerdine, 2004, p. 27). It is supported, she says, through practices of the self that facilitate coping.

> But the ways in which exploitation and oppression are elided within current work and political narratives and discourse, and personal ones in response to a politics designed precisely to elide and obscure them, as well as manage and regulate them, seem to me to demand a politics of constant exposure of the Other of neo-liberalism. (Walkerdine, 2004, p. 27)

Chapter Eight

What Does Feminism Mean to Journalists?

In this chapter I focus on two areas: how feminism and ideas of feminism are deployed in the newsroom and how feminism variously shapes subjectivities of journalists. To do this I analyse how interviewees understand and explain ideas about feminism and feminists in the newsroom. I focus on subjectivities in the newsroom, how journalists create meaning, especially about clearly gendered issues, and explore how the slippery term 'feminism' is negotiated by journalists. Simply, what does feminism mean to journalists and what subject positions do journalists take up in relation to it?

The next chapter moves away from analysis of interviews to an anecdote from my own experience in the industry—one that has much to tell us about the place of feminism in the newsroom. It is here that I move to a discussion in which gendered newsroom politics, feminism, and news content finally come together.

What Is Feminism and How Do Interviewees View Feminists?

Feminism was a theme on which I engaged the discussion of both the male and female interviewees. I was interested in exploring what the term 'feminism' meant to journalists. How did they define the term, and was it a useful concept in their day-to-day work practices? Did interviewees know a feminist? If so, how did that person demonstrate feminist principles? What was the fate of a publicly identified feminist in the newsroom?

Knowledge about 'feminism' ranged from little (or a decision to say very little in response to the question) to an awareness of the plurality of feminism. Knowledge about feminism, however, was not a precursor to having a positive experience about feminist concepts, or indeed feminists themselves. The majority of interviewees variously labelled feminists, both inside and outside the newsroom, with a long list of pejorative terms. Feminists were *'aggressive,'* 'strident,' 'insecure,' 'abrasive,' 'not nice,' 'demanding,' 'over the top' (Jodie); 'full on,' 'emotional,' 'scary,' 'abrupt' (Sally); 'attacking,' (Mark); and 'self-righteous' (Paul). Feminists are also referred to as lacking humour and espousing impractical political positions (Paul); and being overly critical (Jessica). Overall there was a sense that the majority of interviewees understood feminists as angry and extreme in their actions and often pushed their politics 'too far.' One young male reporter (Max) even queried if women who displayed feminist beliefs had 'something happen to them, some emotional sort of thing' to make them believe in feminism—like feminism was some type of psychological disorder.

These definitions are not unlike those found by Cynthia Cockburn in her 1991 study of British workers in a retail industry. Feminists, or 'women libbers,' attracted a similar list of negative terms. Cockburn was told that 'women libbers' were 'harsh,' 'strident,' 'demanding,' 'uptight,' 'aggressive,' 'vociferous,' 'dogmatic,' 'radical,' 'zealots,' 'crusaders,' and 'overly ambitious' (1991, p. 165). Not surprisingly, then, they also 'lacked humour'—a comment that retains common currency today and seemingly across Western countries, and is reinforced in my interview excerpts.

In 1998 Australian women's studies scholar Kay Schaffer offers an insightful analysis of what feminism has come to mean in popular discourse. 'Feminism,' she argues, is a 'scare word.' By that she means:

> A word that has been used to evoke (although no dictionary would say so) the 1970s stereotype of bra burning, man hating lesbians who made up the boiler-maker suit brigade, and now in the 1990s is aligned with the vindictive, puritanical and punishing new generation of 'feminazis.' (Schaffer, 1998, p. 322)

Feminism is not a term that can be easily defined because of the many and varied positions within feminism. Any attempt at defining feminism has always been a contested one, both academically and within the media industry. Liesbet van Zoonen (1989, p. 3), a leader in the field of feminist media studies, suggests that "the current absence of a dominant ideological perspective in the women's movement precludes rigid definitions of feminism." Byerly, however, is very clear about the term. For Byerly (1999, p. 384) feminism "refers to the broad, collective efforts by women of varying philosophies to expand women's rights and to reformulate social norms in terms of women's experiences." Schaffer (1998, p. 321) maintains that there is a distance between popular and academic positions on feminisms. She writes that the ongoing scourge on feminists represented in the media has been a significant factor in reducing the efficacy of a politics of feminism.

There has never been one dominant ideological position in feminism. Rather, there is a multitude of positions and perspectives that both men and

women take up in relation to feminism. Some may not even term a demonstrated perspective as 'feminist,' but they may be understood by others as
encompassing some aspects of feminism and have the experiences of women as
its core focus. Many of the journalists I interviewed about those journalists who
demonstrated some kind of feminist position in the newsroom took up a hostile
position. Journalists are a part of the mix that produces hostile (and other)
media representations of feminism, but importantly, journalists also shape the
experiences of feminists in the newsroom. I am interested in how journalists'
subjective positions about feminism impact on their reporting, and this is further
explored in my analysis of the newsroom anecdotes, in the next chapter.

The distaste that my interviewees demonstrated towards feminists was not
limited by gender. Female journalists were as equally scathing of feminism as
male journalists and, particularly, of feminists—some negatively describing their
physical and emotional characteristics and/or confidently suggesting where they
went wrong in their actions in the newsroom, including their reportage, their
politics, and their approach and demeanour in general. Only one interviewee
pointed to a benefit or changes in the newsroom because of feminism, and that
was to acknowledge that there were more women working in the industry. Of
the three women who identified as feminists (Janet, Susan, Christine) in the
interviews, one (Susan) noted that the changing position of female journalists
today could be due to the second wave feminist movement, but her comment
related more to media content rather than cultural changes in the newsroom.
All three lamented that feminism had not improved a newsroom culture that
still privileged male journalists and male journalists' opinions. Janet noted 'the
backlash' against feminist beliefs and lamented that it was now 'uncool' to be
a feminist in the newsroom.

Paul, a young up-and-coming metropolitan political reporter, makes some
of the most disparaging comments about feminists. I asked him if he knew of
anyone who identified as feminist in the newsroom:

Paul: Well, there's a few yeah, but I mean whether they can claim to be or not,
I don't know, but I mean, yes.

LN: How do you define them as feminists?

Paul: By what they write, by how they talk, their attitude towards things.
Sometimes they would take a really predictable line on an issue and you'd think,
'oh, you know—really.' When they are writing, mainly on the opinion page,
you see things, they are really clutching at straws with a lot of those arguments.
They're just not practical in a sense. But by reputation too, what other people
talk about. It's sort of, there's nothing explicit really, but we are known to have
some pretty self-righteous people who are strong advocates for equal opportunity
and women's rights. I think by and large they often write some decent, very good
stuff, but I think it can go a bit far at times, and it's very easy to detect that

someone's been ultra sensitive or ultra politically correct. I think you need a little bit of a sense of humour and be able to have the ability to take the piss out of yourselves and other people and be more well respected, you know, don't be so serious. And when you are being serious, people will take more notice of you.

For Paul, feminist journalists can be identified not only by what they write—that being their primarily self-righteous, humourless, impractical political position—but also by their '*talk*' and their attitude, and their reputation garnered from what others say about them. Paul then goes on to suggest that there are no '*explicit*' characteristics associated with being a feminist or having a feminist philosophy, but he seems to have little trouble unpacking their politics ('*ultra sensitive or ultra politically correct*') and offering advice on how feminists could gain respect. Paul thinks that if feminists had a better sense of humour then respect would be forthcoming. Who is Paul suggesting would better respect feminists if they could '*take the piss*' out of themselves? Is it the newspaper readers or the male-dominated management? Paul draws on the age-old slight that feminists are humourless, and later in the interview he draws on another common refrain, that of being criticised for opening doors for women.

I was interested to know how Paul's perspective on feminism had developed and why he had such a negative discourse. I asked how he would define feminism and what had been his experience of it—positive or negative. He replied with a story from his university days and explained how he opened a door for two female students. The door was to a campus corridor where, among a handful of rooms, the women's room was located.

> *Paul: I opened it [the door] and saw a couple of women coming [from behind him] and they were like, I wasn't going to patronise them, and held it open like that, and instead of getting 'oh thanks,' they went 'look, you think we can't open a door for ourselves,' kind of thing, and it's like, it's enough you know, like why are you doing that, it's just unnecessary. I mean I would have done it for a bloke. I was just being polite, and things like that get on my nerves and then you see someone who looks the same as them and you think they all must be the same. I try not to have any preconceptions, I probably do, but I try not to and I try to look at what they're arguing and where they are coming from before I make a judgment.*

Although Paul claims to want to be open-minded and not have preconceptions about who is a feminist, he clearly makes the judgment that feminists look a certain way ('*you see someone who looks the same as them and you think they all must be the same*'). So if you can't tell feminists by what they write in newspapers, or by how they talk, or their attitude, you can surely tell them by their physical appearance. Paul has a long checklist for who a feminist is, while paying lip service to not having any preconceptions or the notion that there are 'explicit' characteristics. Paul begins the second excerpt already defending himself before he even explains how and for whom he opened the door. It is clear that the women's response hurt his feelings. In both the excerpts about feminists, Paul never uses the word 'feminist' or 'feminism.' It is always 'they' or 'yourselves' which links me with feminists, even though I have never identified to him in this way. Just asking questions about feminists associates me as a feminist. The word itself taints the speaker, because in the passages I quote, and indeed through all the sections of the interview where feminism is a point of discussion, he does not use the word.

What is the effect of this? What is kept safe for Paul by not using the word? How does his avoidance of the 'F-word' and recourse to women's presentation—humourlessness and lacking manners—contain the challenge of feminism? I think the lack of the use of the term 'feminism,' even though in his opinion he is clearly describing feminist women, keeps him safely distanced from a feminist understanding, knowledge, or discourse. This distance creates a safe place from which he can describe the event without being associated with feminism. He becomes the observer, the knower, the rational man of ideas, offering advice to feminists who certainly need it if they are, in his opinion, to be taken seriously.

Max and Paul have a similar context in which to place a feminist ideology. Feminism is an overreaction, and feminists push too far. Holding a feminist belief is even equated with a psychological disorder:

LN: *How do you understand feminism? What do you think, well how would you define feminism, or someone who had a feminist belief?*

Max: *To me feminism seems to be a reaction against sexism, and implicit in that is—in my perception—that it seems to be an overt reaction, and so much so that, someone stops being someone who is reacting against sexism but is more so pro-feminism and pushing it too far. When you mention feminism, it seems to instil an immediate knee-jerk reaction, like that 'there's no need to be that way,' you know what I mean? I think it is mainly because feminists came up against a very male oriented society, and that's why there's an automatic negative tone to using the word feminism, not necessarily for me, but I think well if someone's going to come out and be very proud about being a feminist, I sort of think, they're immediately going to take some flack for being it.*

LN: *Do you know anybody who is outwardly saying, 'yep, I'm a feminist and that's okay?'*

Max: *No, no I don't.*

LN: *And never in the newsroom?*

Max: *No, not really. I mean, I see women that occasionally adopt the idea, but I don't see anyone that pushes it in everything they do. I knew a few,*

when I was studying, and yet they were so feminist that it almost . . . oh, we
wondered, because we were all teenagers, you know, you often wonder is this
kind of a gimmick that they're going through at the moment? Did something
happen to them, some emotional sort of thing, I mean it's terrible to think that
way, because you automatically assume something set this off, rather than they've
just chosen to be that way.

The idea that feminists go too far is reiterated by Max. He understands feminism,
not in the context of one of many political philosophies that could underpin a
person's life, but as something that is to be 'pushed' every day. For Max, that's
how you know someone is a feminist—they constantly push the idea and demonstrate it in public. Max's subject position is, however, different from Paul's.
Max's comments are contradictory. He does, for example, adopt the words from
a feminist vocabulary, such as 'sexism,' 'male-oriented society' but he then uses the
term 'gimmick' to demean feminism. Max's excerpt also demonstrates a self-reflexive,
defensive subject position, as well as clearly subscribing to an antifeminist discourse.
Initially Max calmly claims that feminism is a reaction to sexism, although he
does not suggest that men are complicit in this. It is only feminists who 'came up
against a very male-orientated society,' rather than women in general. The women
he knows now do not identify as feminists, and consequently those women from
university must have had 'something happen to them, some emotional sort of thing'
to force them into a feminist position. For Max, therefore, feminism is an 'overt
reaction' (and feminists react overtly). It's a position that seems to go too far.
Max offers a reason for the negativity associated with being a feminist, but is it
that the male-dominated society is reacting against the word or the actions of
feminists in exposing the male dominance in the public sphere?

Sally, like Paul and Max, is similarly critical of the only colleague
who she thinks is a feminist. I asked her if any of the female journalists in
her newsroom would consider themselves feminists. Like Paul, Sally doesn't
use the word 'feminist' during the interview, but believes, like Paul and Max,
that feminists often go too far.

> Sally: I think probably one, she's a general reporter, she's pretty full on. She
> gets pretty emotional even with a half picture of half an abdomen or something
> that's not covered, she starts to get really upset about things.
>
> LN: How is she viewed in the newsroom?
>
> Sally: She's full on, she's pretty abrupt, she's pretty emotional too. One minute
> she'll be happy and she'll be okay, and the next minute something will happen
> which we all think is minor, but she just absolutely blows up and she cries, or
> she'll blow up at somebody and absolutely gives it to them.
>
> LN: Would she find it a struggle in the newsroom; she's probably the only
> feminist there. Is that a struggle for her?

Sally: Well people are saying oh [name]'s on a rampage again. . . .

Sally: She throws her weight around. People are actually a bit scared of her.

LN: So feminists are scary?

Sally: Because you never know, you never know, no, not that they are . . . a bit, but she is. You never know which way she's going to go. She's just a bit hard to pick sometimes, you're not quite sure how she'll react to some things.

Jodie takes this fear of the overly emotional, unstable, rampaging feminist whose politics goes too far one step further than Sally, claiming that feminists have hurt men, making them 'disempowered'; a term usually associated with minority groups. A 45-year-old freelancer and a former metropolitan news reporter, Jodie worked in newspapers at the peak of the re-emerging women's movement in the 1970s and early 1980s. Jodie, however, seems to reject the idea that her move into journalism had been underpinned by the feminist movement.

Jodie: What I see are the men—I see the fallout from that [80s feminism]—the men who are just so insecure about what their role is now. I think a lot of that goes back to that strident woman, from the 80s particularly, wanting too much in a not particularly nice way. You know, demanding it. I think men are disempowered now.

Jodie takes on a popular media representation of feminism and feminists. In the next excerpt, Jodie seems happy to have benefited from feminist-inspired legislative and social reforms, but does not want to be associated with aggressive, strident, demanding feminists:

Jodie: I think feminism has gone too far in a whole stack of ways. I never wanted other women to speak for me. So while I agreed with whatever it was that they got through reform-wise, I think at times, they were just completely over the top and abrasive and it irritated me that women thought that all women, would behave like that, would be so aggressive. A lot of them were very strident, particularly in the 80s, and aggressive in what they wanted. I didn't see that so much. What I saw was ruthlessly ambitious women [in her workplace].

LN: Did you see that linked to feminism at all? You were talking about the politics in the newsroom and those bitchy women who were giving you a hard time, do you think they were empowered by the women's movement or they were just like that [ruthlessly ambitious] anyway?

Jodie: I think a lot of them [feminist-identified co-workers] are really insecure. I remember one woman, for example, it's a terrible thing to say, but she was particularly overweight and she was particularly bad at what she did, and she was the editor. She didn't last very long, but you could tell she had this raging insecurity. She used to go around quoting feminism. You know, 'I'm a woman and I'm in power.' I'd look at her and think, 'Well, you know, if you're that empowered, why do you need to tell me'?

So men are insecure about their roles because feminists want '*too much in a not particularly nice way.*' Yet Jodie claims feminists who challenge those stereotypical roles for women are also insecure. This insecurity is understood as being brought on by themselves, and Jodie expresses the opinion vindictively. By contrast, insecure men are the victims of feminism, and she is sympathetic to their pain. Clearly, Jodie doesn't want to be identified as a 'woman,' let alone contaminated as a 'feminist.'

Jessica is also disparaging about how feminists go about their politics in the newsroom. There are 'nicer' ways that feminist opinions should be espoused, ones that are more palatable to co-workers and less disruptive in the newsroom. I ask Jessica if anyone in her newsroom identifies as a feminist and she tells me that there is one feminist in the newsroom:

Jessica: I think she gets shot down all the time.

LN: In what way? What happens to her?

Jessica: She goes about it the wrong way. I remember one day she cut out a whole bunch of things, like all the sport pages from one edition, and she put notes on the board and wrote, 'Where's the women's sport in the sports section'? But instead of . . . maybe she waited until it was too late, until it had been done, she didn't go to the [male] chief-of-staff and maybe she might not have been working, but if she had been working, and she knew things that were on, then she could have said 'oh you know, there's women's soccer going on here, and there's this going on, why don't we do something with that?' Instead, it was just a criticism—she stuck it up on the board and wrote all over it, which people get a bit weird about. Often that's where the subs put up the things that are wrong, or wrong with the paper, and everyone looks at them. It's not something that gets talked about a lot. You put things up there that everyone needs to read but no one necessarily talks about.

LN: So you are saying there's different ways of negotiating those problems?

Jessica: Yeah.

LN: And it's a quieter, it's a more subtle way of doing it?

Jessica: Yeah, I think everyone here gets very upset about people who drag out their soap box and start shouting about things. It's not the way to go.

Jessica has her preferred method of challenging perceived inequity:

Jessica: I have started saying 'oh, it's another warm day is anyone going up to the [the river area] to get a picture of a girl lying on her stomach?' Then they go 'oh no.' So maybe you hope that it starts to get through, that people realise that we know what goes on. Maybe no one's really thought about it either.

Jessica's idealistic notion of how to challenge gender inequity is via sarcasm and keeping faith in the liberal narrative, but it appears to not have been successful. This position is based on being complicit with traditional femininity and an ethic of care—asking 'nicely'—as if it were a favour to women (and female journalists) that the newspaper publish stories about sportswomen. Jessica's reaction to her colleague's complaint about the lack of women's sport in the newspaper also assumes that there was a beginning point before things went bad, and her colleague should have intervened.

I find Jessica's excerpts here particularly troubling, because during the interview she demonstrates a solid understanding of gender politics in the newsroom. In previous chapters I have used excerpts in which she acknowledges a division between how male and female journalists experience the newsroom and the inequity for women and how some of these issues are major frustrations for her. Jessica also tells me that she is pleased there is one senior female sub-editor on staff in whom she can confide and discuss her stories, leaving her feeling positive rather than undervalued, which is how the male sub-editors' criticisms make her feel. Nevertheless, Jessica is very quick to portray a feminist journalist negatively if that woman challenges issues that she experiences as inequitable. When I read this excerpt, Jessica sounds frightened. Then I recall how Jessica negotiated the location of the interview, and my initial reaction seems correct. Jessica was pleased to be involved in the project and happy to be interviewed. She chose to come to the office on her day off and specifically asked that she enter the room in which the interview was to take place via a side door. She said this was to avoid walking through the newsroom, but gave no further explanation. Once I had opened the side door, she surveyed the room making sure that all entry doors to the newsroom were closed 'in case someone might overhear our interview.' This was in complete contrast to two male interviewees from this newspaper interviewed on the same day: one left his office door open, and the other didn't discuss the office geography or feel uncomfortable with others knowing he was being interviewed. Both Jessica and Jodie are frightened by, shamed by, see as disadvantageous to them, the methods and the styles—in fact actually doing anything—that draws attention to the issues they raise.

The pin-board, for example, is a sacred space that (male) sub-editors 'get a bit weird about.' It's their space to use to chastise subordinate staff in writing so that they don't have to talk to them or challenge them directly, and in so doing the hierarchy remains firmly established with little disruption or verbal disputes. It's a board on which subs can put up (serious) notices that affect the newspaper and where sub-editors alert staff to their mistakes. Yet a senior female reporter—and a feminist—who wants to alert section editors to what she perceives as errors in judgment about newspaper content is to be rebuked for using the same communication methods, and not only by the 'owners' of the board, but by one of her female colleagues.

The majority of male journalists interviewed talked about, or defined, feminism in terms of equality. Tony, a 38-year-old deputy sports sub-editor on a metropolitan newspaper, is typical of those responses. I quote at length here to accentuate how uncomfortable he is discussing the term with me, compared to other interviewees who all had very strong opinions.

> *LN: How has feminism impacted on newspapers in general?*
>
> *Tony: Feminism?*
>
> *LN: Yes, if you were to think about feminism would you have a definition for it, or some idea of what you think it means?*
>
> *Tony: What does feminism mean?*
>
> *LN: Yes, to you.*
>
> *Tony: Oh dear, in newspapers?*
>
> *LN: Well what it means in general to you, and then we could talk about what it might have, if you think there are any changes in newspapers.*
>
> *Tony: Well, I might be wrong about this, but I think feminism means the struggle of women to be recognised as equal human beings to males, and that I guess in their work, and in everything, just in their life in general, that's very broad. Is that alright?*

Tony is extremely tentative about interacting with me in a discussion about feminism. Perhaps this is because we had worked together five years earlier as colleagues on another newspaper, and he may have been aware of my feminist beliefs and felt undermined by his perceived lack of knowledge. It's not that Tony wants to slip out of a discussion about the inequality of women, as news subjects or within the newsroom, as later in the interview he talks openly about how his section editor only employs men and throws away job applications from women, and how he cannot understand why. Tony demonstrates an understanding of one of the many versions of feminism—the less abrasive, equity version—which seems to allow for a lack of understanding about the inequity he describes as happening in his newsroom.

> *LN: Are all your sports reporters' men?*

Tony: Yes. I don't employ them though, Louise.

LN: I know, but how does that reflect on the sort of stories that get in the newspaper and is women's sport covered here?

Tony: No. Women's sport is not covered anywhere, not enough, and I notice a few good women sports reporters around as you know. Women in [state] you can have conversations with about rugby and football and cricket, just as well as anyone, any man. But that's talking about men's sports, really women's sport is not really in the public eye. That's in all the media, but we don't have any female sports reporters at the [newspaper title]. We haven't for years.

LN: Do you think that reflects on the content, is that why there wouldn't be much coverage of women's sport?

Tony: It's got to, yeah. The sports editor is in charge of employing sports reporters and I know for a fact that he's had women apply for jobs and he just rejects them on the basis that they're women.

LN: Why?

Tony: Because he's got, I don't know, that's Australian, very Australian, he just doesn't like women.

LN: Can you raise . . .

Tony: I don't understand it, it's strange

LN: Do you ever raise the issue?

Tony: He's a strange guy.

LN: Do you ever raise the issue with him?

Tony: Ah no, not really. He asks me to have a read of that applicant, what do you think of that. But I know for a fact that he takes the women out and just shows me the male ones, because he's not going to employ a woman.

LN: Do any of the women in the newsroom who are in the general news reporting section say 'why aren't we running any women's sports,' or 'why haven't we got a woman writing sport?'

Tony: No. They probably do amongst themselves, but I've never heard it. We have people ringing up all the time, we have letters to the paper, they're not numerous, but you know, every now and then 'why don't you cover women's sport?'

LN: And what's the response?

Tony: The response is 'it doesn't sell.' It's basically it. I have had conversations with my boss and he's interested in women. If women are covered in the sports sections it's because they're glamorous or something like that. Anna Kornikova who's probably never won a tournament in her life—it's the way she looks, and they run a photo of a good looking woman just for the photograph. It's for the perve aspect of it. That's the only reason that they'll run it. It's a very male dominated area.

LN: And that's actually said in the newsroom, 'oh, she looks alright,' or whatever?

Tony: Yeah, sure, all that, yeah. Better use that shot. They have to have their bimbo pages. [Former colleague's name] always had his bimbo page.

LN: He never talked to me about that.

Tony: Well it's not said, you know, it's sort of not really out in the open, but it's what they run. That's what they run it for, it's the perve aspect.

LN: Perve aspect. For half the population? For the men?

Tony: Yeah, that's right.

LN: What happens to the other half of the population?

Tony: No, they get ignored.

This long excerpt does two things: first, it gives a specific account of how female journalists are disadvantaged in accessing certain journalistic jobs that are considered 'male,' making a mockery of the merit principles advocated in EEO polices that this particular newspaper advocates. It also clearly demonstrates homosociality in hiring practices. The excerpt makes transparent the male bias against potential female journalists, while also reinforcing the much-debated (by feminist media theorists) concern about the limited number of acceptable avenues for female journalists. There are no merit principles in action here—it is very clearly 'jobs for the boys.'

Tony's excerpt also identifies a subject position that is rare in my interviews with male journalists. Tony acknowledges that women, as media subjects and as journalists, experience inequality. He explicitly details how and at whose behest inequity takes shape. He also demonstrates an understanding of feminism, or equity concepts. Nevertheless, he is still unable (disempowered, frightened?) to use this knowledge as a basis from which he might address the problems he details and laments. He seems not to want to answer my question about what he might *do* about the wrongs that he observes.

Simon confidently espouses his views about feminism and alludes to a broader knowledge of feminism. He makes the point that there are various strands of feminism and expresses the concepts of gender inequity. Unlike Tony, however, he sees no gender inequity in the newsroom.

LN: How would you define feminism if someone was to come up to you in the street and ask you?

Simon: Feminism as in, what, classic feminism or just . . . ?

LN: However you would see it today.

Simon: Well, I just think it's a push for equality between the sexes; a push from women for equality. That's how I'd view feminism.

LN: Yes. Do you think it's viewed that way in the newsroom by everybody? Is there positive connotations to it, or negative?

Simon: I think positive, on the floor. No one—there's definitely no sort of seeking to denigrate or deny staff members because of their gender. I'm definitely not aware of anything like that. I'm not aware of anyone being denied something that could be traced back to their gender at all, and that goes for both sexes. I think sometimes some people have a bit of a grumble when they miss out or whatever and sort of try to attribute, 'Because I'm this, because I'm that,' but I don't think there's anything that you could—either overt or covert that I'm aware of really [that could] be attributed to any pronounced sexism.

Simon's account of the unproblematic gender dynamics in his newsroom is interesting given that I asked him how other journalists might view feminism, and also in light of Tony's experience and knowledge. Perhaps the different subject positions that Tony and Simon occupy point to industry in/experience, but there are still significant points to tease out here. It's important to place Simon's comments in the context of his earlier defence of sexually harassing behaviour in the newsroom, in which he detailed participating in and condoning sexist jokes (although he did not describe them as sexist), suggesting it was all *'just a little bit of cheeky ribaldry.'* In that excerpt, as here, Simon makes the broad claim that there is no gender inequity in his newsroom because he knows of no one who has discussed it with him, or that he is *'not aware of'* any inequity. It seems to me that Simon is avoiding or attempting to erase the issue of gender inequity/politics. So while Simon uses some words that may allude to knowledge of feminist principles, he paints his workplace as harmonious, and those colleagues that suggest a bias—although he doesn't say a gender bias—are just *'grumblers.'* I find it suspicious, however, that Simon speaks of potential and actual *'grumblers'* in gender-neutral terms. Perhaps Simon has no reason to grumble, because at age 26 he is very highly graded for six years' experience in the industry. During the interview Simon recounts how his colleagues were unhappy about his quick progress through the ranks; he had had seven promotions in five years, which took him rapidly from a third-year cadet to a level 3b on a scale where 4–5 is considered senior.[1]

---

[1] His first promotion took him to a fourth year cadet, then level 1a, 1b, 2a, 2b, 3a, to his current grade of 3b. See Appendix 2 for an outline of the grading system

Mark also has an awareness of feminism and speaks to a debate that feminists have engaged in for many years. He demonstrates an understanding of the white, middle-class criticisms of feminism.

> Mark: Indeed the Anne Summers[2] approach to feminism absolutely annoys the shit out of me. Because it is actually elite, white, and middle class, and only for those who have access.

In this excerpt I am not convinced that this is how Mark actually engages with feminism or whether he wants to appease or impress me with his knowledge. This is evidenced in an excerpt prior to that above. Mark was discussing with me how one of his published stories was badly edited and how angry he was, but that he just got on with his job. Women, on the other hand, prompted a different take on the problem of their stories not being published, or having them changed.

> Mark: There is a view that somehow or other the reason this or that story didn't get in was because there's a plot and part of that plot, is of course, gendered. The people who are making the decisions are quite frequently male. Well, in fact they are also quite frequently women—which is another problem. So they [female journalists] tend to get very vicious about women who are, let's say, in a similar coterie as they are, who are actually in different types of jobs.
>
> LN: Are there women that you know who see themselves as feminist?
>
> Mark: Yes and the obvious one was Susan Mitchell,[3] who gave feminism a bad name as far as I'm concerned. My partner is renowned as being a feminist, so . . .
>
> LN: [laughing] Oh, you must have some great conversations then?
>
> Mark: Well up to a point. She accuses me of all sorts of things, but she still puts up with me occasionally.

Mark then sums up the question about feminists:

> Mark: Feminists are usually women who are very active in groups, and are attacking the world. Oh, hang on a moment, there are an awful lot of people out there who actually, who are feminists in the sense that they want to actually

---

[2]Anne Summers is a prominent Australian liberal feminist, well known for her 1975 classic work on the role of women in Australian society, Damned Whores and God's Police: The Colonisation of Women in Australia. The book was revised in 1994 and 2002.

[3]Susan Mitchell is an Australian author of a number of feminist books from 1987 onwards, and like Summers, has a liberal perspective.

pursue a whole series of goals for women, but they also want to deal within a environment which says 'okay, I want to be a mother.' But journalism doesn't accommodate that.

Mark positions himself here as the beleaguered male, albeit a knowledgeable one who demonstrates a considerable awareness of feminist concepts and concerns. His partner is a feminist, who *'still puts up with me,'* yet his first definition of a feminist includes a derogatory comment that feminists are those who are *'attacking the world,'* before having a quick rethink. Mark's excerpt is rife with contradictions, on the one hand happily detailing women's competitive vicious-ness in the newsroom, yet articulating key aspects of feminism and names of prominent Australian feminists.

It is not surprising that after being told these stories about feminists and feminism that female journalists would not want to be labelled 'feminist.' The oldest woman that I interviewed was 55-year-old regional editor Pat, who was reluctant to take up the feminist label, even though she knows that her actions during her long career have been construed as being underpinned by a feminist philosophy. When appointed in 1988, Pat was one of the first female editors of a daily newspaper in Australia. In the interview she recalls stories from the late 1970s and beyond, detailing at length how she personally chal-lenged gender inequity, stereotypes, and unwritten rules. For example, she tells me a story about how early in her career she had to defend her position as a reporter after being told by a source that he wanted to talk to a *'real reporter,'* that being *'not a girl one.'*

> Pat: *When I first started at the [newspaper name] and I was general reporting, someone came out and said, 'There's somebody out the front who wants to see you—a reporter.' I went out and there was this sort of tall bloody stockman-type. He's out from the bush anyway, had the Akubra and he's pretty dusty looking and he's an older guy and I said 'yeah, can I help you, what's up.' He said 'I want to see a reporter' and I said 'I'm a reporter.' He said 'no, I want to see a real reporter.' I said 'no, I'm a real reporter.' He said 'no, no, I want one—you know, not a girl one, I want one that writes news stories about cattle.' I thought that was hilarious.*

Pat works hard in the interview to deny being a feminist, even bringing her husband into the interview to shore up her position as a nonfeminist, but not antifeminist, for she never chastises feminist women or feminist politics. Rather, she sees herself very individually, challenging a range of inequities. The interview had taken place in Pat's home and her husband had moved in and out of the room during the later part of the interview, only stopping and involving himself in the conversation, at Pat's request, when our talk turned to feminism. We had been discussing some of her ideas about news content and whether there were stories that appealed to women more than men and vice versa. I saw this as an opportunity to discuss her ideas about feminism. Note, too, how I buy into her discourse of feminism (in this and the following excerpt) by sometimes playing down my views and using words that affirm, placate, and reassure her liberal and individualistic position. Generally, I am working to invoke a conservative discourse that is aligned with Pat's to avoid shutting down the discussion.

> LN: *Your ideas are pretty progressive then, so would you go a step further, or maybe not see it as a step further, and call yourself a feminist or is that a term that's very old hat? How do you see it?*
>
> Pat: *I don't think I've ever been a feminist. I think occasionally I've got too blokey, haven't I, a little bit?* [question to husband]
>
> Husband: *No, I don't—other people see you as a feminist, but you don't see yourself as one. You sort of stick up for your rights, I think.*

I'll use another excerpt here from Pat, because I am interested in how far Pat goes to distance herself from a feminist position while at the same time detailing stories from her past that indicate she has a feminist philosophy. Pat tells a long story about how she demanded to be served beer in a pub at a time when women were not allowed into the front bar (in the 1970s) and, angry at the discrimination, she got the police involved. Again she reiterates her position that she is not a feminist.

> LN: *You tell stories like that, and I think I'd probably see that as feminist action in terms of just wanting to be equal.*
>
> Pat: *I suppose it is, but I don't think of myself as a feminist at all.*
>
> Husband: *No.*
>
> Pat: *No, never.*
>
> LN: *Maybe because there's a lot of bad press about feminism and what that might mean.*
>
> Husband: *I don't think it bothers you really, does it?*
>
> Pat: *No.*
>
> Husband: *If you just want to do it, you just go and do it, don't you?*
>
> Pat: *Mmm.*
>
> LN: *A lot of other women aren't as brave as you though. That's where I think perhaps feminism—maybe as a collective thing, as a social movement—has helped other women who aren't as empowered as you.*

Pat: Do you think? It's never worried me. If I'm out somewhere with a whole lot of blokes and a funny situation or wherever, I never think about being in a male-dominated arena anywhere or anything like that. I don't fight—well, not much.

Husband: Mm?

Pat: I said I don't fight that much physically.

LN: Do feminists fight, do they, [Pat]?

Pat: I mean, no, I'm talking about being blokey to the point of having a few drinks and then swinging . . .

There are two points to address in this excerpt. Firstly, I'm interested in how Pat's husband slips into the discussion, initially being called upon for support and reassurance. Then in this last section when I start pressing Pat, her husband speaks for her, reasserting that ideas about feminism don't bother her and whatever she does is an individual choice, effectively taking any links to gender politics out of the situations we have spoken about, even the (political) front bar story. Secondly, when Pat states that '*I never think about being in a male dominated arena, anywhere*' this clearly contradicts her story about the front bar, and also her thoughts in a very specific email that Pat sent to me shortly after our interview. It seems she needed to reassert her opinion about her male contemporaries being a help rather than a hindrance to her career. In part that email reads:

Pat: I really don't think the male put-down has been a serious factor anywhere in my career. We have had the occasional hiccup and they can come from anywhere. I think older men who have had difficulty with a female boss are a small but disappearing problem: more obvious are the young turks who are on their way up and quite gung ho about it. They tend to be a little more dismissive of women around conference tables etc. Or maybe they are dismissive of everyone. The body language etc I have talked about (less avid attention when a woman is speaking) is fairly minimal though. I guess I get a little over-sensitive because I am in a blokey environment so often but for the most part the guys are friendly, courteous and respectful. (email conversation, February 5, 2004)

Here Pat sets herself up in a binary position with her male colleagues. She blames herself for admitting and acknowledging the struggle of being in a gendered minority in the workplace for so much of her career ('*I guess I get a little over-sensitive*') and then puts being '*over sensitive*' down to working in a '*blokey environment so often.*' Pat doesn't want to admit the struggle for women, let alone for herself. It seems for Pat that it is acceptable to be seen as having a feminist perspective in telling stories about the past when she was a reporter in the 1970s and 1980s (when arguably the stories may have been more openly received), but in her role as editor she stays well clear of any newsroom story that would equate her with that apparently ideological position.

Janet clearly articulates why women like Pat might downplay feminist values, even though Pat has been active, individually, in challenging gender discrimination in the past. Janet is talking about a publicly identified feminist in a major city newsroom. At the same time, Janet also offers a reason why Jessica may be so scared of female journalists who challenge gender discrimination in the newsroom.

> *Janet: She's outspoken . . . (inaudible) other women don't support her because they are scared of not getting promoted, feeling threatened (inaudible)*
>
> *LN: But they won't support her publicly?*
>
> *Janet: They don't.*
>
> *LN: But privately?*
>
> *Janet: It's not a case of supporting her. They won't take her position. They won't follow through with her. In a more formal way they are scared of losing their job, I don't know; scared of not being promoted. I don't know. They are threatened.*

Janet 'knows' the way that sexism works. She has articulated that point in previous excerpts in other parts of the book, especially around sexually harassing behaviour in the newsroom. She has been a recipient of it, and she has watched it happen to other young women. Janet is critical of women not supporting this feminist journalist. Janet was one of a handful of women, including the feminist she mentions in this excerpt, who established a short-lived Women in Journalism committee at a newspaper to attempt to address gender inequality. I have had phone and email conversations with the feminist journalist who Janet tells me about. She still works with that newspaper and continues to maintain strong support mechanisms to call upon. These include being involved with the industry union at a very high level, publicly speaking about the difficulty female journalists' face in the industry, and writing articles for international women's media groups. However, I find it interesting that when I speak to her (September 2004) she downplays gender issues and claims that she tries to stay away from talking about gender publicly. It seems that even to publicly identified feminists, the 'F-word' still must be downplayed, if not disavowed to survive as a successful journalist in today's print news media.

Conclusion

In this chapter I have shown that there are a range of positions taken up by the male and female interviewees in relation to feminism. The dominant theme is one of hostility towards feminists both within and outside the industry. Interviewees variously consider that feminists have psychological problems, are overly emotional and insecure. Overall there was a sense that the majority of interviewees understood feminists as angry and extreme in their actions and often pushed their politics 'too far.' A feminist position also disempowers men. With this framework established it was not surprising, then, that many of the female interviewees did not want to be associated with feminism or feminists. The majority of female interviewees, young and older, are inclined to down-play any feminist position, even though as Pat's stories indicate some take up what I and others consider a feminist position. The oppositional themes, then, where a woman takes up a feminist position is shown by my interviewees to be inconsistent with 'being a journalist.' Janet's excerpt, for example, shows how difficult it is for women to have and sustain a feminist position in journalism. Other women, according to Janet and evident in Jodie's comments, do not want to support or be associated with a feminist in her newsroom politics.

Chapter Nine

Feminism and Naked Women in Newsroom Dialogue

I turn now to how news sources and journalists engage with feminism, and in doing so how feminism shapes news content. I move away from an analysis of the interview material and focus on the examination of one particular newsroom story—one that involves the naked female body. I am interested here in teasing out the direct relationship between newsroom culture and news content, a link that's been only implicit in previous chapters.

The newsroom anecdote was gleaned from my time working as a sub-editor at *The Mercury* newspaper in Hobart, Tasmania, in 2003. Several brief newsroom discussions were prompted by an all-women, naked, antiwar protest. Thirty-six Tasmanian women stripped naked to be photographed for a media image to demonstrate their antiwar sentiments in March 2003. This action was part of an international protest, Disrobe for Disarmament, that started in the United States in late 2002 as talk about a U.S.-led war against Iraq gained momentum.[1] By the time the Australian women took action, the war had begun and Australian troops were involved, and the protesters wanted them to return home. The women had positioned their naked bodies on the ground at a secret location in Hobart creating the words 'No War' (see published article, including image, over page). The protesters alerted *The Mercury* of their protest action, and a female reporter was assigned to cover the story (Paine, 2003, p. 5). The anecdote is a paraphrased account of the discussions as I recalled them in my journal later that night. I use the anecdote to discuss subjectivities in the newsroom, which includes a discussion of objectivity (which I have briefly touched on in previous chapters), and here I more thoroughly trace the

---

[1] Italy also took part in the protest. Some protests included men, but predominantly the protests were organised for and performed by women. In Australia the first naked protest was organised by pop singer Grace Knight at Byron Bay in New South Wales. For more information on the worldwide protest see www.sfheart.com/naked_for_peace.html (accessed August 1, 2003).

Chilling out in name of disarmament

By MICHELLE PAINE

WOMEN stripped for peace in Hobart's morning chill yesterday.

The 36 women aged in their 20s to 40s chose a secluded South Hobart paddock for the Disrobe for Disarmament event, named after a protest organised by singer Grace Knight at Byron Bay in , New South Wales.

Participant Linda Seaborn said yesterday most of the women felt uncomfortable about undressing for public eyes, making them feel it was a genuine sacrifice for peace.

"If people want to do it more publicly, they can go ahead, but this is how we felt comfortable doing it," said Ms Seaborn, a member of the Peace Coalition.

"It was what we see as quite an extreme response to an extreme situation.

"Some of these women had never protested. We think going to war without the sanction of the UN, and the Prime Minister making the decision without the consent of Parliament, is wrong."

Ms Seaborn said she did not think the protest was anti-feminist.

"For us it was a feminist thing, to choose to use our bodies in this way. It's reflective of the system in which we don't have a political voice.

We had to do something to have a voice," she said.

There had been interest from interstate and overseas about the women's actions.

"In a way it's like Natasha Scott Despoja and the women who wore their bras outside their clothes. This is what we have to do to get the message

out, not the message about taking our clothes off but the message that we want Australian troops to come home," Ms Seaborn said.

"Australia should be taking the position of Commonwealth countries more like ns, New Zealand, South Africa and Canada, who are

opting for a negotiating role."

The women will wear clothes to take part in the traditional Palm Sunday peace rally.

NAKED TRUTH: A secluded South Hobart paddock allows peace protesters to spell out what they think of the Iraq conflict yesterday morning.

The published article about the 'No War' naked women protestors in *The Mercury* newspaper, 26 March 2003, p. 5. Reprinted with the permission of *The Mercury*.

contours of a long and involved debate both within the media industry and in scholarly research.

The image of the 'No War' naked protesters is a prompt through which I engage with and challenge various feminist discourses about the female body in the area of media representation. I suggest that we cannot simply argue that women who use their bodies for political gain are antifeminist, because clearly, in this case, they are not—these protesters do consider themselves feminists. But neither can we say that the use of the naked female body is not constrained by its long history in Western culture as 'sex object.' As the chapter unfolds I discuss four separate, but often intertwining issues: what journalists think about women who 'get their clothes off' to be photographed; the intentions of the women who take their clothes off; how they are presented in the media; and, finally, how they might be read by audiences.

Newsroom Conversation 1:

A female reporter[2] assigned to cover the naked women's 'No War' protest explained the event to me in the newsroom and asked if I thought it was antifeminist. I replied that I didn't think the women's actions were antifemi-

---

[2]All the journalists paraphrased in these conversations have given written permission to use the quotes.

nist, but that "not all feminists think alike." She told me that a senior female journalist who was directing her to write the story had said to her, and in the news conference, that:

> Women have fought for a long time not to have their bodies objectified, and now they are doing it to themselves.

Newsroom Conversation 2:

The second newsroom conversation involved a senior female section editor who was scrutinising the photograph that the protesters had provided. She had enlarged the image on her computer screen, and when I entered the room she was making disparaging comments about the women's bodies—their size, shape, and colour (two of the women were dark-skinned). She commented loudly that some 'had shaved their fannies.' Then as I passed by her work station she asked:

> You wouldn't do that [be involved in a nude protest] would you, Louise?
>
> Why would you think that? I asked.
>
> Oh, I don't know, she replied.

Newsroom Conversation 2.1:

Another conversation then took place with the newspaper's editor, Garry Bailey, who had overheard this conversation. He came to where I was standing next to the senior female section editor and also looked at the image. It seemed he wanted to elicit a personal discussion when he also asked if I had been involved in the protest. I laughed and said:

> No, I only take my clothes off in the bathroom.

Bailey also laughed and agreed that he was the same. I asked why he thought I might be involved and he replied with a question about what I thought of 'these women doing it.' He answered his own question:

> You know, these are the women who get their clothes off [for publicity I think he was insinuating] and then are the first to complain if it is nudity and women in another way.

I intervened:

> How do you know that they are the same women. Don't you think that's a bit of a generalisation?

He replied:

> *Maybe I am generalising.*

I continued and said that there was a difference between what these women had done and complaints that some women lodge to the newspaper about the print media's objectification of women. I said:

> *The difference is that these women had total control of the image, and that we (the newspaper) decided if we used it or not. You know that many women think the pictures we take are not generally empowering to women, but these women feel in control and empowered by what they have done, so it's positive for them.*

There was no reply.

Newsroom Conversation 3:

The final conversation occurred the day the story was published. An older male sub-editor said to me:

> *I don't understand why they have done it [taken their clothes off]. Was it just for the publicity, a way to make a statement?*

I replied that I did not know the women, the reasons for their actions, or their politics, but it seemed that they had achieved their objectives

In the newsroom discussions women, naked female bodies, and feminism, or conceptions of feminism, are the central concern of all the major players—including myself. There is a shifting and contested collage of subject positions available here: objective journalist; female journalist; feminist; and feminist journalist.

These discussions on the newsroom floor are interesting to analyse, primarily because they reveal the often unarticulated impact of feminism in the news-making process. They, no doubt, also demonstrate slippages in which 'feminism' is deployed to work against politically active female news sources and feminist journalists. There is a contradiction between the sometimes 'negative' dialogues and the end result, which I see as a 'successful' published outcome for the protesting women. As Byerly (2004a) notes, those journalists who interrupt the 'masculine' norm by challenging it, or suggesting alternatives to the mainstream repertoire of news, risk discipline or ridicule. According to Byerly, who spent many years as a journalist before becoming an academic, 'normal' means news that does not offend advertisers and (imagined) readers. Perhaps, it can also be argued that inside the newsroom 'normal' might mean news that doesn't offend the sensibilities or orthodoxies of senior journalists and editors. 'Normal' could also be extended to incorporate the subjectivities of journalists in the newsroom. So in the dialogues presented, these journalists' subjective position as 'objective newsmaker' is reinforced as a stable uncontested one, but becomes unstable when challenged by a feminist perspective both in the newsroom and through feminist news sources.

The dialogues also provide evidence that feminism, and indeed feminists (workers and sources), can and do shape some news content. Although the dialogues could be read as often negative about feminism or feminists, the outcome of this particular story—what ends up in print—offers more positive representations,[3] especially as it reflects the women's concerns about war, a generally masculine narrative, within a feminist framework. It is this paradox that is the central concern of this section. Moreover, I argue that feminism, as Byerly (1999) has noted, is increasingly deeply embedded in media messages and the industries that produce them.

Feminism or its implication as newsroom discourse is generally met with public silence. Few, if any, want to be publicly aligned with a feminist perspective, especially female journalists; the repercussion for public disclosure is known in the industry to stymie careers (as indicated in previous chapters, see Yallop, 2004f, pp. 41, 43). It's a point that many of the female interviewees noted. This 'alternative knowledge' (Lewis et al. 1998, p. 67) of feminism is understood as irrelevant to journalism and indeed as impinging on journalistic objectivity. But people's identity positions are strategic (Jeffreys, 1991). That is, according to Sue Lewis et al. (1998, p. 61), "they construct, change and deploy their notions of who they are in order to achieve their chosen goals in a variety of contexts." It is my experience that there are many women in the industry who hold feminist beliefs, but rather than construct their identities around feminism or label their often private concerns as feminist—already alert to a fear or misunderstanding of feminism by the dominant newsroom culture—they merely attempt to fit in, rather than challenge dominant orthodoxies.

There are many questions that arise from the anecdotes I have presented. They include: how did an antiwar protest get reconfigured as a feminist/women's protest, and what part does the nakedness of the women play in the assumption of a 'feminist protest'? Also of interest are other questions, such as: how do protesting women become 'complaining' women and become overwritten with feminism, when that was not the basis of their protest? What subject positions do female journalists take up in order to fit the dominant newsroom culture? How do subject positions in the newsroom get shaped by engagement

---

[3]Positive versus negative representations have been a central concern of feminist theorists for the past 30 years. I am aware of the critique of the simple notion of "positive" images as a solution to the problem of the representation of women, but I do not want to engage in that debate here.

with news stories? Is there an underlying fear of covering what is perceived to be a women's issue? How do constraints and negotiations over feminism shape subjectivities in the newsroom?

Multiple Identities and Objectivity

These discussions also reveal my multiple identifications as journalist, feminist, feminist journalist, and academic. During the research and writing of this book there has been a constant underlying tension between these multiple identities.[4] This is largely due to how I have envisaged and experienced that loaded notion of objectivity in both my early journalistic training and later academic education. Journalists are well known for prizing their reputation for impartiality, and this was a position I found difficult to let go of when I began academic study. To accuse a journalist of bias is to impugn his/her journalistic integrity: "For it is to claim that a journalist is, intentionally or otherwise, not adhering to the truth-respecting methods required for him [sic] to achieve the proper goal of journalism: arriving at the truth of the matter" (Kieran, 1998, p. 23).

In news journalism pursuing institutional goals, the constraints of organisational routines, relations with sources, editorial policy, and the like are embodied in a professional ideology that prescribes that journalists are detached outsiders who cannot promote specific interests (van Zoonen, 1998a, p. 135). The guiding principle of Western journalism, which has prided itself on 'objectivity' and neutrality in reporting, claims to discourage journalists from demonstrating their personal political convictions inside or outside the newsroom. This professional value system denies the fact that reporters may be politically active or that they may be personally affected and motivated by the very news events that they cover (Byerly & Warren, 1996, p. 3). It also denies the idea that their personal histories shape their view of the world and that they become journalists through particular cultural and social contexts.

The idea of objectivity (meaning distance and neutrality) in journalism has come under siege, from both inside and outside the industry, and has been shown to be built on specific methods that tend to favour dominant institutions, positions and people (see, for example, Hall et al., 1978; Schudson, 1978). Van Zoonen (1998a, p. 139) argues that objectivity in journalism has come under attack for various reasons including "its epistemological and ontological untenability; its practical impossibility; its effects as an instrument of domination, etc; nevertheless, the term itself has maintained its value as a marker of good

---

[4]These multiply identities are also noted by other media researchers who were formerly journalists; for example, see Byerly (2004a).

journalism" and journalistic integrity. This is the case even though one of the consequences of the pursuit of objectivity is that it makes reporters hesitant to inject issues into the news that aren't already there (Cunningham, 2003). Therefore if an issue isn't already in the news, it is more difficult to sell to editors. It is evident from this perspective that feminist issues and/or feminist sources may find it difficult to be included in the values associated with 'news,' even though feminist issues have been around for 30 years.

The following excerpt from Susan, an experienced metropolitan reporter, shows that she knows that the 'news' is subjective. For Susan there is pressure to write to the 'agenda' of the newspaper.

> Susan: When I write I try to make sure I get all those balances in there and everyone's had their say. But I have an opinion about it before I start writing. I know now that's going to affect how I write that story, how I weight certain paragraphs, what's the opening paragraph, what's the end paragraph, the two most powerful ones, you know all those sorts of decisions you make. I know I'm going to make subjective judgments about it, not necessarily only my subjectivity, but also perhaps what's coming down the line from my employer as well—what they would consider the most interesting aspect or where they see the tilt for that story.
>
> LN: So you are saying that when you write your stories; you have got that thing in the back of your mind that you know what angle they're going to be wanting?
>
> Susan: Absolutely.
>
> LN: They know what agenda is there.
>
> Susan: Yes.
>
> LN: And you know that you need to fulfil that because they're employing you?
>
> Susan: Yes.
>
> LN: And you write accordingly?
>
> Susan: Yes, or I would be wasting my time because I know it wouldn't get a run [be printed]. Or I would be wasting my time because I would be sitting here re-writing it at 7 at night, because I know it would get to the desk and they would say 'this is not what we wanted,' or 'this is not what we were discussing,' or 'this is not what we thought we were going to get, can you change it accordingly?'

Stuart, a first year cadet, has a similar take on how 'the paper' sets news agendas, and therefore has an awareness of the subjectivity of news. I was asking him about some of the frustrations of being a journalist.

*Stuart: Having to compromise between what you know the people want to hear,
and what the paper wants to put out there—I guess that's a frustration. And then
you feel that you are not actually doing your job if you don't stir up trouble.*

Susan and Stuart both speak to a form of newsroom socialisation. More than
50 years ago American sociologist Warren Breed (1955) wrote about how 'policies,'
defined as the more-or-less consistent orientation shown by the newspaper, come
to be maintained, or bypassed, via social control in the newsroom. He was not, of
course, interested in how practices of gender impacted on newsroom culture because
female journalists were rare at that time, but he was one of the first to identify how
news culture is learned—by 'osmosis.' Breed's historical account is invaluable in
helping identify the changing nature of journalism practices today. Journalists learn
'policy,' says Breed. "When a new reporter starts work he is not told what policy
is. Nor is he ever told. . . . Yet all but the newest staffers know what policy is. On
being asked they say they learn it 'by osmosis' " (cited in McChesney & Scott, 2003,
p. 229). Tasmanian journalism academic Libby Lester (2007) reinforces this
notion that journalists learn the news agenda via 'osmosis' in her discussion
with journalists involved in the 1983 coverage of the controversial Franklin
dam blockade in Tasmania. One reporter Lester interviews recalls that *The
Mercury* newspaper was clearly supportive of the state government's position on
the dam—that it go ahead. The reporter, Lester notes, had an awareness of the
newspaper's political position on the issue and he acknowledged it "was an innate
part of being a journalist at *The Mercury*" (in Lester, 2007, p. 61). Although the
reporter was never pressured to write the newspaper's agenda on this issue, it is
clear that he knew what it was.

Susan and Stuart show how journalists anticipate what is required of
them so as to win rewards and avoid punishments. The reward is, firstly, having your story published, having it bylined, and preferably having it used as a
page lead or on the front page of the newspaper. Punishment is having your
story 'spiked' (an industry term for 'deleted'), cut (reduced in size), or placed
towards the rear of the news section. In this way journalists learn to identify
newsroom norms and values and in the process learn and internalise their
status and obligations.

In my interview with Mark, however, it appeared that eschewing objectivity was a method of separating himself from the other 'objective ' reporters and
maintaining some distance from a management he was critical of. In detailing
his long career, he discusses various jobs out of journalism where he worked
for various state Labor governments. He proudly asserts:

*Mark: I'm a Labor [Party] person [supporter] and have been for 35 or probably
about 45 years.*

LN: You wouldn't acknowledge that publicly too often would you?

Mark: No, but everyone knows that I'm a Labor person.

Mark acknowledges his subjectivity and frees himself of concerns about a lack of objectivity by stating that even though he had this personal conviction, he was very critical of a particular state Labor government over certain issues. In this way he acknowledges that objectivity in news is still held up as possible and also believes that he could separate his personal beliefs from his role as objective reporter. I have found from the interviews, however, that the same confidence is not entrusted to feminism or feminists. Mark notes that if a known feminist were to apply for a job at the newspaper where he worked, she wouldn't be successful because she would be pigeonholed as subjective.

The opposite of 'objectivity,' 'subjectivity' (defined as personal interests and opinions), even when openly advocated, especially in sports journalism, is difficult to envisage in a positive light (van Zoonen, 1998a). But for van Zoonen it's the denial of subjectivity in journalism that is problematic.

> The current descriptive and prescriptive denial of subjectivity and structural constraints undermines the credibility of journalism, and fools no one any more. . . . In other words, journalism should become more open about its own constructedness, subjectivity and structurally, to maintain its status as a core institution of democratic societies. (van Zoonen, 1998a, p. 140)

Inherent in this notion of democracy is the belief of the mass media that it constitutes a 'fourth estate':[5]

> An independent and impartial public sphere through which the polity gain insight and information about local, national and international affairs and where, through the diligent ministrations of the corps of journalists, the government of the day (and any other appropriate target) is held to account. (Ross, 2002, p. 112)

---

[5]The 'fourth estate' is a term most often used to refer to the 'three powers' in a modern democratic society, principally the legislative power that makes the laws (for example, the parliament); the executive power that makes executive decisions on a day-to-day basis (for example, the Prime Minister); the judiciary who interpret the laws (for example, the Supreme Court). These powers supposedly counterbalance one another. This system of 'checks and balances' works to ensure that none of the three powers become too strong. The media often argues that it constitutes the fourth estate, watching for wrongdoings of the other three.

Here it is worth delving into a short history of this relatively recent journalistic pursuit of objectivity that evolved from controversies surrounding news coverage around the turn of the twentieth century (Gamson, 1984). Richard Harwood (1997), the *Washington Post*'s media columnist, argues that a concern for objectivity arose when "owners saw more money in making their papers more accurate and non-partisan." Objectivity, far from being an idea emanating from the thoughtfulness and concern of journalists, was a judgment from the top. "Several very famous owners—[Joseph] Pulitzer and E. W. Scripps and [Adolph] Ochs—decided that it was in their economic interest to have credible newspapers, so they began demanding a far greater degree of accuracy than they had been accustomed to" (Harwood, 1997, n.p.):

> I'm going to quote Pulitzer. 'It is not enough to refrain from publishing fake news or to take ordinary care to avoid mistakes. You've got to make everyone connected with the paper believe that accuracy is to a newspaper what virtue is to a woman.'[6] (Harwood, 1997, n.p.)

He noted that Ochs talked about the need to give the news impartially 'without fear of favour' and that Scripps instructed his managers to 'always see that the news report is handled objectively. You must not be biased or take sides in controversies.' This was revolutionary language for the beginning of the century, because it referred to a business and to practices that had been famously partisan and unreliable since the first newspaper appeared in the United States (Harwood, 1997).

> Nevertheless, the need for objectivity became a popular theme in those early trade publications and early journalism schools at the start of the century, and the idea became a cardinal and often unexamined principle in most of the newsrooms of America. (Harwood, 1997, n.p.)

Feminist media theorists have been much more critical of the idea of objectivity, seeing it very much defined by the rational, all-knowing man. Creedon (1993) argues that, as yet, no one has been able to define the parameters of objectivity or procedures in place in order to guarantee that it is always a part of the news judging process. "This ambiguity actually may be a tacit acknowledgement that journalists can't report facts objectively because news sources represent the dominant interests in society" (Creedon, 1993, p. 15).

Michael Parenti argues from a structuralist Marxist view that:

> Opinions that support existing arrangements of economic and political power are more easily treated as facts, while facts that are troublesome

---

[6]We can see here that 'virtue' and 'womanhood' are relegated to the private and emotional sphere and 'accuracy' (read objectivity) and manhood sit in the rational public sphere.

to the prevailing distribution of class power are likely to be dismissed as opinionated. And those who censor dissenting views see themselves as protectors of objectivity and keepers of heterodoxy when, in fact, they are the guardians of ideological conformity. (Parenti, 1986, p. 50)

If journalists enter the profession, as most researchers confirm, as a means of 'changing the world'[7] and choose the mainstream media in which to work because it expands the possibility of reaching wider audiences, why are journalists so concerned with claiming objectivity? Margareta Melin-Higgins (1996, p. 159) finds that the notion of objectivity is not a central concern for all journalists. Her research of Swedish journalists indicates that most enter the profession because they are interested in expressing *themselves*.[8] Many journalists that I have spoken to over the course of my career are sceptical of the notion of objectivity; firstly that it can be obtained in news reporting, and moreover that it is even a serious consideration of many senior editors and media owners. Some claim that biases towards certain political stories see many stories 'killed,' only to reappear, written by another journalist and published by the same newspaper when a different (or more sympathetic) night editor is heading the news desk. Still, the idea of adhering to the principles of 'objectivity' are regularly dragged out by media managers as a claim to 'serious' journalism; there appears to be an expectation that less serious or 'soft' news is 'subjective,' and this is also acceptable.

Why doesn't the industry, then, acknowledge, as certain strands of the academy do, that objectivity is an intent that is and has been a lofty, idealistic, and unattainable goal? Maybe that's where the clash comes between feminism and the media: as Angela McRobbie (1982), suggests "feminism forces us to locate our own auto-biographies and our experience inside the questions we might want to ask" (1982, p. 52). Yet media owners and editors are so entrenched in the idea that they can and do achieve objectivity in their selection and presentation of news.[9]

---

[7]See for example Steven Reese (1990), who also lists other researchers who agree.

[8]Although it should be noted that Swedes seem to stress neutrality far less than other journalists in, for example, Britain and Germany (Melin-Higgins 1996, p. 161).

[9]Although this is the attitude for general news, it should be noted that in sports reporting subjectivity is accepted and indeed openly encouraged from reporters. Sports journalists produce a daily work routine that is characterised by closeness to the source and the recognised mutual interest of journalists and sources; "by love or fandom of the topic (sports) rather than distance; and by siding with the audience and asking their questions rather than trying to inform them on the basis of objective standards" (van Zoonen, 1998a, pp. 131–132). Because most sports journalism is about men, it is masculinity that is a key element for professional understanding. Yet any apparent partiality on gender, for example being pro woman, is denounced as unobjective. This demonstrates how the media allows for subjectivity only when more or less in line with accepted masculine goals.

Objectivity has also significantly been linked to rationality and in Western tradition the rational mind is one belonging to a male. Female journalists, as such, enter the industry cloaked in the rational man's opposition; the irrational, subjectivity of woman.

Feminist Debates About the Representation of Women

At this point, I make a detour through an analysis of the female image to explore further the gendered contest over feminism (and media representations of it) in the newsroom. In laying out these debates I can then return to the 'No War' naked women news story from earlier in the chapter and to an analysis of it, asking two key questions: how do naked protesting women challenge the objective journalist; and do male and female journalists experience the challenge differently?

The body is not only the physical form: flesh, bone, and blood and constrained by its biology. As Susan Bordo (1999, p. 26) suggests, we need to think about the body not only as a physical entity, but also "as a cultural form that carries *meaning* with it" (emphasis is original). When we look at bodies there is more than just biology at work, but "values and ideals, differences and similarities that *culture* has 'written,' so to speak, on those bodies" (Bordo, 1999, p. 26). And as we shall see, it is evident that bodies are not simply the loci of power, but also of resistance, and, as Elizabeth Grosz suggests, particularly of resistance because of their excess.

> Bodies exceed whatever limits politics and representation, management or desire dictate: the bodies of women, even the depicted bodies of women, are no more passive, no more exhibitionistic, no more objects of consumption, than male bodies, animal bodies or natural bodies. (Grosz, 2001, p. 219)

Early feminist attempts to demonstrate the sexism of images of women in the media, especially in advertising, centred around 'turning the tables' on the perceived sexist images of women. Patricia Edgar and Hilary McPhee in 1974 produced a book, *Media She*, that replaced the images of traditionally exposed and objectified female bodies with that of male bodies. By demonstrating the sexist and stereotypical images of women, Edgar and McPhee (1974, p. 1) argued that the images women are taught to have of themselves from birth, and the extent of the exploitation of these images, becomes clearer. The media, they claimed, needed to portray women in a more 'realistic' manner and reflect women in their many and varied roles in life, rather than as just objects for the male gaze. Problematically, however, this thesis suggests a uniform category. As Charlotte Brunsdon (1988, p. 149) argues: "for feminists to call for more realistic images of women is to engage in the struggle to define what is meant by 'realistic,' rather than to offer easily available 'alternative' images. . . . Arguing for more realistic images is always an argument for the representation of 'your' version of reality." Van Zoonen (1996, p. 41) also suggests that a related problem of the 'reality reflection thesis' is the implication that media output has unequivocal meaning: that is either real or not real. This of course denies the very complex nature of images and the multiple meanings associated with them and the acknowledgement of the media as a central site over which there is an ongoing struggle over meaning. As well, this position reinforces the idea of passive audience reception.

The tide had turned on this overly simplistic analysis by the 1990s. Feminist theorists began to present an alternative view of women's representation in the media. Some claimed that feminism had produced its own set of limitations for women: at worst, a kind of prescriptive orthodoxy, and at best a list of well-meaning expectations. Catharine Lumby (1997), a vocal critic of the 'objectification of women' argument, suggests that women need to reclaim the power of their sexuality and not be oppressed by the media's use of it. Lumby argues that second-wave feminism's prudish arguments over sexist media images is a central tenet in the Christian right's rejection of sexually explicit images of women. Lumby (1997, p. 17) claims that 'unwittingly' secular liberal feminist arguments often share a narrowly normative and limiting idea of what it means to be female with those of traditional Christian moralists. A more viable feminist approach to media images needs to recognise, develop, and enhance women's abilities to negotiate images (Lumby, 1997, p. 25). Although I agree that women variously receive images and negotiate and often reject the dominant or preferred reading, Lumby's argument presents another stereotypical view: one that considers that it is women themselves who need to 'get over' their problem with the images of women in the media.

Lumby is not the first to link so-called 'antisex' feminists to the moral right. Pat Califia (1994) and Gayle Rubin (1984) have similarly also condemned U.S. antipornography feminists such as Catharine MacKinnon and Andrea Dworkin. The 1990s and beyond has seen the re-emergence of a prosex position in postfeminism.[10] The tragedy, for Lumby, is that feminism is becoming complicit with an ideology that wants to deny women the right to control their own bodies and to expose them if that is their choice.

I argue that the representation of naked or seminaked women is different from earlier representations in the 1960s and 1970s because of feminism. The naked protest, for example, is clearly a strategy enabled by feminism, and in

---

[10]The definition of postfeminism is a varied and contested one among feminist scholars. It is a term that I think often limits the currency of feminism by placing it in history, as if the aims of feminism have already been achieved.

that sense, is far less 'innocent' than earlier sexualised depictions of women. There's an irony here in the 'No War' protesters drawing on a feminist consciousness to expose their bodies to the media. British scholar Rosalind Gill (2003) suggests that there has been a highly visible shift in recent years of the knowing and deliberate resexualisation and recommodification of women's bodies, by women, in the wake of feminist critiques that neutralised at least the more overt examples of objectifications of women bodies (Gill, 2003, p. 101).[11] I would suggest that the 'No War' naked women were well aware of concerns over objectification of their bodies (some said they felt uncomfortable about undressing for 'public eyes'), but that they as knowing female and (at least some) feminist subjects consciously use irony and a knowing of the history of the objectification and sexualisation of the naked female body from which to base their protest.

This is a shift in how women present themselves to the media: it is a move away from the notion of the passive objectification of women (women as victims of the media) and an embracing of the autonomous feminist subject (utilising their liberated bodies). As Gill (2003, p. 103) asks, however, can this shift be the rise of the "assertive liberated subject of the feminist imaginary?"

This is an area of contention among feminist scholars. Firstly, it needs to be considered that not all women are constructed as equally desirable sexual objects. There is a certain type of woman who is put up for the male gaze; predominantly she is heterosexual (although lesbian imagery is also used to appeal to general readers). Also there is a narrowness in the type of bodies that are constructed as desirable—predominantly thin, white, young women. It is hard to ignore, however, the argument of women pleasing themselves and choosing to partake in naked or seminaked mediated images, whether it be in the context of protest or aesthetics (for example, sports calendars with sexy, sweaty, fit bodies and calendars of older women in various states of nakedness).

Australian academic Kath Albury suggests that women's participation in images of nakedness blurs the moral boundaries between good and bad women by refusing to be categorised as either wife/mother or whore (2002, p. 124). Here she is talking about 'Home Girls' who send in photos of themselves naked or seminaked to be published in a magazine. Albury posits that 'Homies' challenge classic feminist theories about what porn is and what it does to women who help produce it and consume it. However, as Gill (2003, p. 104) says, this 'pleasing ourselves' concept "simply avoids all the interesting and difficult questions about how socially constructed ideals of beauty are internalised and made our own."

---

[11]She raises this point in response to the increase of 'fashionable' t-shirts for women with sexualised comments written on the front.

Is it possible that this shift in how women represent themselves (like Homies for example) is a move from an "external male judging gaze to a self-policing narcissistic gaze"? (Gill, 2003, p. 104). Gill posits, as did many feminists in the 1980s, that there is a limitation of power in the position of object. She sees this more recent shift in the way women 'choose' to represent themselves as a deeper form of exploitation than objectification: "One in which the objectifying male gaze is internalised to form a new disciplinary regime" (Gill, 2003, p. 104; see also Bordo, 1993.).

The academic study of the representation of women stems from the women's movement of the 1960s and 1970s, which influenced feminists in academia and spawned a feminist critique of the mass media (Meyers, 2000, p. 10). This focus, according to Helen Baehr and Ann Gray (1996, p. 1), "deeply implicated (the media) in the patterns of discrimination operating against women in society." Scholars such as Elayne Rapping (1994) and Byerly (1999) acknowledge the limits in the material existence and mediated representations of women, but refuse to take up the backlash theory. They highlight that the popular media's treatment of women has dramatically improved since the second wave of feminism. Rapping laments the focus on the fear that women's gains over the past 30 years are in danger of being swept away by a renewed political conservatism:

> The backlash model of media dynamics assumes an ahistoric, one dimensional, either/or, them/us, then/now (in current academic jargon, 'binary') playing field. According to backlash theorists, feminists made certain strides in the late 1960s and then, in the early 1980s, were pushed back to point zero by the monolithic, misogynist focus of the backlash. (Rapping, 1994, p. 9)

In the case of the 'No War' naked women, Lumby's antibacklash position that women are empowered by their own sexuality, not victims of it, is certainly appealing. However, I think this appeals only because of the women's rare control over the image more than broad assumptions that all women are empowered by such images.[12] When I say rare control of the image, I refer to the fact that because *The Mercury* was unable to meet a request from the protesters to provide a female photographer—because the newspaper, at the time, didn't employ any full-time female photographers—the protesters then organised a woman to take the image and thus they had control over image content. The naked 'No War' women had the same control over the image that the Homies

---

[12]Lumby made the comment, after hearing a paper based on this chapter, that her point was that not *all* women are disempowered by such images.

have; both groups of women decide how the image is constructed. Yet the 'No War' protesters also acknowledge in their story that although they choose to strip naked, they can see no other way to 'have a voice.' So the women's 'choice' must be understood within their noted confines. This notion that women freely choose to expose themselves or be empowered by this exposure fits with a broader postfeminist discourse that presents women as autonomous agents no longer constrained by any inequalities or power imbalances (Gill, 2003, p. 104). But being motivated to protest in this way against the war is hardly 'free choice,' unlike Albury's forever empowered Homies.

Naked Female Bodies and Protest

I now turn to a discussion of specific debates around naked women's bodies and protest to ask what might we make of naked protest and media representation of it, as distinct from images of naked women in general. In this section I also consider the words of the naked women protesters and provide an analysis of some of the discussions that occurred in the newsroom. Before doing so, however, it should be noted that there has been a long history of debate about the use of the words 'nude' and 'naked.' Art historian Kenneth Clark's (1956) book *The Nude* is often drawn upon as a starting point for debate (also see John Berger, 1990/1972). Clark highlights the difference between the nude in art and the naked body outside of art by arguing that the naked body is simply one which has been divested of clothes, while the nude is a naked body which has been invested with social significance. According to Negrin (2004) there are problems with conceptualising the distinction in this way because it presupposes that the naked body is without cultural or social meanings; that is, it is seen simply as a biological/physical entity. Negrin (2004) argues that the naked body is equally coded with cultural meanings as is the nude in art. "Rather than see the naked body as pre-social and the nude as culturally coded, it would be more accurate to see both the naked body and the nude as invested with social significance, but the meanings associated with each as different" (Negrin, 2004, p. 2). She maintains that while public exposure of the naked body is usually considered offensive because of its primarily sexual meaning in Western culture, the nude in art is regarded as a culturally elevated form of presentation of the naked body in which its erotic connotations are veiled by a higher spiritual meaning.

Even though nudity as a form of protest is often viewed as an antisocial mechanism, naked protest appeals to women for a range of reasons. Barcan (2002, p. 74) suggests that naked protest is nonviolent, it uses the body as a form of theatre, it requires no financial resources, and "it is subtended by powerful mythical and/or religious connotations that have historically been one pathway to female virtue and even heroism." The myth of Lady Godiva is an historical case in point.[13]

Problems with Using the Female Body to Inscribe Protest

The action of the 'No War' naked women can be viewed outside the parameters of the traditionally sanctioned erotic contexts because they chose to use their nudity to challenge a historically masculine event—war. A possible reading of their actions could be that the women may have been challenging the broader notion of hegemonic patriarchy. Yet, as Barcan (2002, p. 62) notes, women who seek to use their naked bodies in protest face complexities and dilemmas "that reveal the limits of what female nakedness can mean within a patriarchal hegemony." Margaret Miles (1991) argues that in many early accounts of naked female martyrdom in the Christian West there is (and I suggest that this can be applied to the 'No War' women) a tension between respect for them, interest in their bodies, and the concern to establish the inferiority of their sex.

Is my position to the editor—that the women were empowered by their method of protest—a suitable explanation when the historic hegemonic framing of the female body is considered? Barcan (2002) argues that although harnessing the power of the association between femininity, beauty, and eroticism does little to challenge dominant meanings of femininity, it has strategic value, "especially given the power of female nudity to capture media attention" (2002, p. 68). Barcan continues that the ascription of agency to an ornamental type of naked beauty is a postfeminist strategy used by advertisers as well as protesters:

> While it may be of strong strategic value and provide individuals with a sense of empowerment, it doesn't contest a hegemonic framing of the female body, and for that reason may perhaps be of limited use as a mode of collective protest. (Barcan, 2002, p. 68)

Similarly, Janet Wolff argues that there are problems in using the female body for feminist ends. "Its pre-existing meanings, as sex object, as object of the male

---

[13]In the 11th century, Lady Godiva, as myth would have it, rode naked on a horse through Coventry in a bid to reduce taxes. Her husband, a powerful nobleman, Leofric, Earl of Mercia, said if she rode naked through Coventry market-place at midday, it would be a celebration of the perfection of God's work, and he would in return abolish all local taxes, save those on horses. On the day, flanked by two fully clothed horsewomen, Lady Godiva rode naked through the market, unashamed of her nudity. The taxes were duly removed (www.harvard-magazine.com/on-line/070377. html, accessed August 7, 2006).

gaze, can always prevail and reappropriate the body, despite the intentions of the woman herself" (1990, p. 121).

Are erotic associations, however, always a hindrance to female protest? And what happens when the female body is affirmed and displayed in defiance of the dominant ideals of the passive and ornamental norms? Although there is reason to suspect that the dominant construction of female nakedness as ornamentally erotic might limit its potential as a subversive tool, and the political effectiveness of one-off protests is open to doubt, "the fact remains that in a world in which the exposed female body is almost inevitably erotised, female nudity presents not only a predicament, but also a resource" (Barcan, 2002, p. 73). There is little wonder why women resort to their naked bodies as a symbolic site, when Western thought and practice have long encouraged women to dwell on their bodies.

The silent form of protest of the naked 'No War' women is common to disempowered groups. The body is, as Barcan (2002) reminds us, one of the best resources for those denied access to other modes of public discourse; a point the Tasmanian women actually make in the article. In this case, what makes such an impact is the women's own claim that they had no other choice if they were going to be heard. Although they were uncomfortable with *undressing for public eyes* it was a *genuine sacrifice for peace.* They *chose* to use their *bodies in this way.* *'It's a reflection of the system in which we don't have a political voice,'* the spokeswoman is quoted as saying.

Not only is the group fighting for a political voice, but the spokeswoman is forced to defend the method of protest and reject the reporter's claim that their action was antifeminist. Early in the article the reporter writes: *'Ms Seaborn* [the spokeswoman] *did not think that the protest was anti-feminist.'* On the one hand, this very statement is an inherent assumption that the method may have been antifeminist and detracts from the power of the women's actions. Alternatively, the statement also could be read as giving the spokeswoman an opportunity to locate the group's central values: a feminist value. (*'For us it was a feminist thing, to choose to use our bodies in this way. We had to do something to have a voice.'*) She said it wasn't about taking clothes off, rather it was about wanting Australian troops to come home. Yet their small protest was never going to bring the troops home; it was a symbolic protest in which their power came from manipulating an insatiable media hungry for images (of any kind) of naked or seminaked women. Feminism, or a feminist concern verbalised by Bailey and the senior staffer was used as a 'spoiler' for the ultimate hegemonic discourse.

The 'No War' naked women used the feeling of powerlessness in the most powerful way they could envisage: stripping. Their nudity offered the women public exposure in more ways than one. No longer were they muted from public discourse, they became public discourse. According to Miles (1991) the most accurate test of whether a social group has political power is to ask whether that group enjoys the power of self-representation, which the 'No War' women certainly achieved (albeit in a limited way). "People who do not represent themselves live under conditions in which their subjective lives—their feelings, concerns, and struggles—are marginalised from public interest; they also live in constant danger of misrepresentation" (Miles, 1991, p. 170). Instead of being represented as 'other,' Miles continues, misrepresented people can use self-representations as an important strategy for maintaining power in suspension and circulation. The 'No War' women acknowledge themselves as marginalised, or muted, by the media, but their actions, their method of self-representation, produced a moment of empowerment. The method of their self-representation ensured they had a public 'victory': they were represented as they wanted; they used their nudity to attract media interest; and the group controlled the image the media used. The result—a large space allocated on page 5, and a colour image—was the perfect outcome for a small-scale protest.

Ardener (1974, 1983) notes that public displays of nudity are often adopted by what she calls 'muted groups' who eschew violence "or who do not have fluency in, or access to, the dominant modes of communication by which to express their grievances, and redress their perceived wrongs" (1983, p. 261). Of course this position reinforces the notion that women are often forced to act in ways that they would not normally wish to, or act in this way because they are victims of a system in which their voices are marginalised. Yet, paradoxically, these women were able to use the system and had a fleeting moment of (media) empowerment, because the media wanted the picture. The magnetic pull of that old (some might say still current) remnant of tabloid newspapers—the seminaked page 3 girl—was still there, as indicated by the senior staffer's comments, above, about women.

Miles (1991) has similar concerns to Barcan (2002) about the usefulness of public nudity for women. She posits that because the act of seeing does not occur independently of the associations provided by public meaning, that female nakedness as a method for redressing the power imbalance is limited. For Miles (1991) the female body is too assimilated to the male gaze to permit inscription with new meaning. However, exposing the female body publicly is not always assimilated to the male gaze. Iris Marion Young (1988) maintains that women, whose visual training by the media has been virtually identical to that of men, have, like men, a subjectivity that is "crucially constituted by relations of looking" (1988, p. 146). Women, like men, acquire "a sense of subject set off against objects through active looking," so that women insofar as they develop subjectivity, do so by occupying "the position of the male gaze" (1988, p. 147). So for Young the subjectivity belongs to the one who looks and objectivity to the one looked at, and in this case it becomes difficult for women to change, not only in society, but, as Miles (1991, pp. 177–178) suggests, in our own visual practices. For the 'No War' naked women, their protest, in Miles' view, is a reactive attempt to reclaim power, but the idea of reclaiming it is lost in the very method in which they attempt to have a voice. I want to suggest, however, as Grosz (2001) does, that the ways in which women, as well as men, look—the ways in which they engage with images and representations of bodies—is not singular or monolithic. Grosz (2001) argues that art has always elicited looks other than the gaze. It could be argued that the image in the newspaper of the naked women is a work of art, produced by the women for public consumption. Grosz suggests that this idea of the look is not unknown by the artist, "whose work is commonly an attempt to engage with, and perhaps produce other ways of looking that move beyond the mundane and the habitual, and hopefully beyond the apparatus of the gaze" (Grosz, 2001, p. 219).

The male gaze theory asserts that although the individual woman may believe that she is freely choosing to be naked, she is in fact responding to internalised masculine culture pressure. According to this theory a woman who takes on the male view fears that if she doesn't exist in the eyes of men, she'll cease to exist at all (Albury, 2002, p. 111). To gain male approval, she has to see herself through 'the gaze,' ensuring that she meets the standards of sexual beauty at all times. Laura Mulvey's (1975) influential hypothesis, that the spectatorial look (in mainstream cinema) is implicitly male and active whereas the object of the look is female and passive, has become common cultural currency. But the male gaze theory has been criticised, especially by those who raise the question of women's agency. This reading assumes that there are only ever two ways for a woman to see and be seen (Albury, 2002, p. 112). Albury argues that: "The idea that males look and women are looked at denies the possibility that some males may not look in this way, and that some females may get pleasure from both looking *and* being looked at" (Albury, 2002, p. 112, italics are original).

So what is it that really gets under the skin of media managers about exposing protesting female flesh to their readers? (This, however, is certainly not the only concern for the editors. I would argue, in this case, that there was similar concern over the control the women had of the published image.) Is it the political nature of the protest, or is it that political women are automatically considered feminists and feminism carries some inbuilt irritant?

There are a variety of complexities in attempting to address these questions, not the least being the paradoxical nature of female exposure, so prevalent as to be almost invisible (Barcan, 2002). Rarely is intentional public nudity seen as an act of madness, extreme immorality (although the 'No War' naked women were variously understood in this way), and criminality, as it once was. (See, for example, Douglas & Rasmussen, with Flanagan, 1977). In our consumer culture female nudity or seminudity is everywhere: on television screens, public billboards, works of art, advertising, and in movies. As Bordo posits, the naked female body is "common cultural property" (1993, p. 698).

Barcan (2002) argues that the female body is seen as 'naturally' more beautiful and therefore more acceptable than male nude bodies. But this position also denies the eroticisation of the male body in many cultural forms; for example, works of art both historically and more contemporarily, and in advertising and television programs in which seminudity helps to sell products, in much the same way as women's exposure has, although the exposure of the male body to the consumer gaze has a much shorter and different historical context. Perhaps the position on female nudity in newspapers is more about the predominantly white, heterosexual male media managers' view about female nudity being acceptable (even encouraged) to the male gaze. This doesn't, however, exclude the complicity of the female gaze, which I discussed previously. Certainly, female nudity is more often tolerated and actively applauded or encouraged (and more likely to be financially rewarded—except in sporting contexts in which seminaked men earn more money than women; for example, surfing, football, running) than exposure of the male body (Barcan, 2002).

The 'No War' women were not as easy to slot into a 'news' category. *The Mercury* understood the protest as a feminist strategy, and it was met with mainly confusion and some ridicule from key decision makers. It was clear that the women needed media coverage to get their message across, and without it their protest would have been in vain; they needed the media as much as the media needed them. The 'No War' women knew that the photograph was the key selling point to the media. Without the photograph their 'story' would have been, at best, a few paragraphs on a back news page.

Gender Politics in Newsrooms

In the dialogues that took place about the 'No War' naked women, each of the participants was engaging in a dialogue about what feminism means. Clearly the journalist's comment that *'Women have fought for a long time not to have their bodies objectified, and now they are doing it to themselves'* brought a particular set of meanings of feminism to the fore. These were implicit in the comments made by the reporter who queried that interpretation with me and Bailey who subscribed to it and then went further to link feminism to complaining women.

The senior female journalist's comments in the news conference carried a lot of weight. For example, the reporter was told to ask the protesting women if their actions could be considered 'antifeminist' based on her understanding of feminism, and this then became the main frame for the story. Because her immediate superior had taken a position that challenged women who used such a method of protest, the less senior reporter was told to ask the 'antifeminist' question. Once the question was asked, the protesting women's articulate rebuttal became the key focus of the article, which inevitably worked to link protesting women to feminism. Yet, even though this linkage could be read as a negative, in terms of how feminism has shaped news content, the women's 'feminist' beliefs, and defence and definition of what feminism meant to the protesting women, were actually allocated a good deal of news space.

The senior female journalist's comment that women *'had fought for a long time not to have their bodies objectified, and now they are doing it to themselves'* certainly derives from a feminist position, but one that is, at the same time, critical of it. It could be argued that she draws on an antifeminist or postfeminist frame that works to suggest that women are often 'their own worst enemies.' The journalist's comment invokes a history of struggle, and in so doing acknowledges that women's bodies have been objectified in the past. The comment also demonstrates an acceptance of feminist terminology ('objectified bodies'). Yet this is a feminism that is concomitantly used as a tool of judgment against other women (*'now they are doing it to themselves'*—making objects of themselves). She turns a feminist position around to an 'acceptable' antifeminist position, thus effectively letting the male media managers, and herself, off the hook and reinforcing her professional status as a rational, objective journalist. It could be that the protesting women and their naked bodies have challenged the senior female journalist, because she—the rational, objective journalist—becomes located in the same subjective female body as the protesters. There is a fear, for her, of being imbued with (female) gender.

Her comment was critical of the women's method of protest, their agency, and their feminist claims. Women who succeed in journalism where male values dominate do not necessarily have to disavow feminist beliefs. But the outcome of female journalists' negotiation of the subject position 'journalist' must still fit with an objective, rational journalistic discourse that, historically in Western tradition, has been mostly male. Perhaps because there are so few women journalists in positions of authority at *The Mercury*, female journalists become focussed on being 'as good as a man,' disavow their gender, and are critical of others who then use their femaleness (or feminist beliefs) to elicit media coverage.

McLean et al.'s discussion of the effects of a dominant masculine culture among engineering undergraduates is helpful in exploring this idea. They found that:

> Given the persuasiveness of the dominant discourse and the sanctions applied against those who challenge this, it is not surprising that the majority of the female students we interviewed strongly denounced feminism and disassociated themselves from any strategies identified with the women-in-engineering program. (McLean et al., 1997, p. 154)

This is reflective of the point made by Leonie Huddy's (1997) empirical work in the United States that shows all journalists are pressured to limit their feminist-identified news sources and to greatly simplify definitions and perspectives in their stories. Because the majority of people learn the meaning of feminism through the media (Huddy, 1997, p. 183) this raises concerns about how feminism is represented in the media. Problematically, the terms 'feminist' and 'feminism' are rarely defined as a broad of ideas; indeed, as Huddy (1997, p. 193) suggests, they often remain undefined. This is evident in the 'No War' naked women article, in which there is an expected preconceived knowledge of what feminism actually means. So although it is expected that the audience will understand what feminism means, this is at odds with the newsroom, where the producers themselves are in conflict over it.

According to Byerly (2004a) such industry censorship continues to marginalise women as social actors and renders their activities less important than men's. News content has been more likely to incorporate feminist themes and sources when feminist movements have been strongest (Byerly, 2004a). On the other hand, if you do decide that 'feminist' is a label you are willing to wear, the 'female perspective' is all that you become. As English journalist and novel writer Zoe Heller (1999, p. 15) posits, you then are required to pretend that your femaleness is all; "that every one of your opinions is refracted through the lens of gender." This is the case even though the male-dominated sports pages, for example, are never seen in terms of male gender.

Bailey's dialogue on the 'No War' story also indicates that he took on board the senior female journalist's position on feminism when he asked what I thought of *'these women doing it.'* Was he attempting to link my feminist position with her antifeminist position? Did he think all feminists had the same ideological position? What is clear is that he asked me because I was a feminist, but then concluded by categorising me with 'complaining women' when he said: *'these are the women who complain when it is nudity and women in another way.'* But I did not see the image in this way, and this is when the discussion changed. Was Bailey's comment deliberately obtuse? Was it only a certain type of woman—perhaps a 'complaining' feminist—who criticised the way that women were represented in the newspaper? The editor's comment was even more interesting because I had rarely heard of women contacting the newspaper to challenge the way women had been portrayed, and certainly those complaints were never passed on to journalists, even though other complaints from the public and the editor about reporting are pinned to a staff noticeboard.

I felt under a great deal of pressure to *speak for* these women. There was an unspoken assumption that the protesters and I would share a common sisterhood because we were women and also because we identified as feminists, yet I knew none of the women or anything of their protest or gender politics before I walked into the newsroom that afternoon. The balancing act in these discussions between my subject position as feminist and 'objective' journalist was, for me, tenuous: not relinquishing my position as an 'objective' media worker yet completely submerged in the position, created by me and reinforced by others, of 'feminist journalist,' which lessened the validity of my professional position. While Bailey was seeking my opinion as a feminist to make sense of the women's protesting action, he was also associating me as one of those feminists 'who ring up and make complaints.' As a journalist I had become invisible; and as a feminist, I was categorised with these protesting 'complaining' women.

Finally, what of the older female journalist? Why was she so concerned that some of the women had 'shaved their fannies'? And why was she loudly involved in objectifying the protesting women's bodies? I suggest that her objections absolve her of any feminist connection. By ogling the women's bodies, she is located more safely as 'just one of the boys.' Margaret Gallagher (2002, p. 5) argues that male attitudes in the newsroom are by far the most common obstacles to advancement that women media professionals report. One of the most important implications of the male dominance within media organisations is that women are judged by male standards and performance criteria. As Gallagher (2002, p. 5) states: "Often this means a constant effort to be taken seriously, and 'to prove that you are as good as a man.'" Perhaps for this older female journalist it is not that she needs to prove she is 'as good as a man' in terms of professional competence (she was, at the time, one of the few women on the 90-odd editorial production team who actually had more authority than many of the men). Perhaps because of her isolation, her desire to be 'one of the boys' rather than 'as good as one of the boys' is central to her actions.[14] Similarly, it could be argued that her position at the top may depend on her being a 'man.' Byerly (1998) suggests that a few women are allowed into male ranks if they behave like men.

Why is it that the act of women seeking publicity by unusual methods is so complicated for all of these journalists? When the older male journalist called on my 'feminist' position to make sense of the women's action, he was similarly concerned, as was the other older female journalist, about whether they 'did it just for publicity.' But many stories published in newspapers are 'just' publicity for an individual or institutional cause. Is it that women are rarely willing to strip naked for media exposure, and this rarity is what surprised the editors and caught them off guard? The many images of naked or seminaked women often published in newspapers suggest this is not the case. In recent years The Mercury has published a series of prominently positioned news stories and images of older women stripping for a 'girlie' calendar (Paine, 2002, p. 5; Read, 2001, p. 1; Wood, 2002, p. 3), women in the theatre production The Best Little Whorehouse in Texas

---

[14]Neither of these actions, it seems, proved helpful to her career progress. She has since been relieved of her senior role and returned to a middle-ranking editorial position.

(Bailey, 2001, p. 1), and women stripping for Miss Nude Tasmania competitions (Lovibond, 1998, p. 5). I am also guessing that the publication of these stories would not have been preceded by a similar kind of discussion I detailed here about the naked protesting women. But the 'No War' naked women were political women, they were challenging war, and it seems political women are read as feminists and their politics reduced to a statement about gender, even if the protesters had not initially promoted themselves as such.

The Politics of Nudity

There is also another angle to consider in the reticence of the senior journalists to see this story simply as one of protest, rather than one about women and/or feminism and gender politics. Although the 'No War' naked protest was not in a news sense particularly exciting—after all, there were only 36 people protesting and there was no conflict, physical or otherwise—it was an exceptionally enticing picture. The female nudity was the only aspect of the story that was 'news,' and it added a much needed fresh and local angle to the constant war stories emanating out of Iraq. Although the freely offered nudity was appealing, the paradox for the decision makers was that the nudity came with a strong political message that ran counter to the political position of the newspaper, which was prowar. According to a report in the trade press magazine *The Walkley Magazine*, which quoted the U.K.'s *Guardian* newspaper, all 175 of Rupert Murdoch's News Limited media outlets worldwide (of which *The Mercury* is one) were biased towards the war (Malone, 2003). Not one, according to the report, was antiwar. The author notes that this was "a somewhat surprising statistic . . . given that in countries such as Australia and the UK the population was roughly divided on the issue" (Malone, 2003, p. 16).

The point is that these were women protesting the war in Iraq and wanting Australian troops to come home; they were naked but political, rather than the conventional nude but passive female image. Yet this political (antiwar) position was not mentioned by key editorial decision makers as a reason for having concerns with the story. Rather, it was the female nudity that seemed to be the problem. I would suggest that it is female nudity that allows disavowal of the protesters' antiwar politics.

So did Bailey believe the picture objectified women, and was that a consideration in whether to publish it or not? He had said the issue had been raised in conference. Bailey's concern with using a feminist framework to decide on publishing the story seems a little exaggerated if the finished product is considered. The story was placed on the third most important news page (after the front page and page 3), on page 5, in colour, and took up the most space on the page of any story, even the lead story. The text becomes almost insignificant compared to the size and central location of the image, indicating that the image is more important.

Conclusion

In this chapter, which explores how feminism and ideas of feminism work in the newsroom, I have been particularly interested to probe the direct relationship between newsroom culture and news content. I did this through an analysis of the naked female body, particularly via a series of newsroom discussions that took place in *The Mercury* newsroom. That newsroom anecdote fleshed out established ideas about feminism by some journalists. In a culture that openly commodifies female nakedness, and even applauds it, the idea that there might be circumstances in which female exposure is perverse, or deviant, becomes linked to feminism. Yet although the display of female nakedness is encouraged in presentation (television, billboards, art) and erotic performance, other forms of public nakedness—those with a political message—are outlawed (protesting women).

So how do naked, protesting women challenge the objective journalist? And do male and female journalists experience the challenge differently? I think that naked, female protest is particularly troubling for many female journalists because, in theory, they need to attain the status of the objective (male) journalist. In practice, however, their bodies imbue them with a female subjectivity that makes it difficult to challenge this particular story if they are to retain their objective status. So, although this newsroom encounter indicated confusion about what feminism means and some dissension among its workers who took various positions on female nakedness and feminism, the final outcome was a victory for the protesting women: they were vocal, they were visible, and they were political, and perhaps that does contest a hegemonic framing of the female body. What is so interesting about this dialectic is the disjuncture between the debate in the newsroom, where many of the players were critical of feminism, and the 'successful' news story. It's clear that one doesn't determine the other fully or predictably. "What a complex amalgam, then, the naked body of the protester is—shocking (but natural); aggressive (but innocent); criminal (but free); anti-social (but true)" (Barcan, 2002, p. 69).

There is no doubt that harnessing the power of the naked female body and using it to attract media interest has strategic value and often provides women with a sense of empowerment. That empowerment obviously comes from the challenge they make to dominant discourses about the female body. Female nakedness, as used by the 'No War' women, can be understood concomitantly as a subversive tool. Their method of protest drew on a strategy enabled by feminism and as such cannot be understood in the same way as the more 'innocent' sexualised depiction of women in earlier decades. I like the irony in their protest, which draws on a feminist consciousness. The protesters understood that they were a muted media group and that they had little chance of getting their message out without a news 'hook'—their naked bodies. The women then used their media exposure to explicitly challenge women's general lack of representation in the media and the typically sexualised images of women's bodies in the media. In this one fleeting media moment the 'No War' women had the power of self-representation, but only by going to the extreme. What initially began as a brave strategy to induce media coverage then became a platform for a feminist dialogue about women's lack of voice about the war and in the media in general.

In this chapter I have attempted to probe the micropolitics of subjectivity negotiated around 'feminism' in the newsroom. What has proved so fascinating to me is the interrelationship between newsroom dynamics and news content and the ways in which the journalists in the anecdote take up various subject positions about feminism. Journalists do produce a variety of media representations of feminism, arguably many of them hostile, but importantly, journalists also shape the experiences of feminists in the newsroom. Journalists' subjective positions about feminism, however, seem to not always impact greatly on the outcome of news stories about feminist topics. Journalists' views about feminism appear to impact more on newsroom culture than they do on news content.

Chapter Ten

Conclusion

In this book I have explored the gendered production of news in the Australian print news media, and in particular focussed on how female journalists experience newsroom culture. The Introduction details the past 30 years of feminist research, which has critiqued the representation of women in the media. Feminist media researchers have also been engaged in a 'body count,' finding that women are few in number in the higher ranks where editorial decision making affects news content. In the past 10 years some international feminist media scholars have, importantly, taken this research a step further to probe the gendered dimensions of media production processes. In Australia, however, feminists have so far failed to follow this trend to analyse media production processes in any significant way. We cannot assume that the experiences of Australian journalists are the same as international journalists. Part of this book has been to document and analyse the specificity of the Australian journalists' experience in the newsroom.

The small-scale nature of my research in which I interviewed 17 print news media journalists allowed me to attend to a close reading of the interview transcripts and explore a series of overarching themes about how Australian journalists experience and negotiate newsroom culture. I considered 'What is journalism and what is a journalist? How do female journalists experience newsroom culture? How is newsroom culture embodied? What are women's embodied responses to newsroom culture? How has global industry change impacted on the workplace and what does this mean for journalists? How does feminism get played out in the newsroom? What is the relationship between newsroom culture and news content?

As noted in Chapter Two, I do not assume that 17 interviews allows for definitive statements generally applicable to all Australian journalists or the industry as a whole. The research project was set up to be a small and diverse sample through which a close reading of the transcripts would allow for the identification and exploration of key themes. My aim was to collect stories, accounts, and narratives that would present me with some journalists' experiences in newsroom production; some of the themes that arose surprised me, others did not. For example, I was surprised that the majority of female interviewees raised issues around, or talked explicitly about, sexually harassing behaviour by men in the industry and its impact/or not on their embodied experience in newsrooms. Although the pervasiveness of cynicism among older journalists did not surprise me, its presence in discussions with cadet journalists did. I don't suggest that everything that the interviewees discussed with me can be understood as 'truth,' but I do understand it as part of their individual 'truth' produced in response to their experience of the occupation of journalism within very complex organisations. As part of that debate Chapter Two also engages with questions of objectivity and subjectivity in the interview process.

In Chapter Three I asked 'who is a journalist?' and what has to be done to 'be a journalist.' All interviewees agreed that men dominate in positions of power in print media newsrooms in Australia. One repercussion of this dominance in positions of authority is that men's superiority to women is asserted and women are viewed as and experience the workplace as outsiders, or inferior others. It is more than just numerical gender inequity at the top, however, that creates an uncomfortable newsroom environment for the female interviewees. More importantly, women's inferiority is an effect of a masculine newsroom culture that privileges dominant discourses or ideologies. Not everyone, however, identified women's situation in journalism as a sign of their subordination. Some men saw women's position as one of privilege. It appears to me that many of the male journalists interviewed, particularly those in positions of authority in newsrooms, often don't experience a 'newsroom culture.' They are the 'culture,' the newsroom is 'theirs' and they guard the parameters from 'outsiders,' allowing some in, but rarely to the core, where power is experienced, wielded, and often homosocially shared.

The prevalence of discussions by female interviewees about sexually harassing behaviour by men was an aspect of embodied newsroom culture that I did not expect to find, or indeed have as a theme area for discussion in the interviews. In my analysis of the interviews I found that the female interviewees experienced constant reminders of how their bodies did not 'fit' and/or where and how they did fit in the occupation of journalism. The interviews revealed that sexually harassing behaviour was a defining part of the occupational culture of journalism. In Chapter Four, I reflected on how sexually harassing behaviour was remembered and told in interviews, how feminist discourses, government legislation, and company policies about 'sexual harassment' had great costs, or at best, limited benefits for female journalists. This was the case because the term itself, established within a liberal framework and captured by antifeminist sentiments, has begun to mean things that minimise and mock its original challenging potential. The distinctively Australian discourse of sexual harassment was shaped by three very public cases during the past 30 years. It was Helen Garner's best-selling book *The First Stone*, however, that engaged the public and the media in the most lengthy and at times vitriolic debate about sexual harassment since laws were introduced in Australia that made sexual harassment in the workplace illegal. The Garner debate, in particular, served to remind us that sexual harassment does not have a fixed meaning but, rather, in the process of public debate, among other things, is reconstituted and reshaped. As a result of my analysis of the interview material I argued that women were rarely inclined to take up the discourse of sexual harassment because it would be used against them. If women identified and named sexual harassment, they feared they would be labelled as whinging feminists, or victims, or unable to accept 'normal' gender relations. 'Sexual harassment' then is a discursive object that feminists identify, but which the majority of women in newsrooms—especially younger women—do not.

There have been massive changes in the way that news is produced in the last 30 years, and Chapters Five, Six, and Seven attend to the changes that have occurred in global news practices—albeit analysed in different ways. I wanted to know how journalists lived these changes. How did they tell the stories of change? How did they challenge the effects? We know that there has been a dramatic and increasing concentration of media ownership, there are a decreasing number of journalists employed by media companies and they work with fewer resources then ever before, and technological changes have changed the way that news is produced, practiced, and consumed. One of the most obvious changes within the industry, however, has been that more women work in the news media then ever before, and I explored some of the repercussions.

In Chapter Five I questioned whether the increasing number of women entering the industry was changing the news genre—was there a feminisation of news, as some have asserted? I argued that the convergence of media interests by media owners was changing news content (and journalistic practice) and I suggested this added to the trend of more 'feminised infotainment' news.

In Chapter Six I turned to the interviewee material to probe what was a 'journalist.' Female interviewees who had children found it increasingly difficult to perform/manage the tasks that were expected of 'journalists.' Many, however, did manage to make the industry work for them. Sally's example of being prepared to do 38 hours' work in 25 hours and be paid for 25 (and be underpaid by not being paid casual rates) is a result of global industry changes that affects female journalists differently than male journalists. Sally spoke through a neoliberal subjectivity in describing the gendered implications of work intensification. This chapter also found that the intensification of work practices in the media had aided in creating a cynicism among many of the journalists, from cadets to senior section editors. I identified a gendered dimension to that cynicism, with more female than male interviewees discussing this as one of the pitfalls of working in the industry. Nevertheless, the majority of interviewees said that a career in journalism had increased their personal and/or professional confidence. There were, however, also gendered differences in this experience. Male interviewees often stated that their professional confidence was increased because they had more access to people of influence, like politicians. Female interviewees were more likely to explain their increased confidence as primarily benefiting their social worlds. For example, they were 'humbled' by their role in journalism, were privileged by access to 'people's homes and hearts,' and were more 'compassionate' towards people because of their experience in journalism.

The effects of globalisation in the Australian print media turned up a complex terrain of change across individual, social, union, government, and industry dimensions. My investigation then turned, in Chapter Seven, to three important Australian legal cases in which senior female journalists all claimed pay discrimination on the basis of their gender. The reports were in the Australian print news media in 2000, 2003, and 2004, and they provided an opportunity to consider the outcomes when women journalists actively challenge their employers. None of the cases could be understood as successful for the women. One woman left the industry after a payout that included a 'gag' rule, one was effectively silenced and disempowered (and made ill) by being taken off important stories and eventually withdrew her claim, and another had to endure personal public attacks from colleagues and an ongoing legal appeal by her employer against her 'win' on a single claim. In December 2005 she resigned from the newspaper, and the appeal has not been reported since.

To bring the book to a rounded conclusion Chapters Eight and Nine explored how gendered news practices affected news content. I considered what interviewees had said in the interviews about 'feminism' in their workplaces. I found that the interviewees' knowledge about 'feminism' ranged from little (or a decision to say very little in response to the question) to an awareness of the plurality of feminism. Knowledge about feminism, however, was not a precursor to having a positive experience about feminist concepts, or indeed feminists themselves. The majority of interviewees labelled feminists pejoratively, both inside and outside the newsroom. Overall there was a sense that the majority of interviewees, male and female, understood feminists as angry and extreme in their actions and often pushed their politics 'too far.' With this framework established it was not surprising, then, that the majority of the female interviewees did not want to be associated with feminism or feminists.

In Chapter Nine I expanded on the interview material and analysed my own newsroom anecdote, garnered from my time working as a casual sub-editor at The Mercury in Hobart, about the publication of a story about naked women. The newsroom discussions were prompted by an all-women antiwar protest by 36 Tasmanian women who stripped naked to be photographed for a media image to demonstrate their antiwar sentiments about the then imminent U.S.-led war against Iraq. It was assumed by some senior journalists that the protesters were feminists, and questions were then asked by those in the newsroom who saw the image about why feminists would strip naked in public. I used this anecdote because I wanted to explore the link between news content and concerns about feminism in the newsroom. The overarching question here was 'what did feminism mean to journalists and what subject positions did journalists take up in relation to it?' I was concerned with how interviewees understood and explained ideas about feminism and feminists in the newsroom. How was 'feminism' negotiated by journalists?

The story was published on a major news page with enough allocated space for the protesters to tell their story and answer the journalist's concerns that their protest was antifeminist. The image was one that the women themselves had organised and made available to the media. The protesters had found a method to secure a voice in the media, and get their antiwar message public. Although this newsroom encounter indicated confusion about what feminism meant and some dissension among its workers who took various positions on female nakedness and feminism, the final outcome was a victory for the protesting women: they were vocal, they were visible, and they were political. What was so interesting about the No War women anecdote was the disjuncture between the debate in the newsroom, where many of the players were critical of feminism, and the 'successful' news story. It's clear that one doesn't determine the other fully, or predictably. What the anecdote and my analysis of the interview material about feminism reveals is that feminism is a contested term in the newsroom, but that content, even when avowed feminists are on the back foot, doesn't always mean antifeminist content.

Is Change to Newsroom Culture Possible?

The concept of change in the Australian print news media (more women in the industry, ideas about feminism, feminisation, technology, globalisation, and personal narratives) has been the backdrop to my research. In the process of researching and writing this book I too have been deeply changed as a journalist and now an academic. During my research I worked casually in the media and academia—the two never sitting comfortably. How could they? I was researching a culture notorious for its ambivalence towards academia and academics. Perhaps this, among other things (like 'fashion' within the academy), contributes to the lack of research into production processes in the Australian print news media—that actually accessing journalists is a very difficult task. As I have previously mentioned, it was my links and role within the industry at the time of the research that enabled easier access to participants; I was seen as an 'insider.' By the time the thesis was completed and the book written I had started to think like an academic rather than a journalist.

Angela McRobbie (1997) has written about teaching feminist media theory to many women who now work on women's magazines in Britain. This, she claimed, could lay the foundation for enabling change from 'within' the media industry. That is a moot point, but in Australia so few journalism courses attend in any depth to feminist media theory. Gender Studies students have the benefit of this research, but not the majority of students who will enter journalism. So what might a Gender Studies focus bring to a journalism course? At the very least I would argue for a unit that explored contemporary gender issues in the media, addressing both news content and production issues. Topics to be covered in such a unit could include an overview of the rise of women in journalism historically and numerically both in Australia and internationally; an analysis of where women are located in the newsroom and the broader debate about the feminisation of the news; an examination of newsroom culture probing issues of power, masculinism, and objectivity in journalism; and an investigation of the impact of feminism on news content and how gender makeup in newsrooms effects content. If such a unit formed part of a journalism degree program, potential young journalists would be better prepared to understand, negotiate, and perhaps challenge gendered (and raced) work practices.

Carolyn Byerly and Angela McRobbie are two of the influential theorists who have called for a return to media production studies. For Byerly, this information would provide strategies for how feminists could be in dialogue with the media about its content and identify where feminist media workers were making inroads. What does my project then say to their call? My research found that of the feminist journalists I interviewed all are at best cynical about the benefits of feminist identification or ideology in challenging news content. Indeed, of the three interviewees who identified as feminist two have left the industry and the third struggles to find satisfaction in her career. Nevertheless, the efforts of publicly identified feminists, or antifeminists, in the newsroom are not the beginning and end of determining the outcome of published news stories, as the No War naked protest indicated.

The majority of print news journalists in Australia work under the News Limited banner and learn how to write the News Limited agenda. This agenda is learnt via a series of rewards and punishments, not all related to how well journalists do their jobs writing or producing the news. One just has to ask why men dominate in the editorial hierarchy, why sexual harassment is a continuing problem in the newsroom and effectively unaddressed by media organisations, why there is a disproportionate number of men graded higher than women of equivalent industry experience, why there is no formal process of assessing and promoting journalists, and why women are more cynical about the industry to find what it takes to be 'a journalist' in the Australian print news media.

The question remains: What strategies need to be put in place so that female journalists/feminists can better survive the changing newsroom? I think this question begs the response that there needs to be much more research with a wider scope into gendered news production practices in the Australian media (including broadcast and radio sectors). A larger-scale project would provide a more representative sample with which to work and make more definitive claims and recommendations that could be taken to the industry and union for discussion.

Also, further research on the gendered production of news would benefit from a more directed questioning of participants. My project's broad theme list provided an overall sense of the news media and raised some fascinating aspects of newsroom culture. The next step, however, would be more specific questioning about gender inequities in the industry and asking journalists how they think these could be addressed.

Although government legislation and company policies established to address problems such as sexual harassment and gender discrimination on the basis of pay and promotion have provided an important framework for acknowledgment and negotiation, gender discrimination is still very much a part of the newsroom experiences of female journalists. It is, therefore, evident that strategies will have to involve more than legislative and policy change.

More specifically, the Australian industry union, the MEAA, needs to be more involved with and interested in changing the gendered inequalities in our industry. Since 1996, when the IFJ and MEAA published a groundbreaking report that clearly demonstrated the lack of women in decision-making roles in the newsroom, the prevalence of sexual harassment, the lack of promotion opportunities for women, and the fact that women are clustered in the lower paid, less prestigious positions, the union has taken no action to effect change. It hasn't even undertaken another report. My two emailed requests to the union asking if another report would follow have gone unanswered. The broader problem that partly underlies these gendered inequalities is also ignored. It is clear from the 1996 report that the union is aware of the inequalities but is loathe to acknowledge that they stem from a privileging of a hegemonic masculinity in the newsroom.[1] I'll recount here a story that can tell us a lot about how an aggressive, hegemonic masculinity is privileged in the news media, and then outline how the union ignores this type of masculinity as problematic for the industry.

The Australian journalism industry's prestigious awards night, the Walkley Awards, was held in December 2006, and as has been the case for the past four or five years it was televised on SBS television. The cofounder of the news website crikey.com, Stephen Mayne, was a presenter on the night. Mayne has in recent times incurred the wrath of some 'old media' journalists because he

---

[1] Desiree Savage's 2003 article printed on the last page of the magazine in its Autumn issue no 20 is the exception. In the four years since that article was published there have been no further articles that attend to an analysis, or problematising, of hegemonic masculinity in the newsroom.

had on occasion used his website to criticise his former colleagues. But no one expected a public assault to occur on national television—and later replayed on websites all over the country. At the awards night senior News Limited reporter Glenn Milne came unexpectedly onto the stage during the broadcast and shoved Mayne to the floor. Clearly intoxicated, Milne followed Mayne, who had jumped off the stage, and labelled him a "disgrace" to the industry. SBS production crew attempted to restrain an angry and flailing Milne, who tried to break free and move again towards Mayne—all while the cameras continued to roll. All forms of media published detail and opinion on the now infamous event. Milne also wrote a column claiming a migraine tablet he had taken mixed with alcohol consumed on the night fuelled his behaviour (Milne, 2006, p. 2). It was *the* 'water cooler' topic of discussion in newsrooms around the country for days. No one remembered who won the Gold Walkley, but most had a good laugh as they watched the online replays of a stumbling, bumbling Milne. The mass coverage of the incident went on for a week or so, but as is the way with our short-term fixations, the industry moved on.

The analysis by his colleagues, in the end, was shallow. No one named the incident as the gender specific act that it was and/or linked it to an industry that privileges masculinity, both within and without its newsrooms. Generally the reporting of the 'incident' went like this: Milne was the *Sunday Telegraph's* "Saint of the Week" (not surprising given that he writes a column for the newspaper) because he did something "many others [presumably male journalists] have wanted to do for years" (Rothfield & Wilson, 2006, p. 57). The industry had "got a bit soft" of late, and the incident was "truly inspiring stuff" and "good clean fun," even though Mayne "ran away like a girl" (Hildebrand, 2006, p. 87). It was just "a bit of biffo between friends," (Day, 2006, p. 20), another said, with the only tongue in cheek part, 'friends.' After the initial gossip columns, then some started questioning whether Milne should be sacked for such behaviour, but his bosses at News Limited said even though they were "very disappointed" by Milne's outburst (Ricketson & Harrison, 2006, p. 3) they accepted his apology. Two News Ltd columnists did digress and suggest that the 'event' 'reinforced journalism stereotypes' (Powell, 2006, p. 11) and the 'intrusion' 'would heighten the perception that all journos are drunken buffoons' (Day, 2006, p. 20). Did they mean stereotypes of male journalists?

Milne's drunken, abusive assault is a prime example of a masculinised newsroom culture spilling into a public forum. This type of 'incident' is not an unusual feature of many newsrooms and/or journalists' social gatherings, as I have indicated via much interview material (especially Susan) and evident in a series of published 'incidents' valorised by the media (see Chapter Three). That is why Milne was never going to be sacked—one of the central themes in the media discussion. The industry accepts and privileges a masculine hierarchical dominance in newsrooms, so it can hardly disapprove of such masculine displays such as Milne's in public. I was left pondering how an outburst such as Milne's would have been read by media commentators if it had been a high-profile female journalist, such as Michelle Grattan (who incidentally won a Walkley that night), who drunkenly tried to punch a show host on national television.

After reading the media 'analysis,' I decided to offer the union magazine, *The Walkley Magazine*, a no-fee article that reflected on the nature of the media debate around that story and how it failed to examine the masculinised media culture that spurned such an outburst. I was told by the magazine editors that: "In terms of the story and the nature of the magazine as a union journal and the vehicle for the Walkley Awards, it is a story that is quite sensitive for us and we are taking quite a thoughtful approach to the situation" (email conversation January 10, 2007). That thoughtful approach was to ignore the entire incident, save a small brief on page 7 of the next edition, which mentioned what they called an "onstage spat" and to note that the clip of the assault received almost 200,000 hits on YouTube ("Top Gongs," 2007, p. 7). The union magazine had 'thoughtfully' framed the assault as a media spectacle, and an insignificant 'spat' at that, not the 'assault' that it was. The union and the media thus managed to naturalise male aggression by suggesting that it was 'a bit of biffo' (Day, 2006, p. 20); an 'on-stage biffo" (Byrnes, Grant, & Barrett, 2006, p. 27); a 'stoush' and 'outburst' (Mitchell, 2006, p. 14); a 'fracas' (Ricketson & Harrison, 2006, p. 3); and 'a good old fashioned go' (Hildebrand, 2006, p. 7). Only once was it refereed to as an 'assault' and that was when the News Ltd website published a story detailing its staffer, Milne's, apology (www.news. com.au December 1, 2006). Crikey.com, which had run pages of copy from Mayne and others, also refused a similar article idea from me. After outlining the article focus I was told: "We'll pass on this one because we are endeavouring to put the Milne thing behind us now" (email conversation January 15, 2007). So just six weeks after the event the shutters were brought down on public and even industry-only debate that promised a deeper and broader reflective and feminist analysis of the 'incident.'

The central debate in Australia about our media generally centres on media ownership and associated issues of democracy. The industry and the union, however, have failed to seriously consider the implications (both in terms of content and work culture) of a mainstream news media in which the key decision-making roles are dominated by men and a blokey culture persists. I would argue that the union needs to be more willing to face up to the problem of a masculinised work culture. Through its inaction it continues to privilege a certain way of 'being a journalist' in the Australian print news media.

At the end of this project I am also left thinking that the domination by one media conglomerate—News Corporation—of the Australian print news media stymies so many aspects of news practice and production. It is this domination by News Corp that aids in creating a particular newsroom culture, and one that is rarely challenged, successfully at least. It is difficult to envisage that domination changing in the near future, or that individual journalists with a feminist philosophy can make a major impact in the overall direction of Australian news content. When working in the industry I often satisfied myself with the fact that, as a feminist journalist, I was making small differences to the news by bringing my philosophy to news production and to some extent news content. But I know my jobs were sustained by maintaining the dominant ideology, and when I did challenge it, and perhaps even shape it, it was in such a small way—and it came at a personal and professional cost.

In an industry that seems to require that its workers develop cynicism to survive, one wonders about the fate of newly employed journalists and how they see their future in the industry. If my research reinforced anything to me, it was that journalists enter the industry with idealism and after a very short time become cynical about the profession and what they have to do to survive in it. There are gendered dimensions to this point, but I close with the thoughts of one of the interviewees, Stuart, a 19-year-old regional cadet who had been in the industry just a year when we first met for an interview for my research. He was full of hope and belief that he could give voice to people who didn't normally have representation in the media. I mused privately about how long his innocence would last. Two years later he replied to an email from me asking how his career in journalism was progressing. The final sentence summed up my concerns:

Stuart: My eyes are open a bit wider to the big bad world of newspapers and I have developed a healthy cynicism towards most aspects of life as a result (email conversation January 16, 2006).

Appendix 1

MEAA (Journalists) 12-point Code of Ethics

1. Report and interpret honestly, striving for accuracy, fairness and disclosure of all essential facts. Do not suppress relevant available facts, or give distorting emphasis. Do your utmost to give a fair opportunity for reply.

2. Do not place unnecessary emphasis on personal characteristics, including race, ethnicity, nationality, gender, age, sexual orientation, family relationships, religious belief, or physical or intellectual disability.

3. Aim to attribute information to its source. Where a source seeks anonymity, do not agree without first considering the source's motives and any alternative attributable source. Where confidences are accepted, respect them in all circumstances.

4. Do not allow personal interest, or any belief, commitment, payment, gift, or benefit, to undermine your accuracy, fairness or independence.

5. Disclose conflicts of interest that affect, or could be seen to affect, the accuracy, fairness or independence of your journalism. Do not improperly use a journalistic position for personal gain.

6. Do not allow advertising or other commercial considerations to undermine accuracy, fairness or independence.

7. Do your utmost to ensure disclosure of any direct or indirect payment made for interviews, pictures, information or stories.

8. Use fair, responsible and honest means to obtain material. Identify yourself and your employer before obtaining any interview for publication or broadcast. Never exploit a person's vulnerability or ignorance of media practice.

9. Present pictures and sound which are true and accurate. Any manipulation likely to mislead should be disclosed.

10. Do not plagiarise.

11. Respect private grief and personal privacy. Journalists have the right to resist compulsion to intrude.

12. Do your utmost to achieve fair correction of errors. (www.alliance.org.au/hot/ethicscode.htm).

Appendix 2

MEAA (Journalists) Grading System

MEAA documents provided by the union to me indicate that all media outlets in Australia (print, radio and broadcast) loosely follow a grading system. Many organisations use margins (an industry term for half grades or negotiated amounts of money above a grade) to promote staff but not to the next full grading. Hence some interviewees in this book have mentioned being graded a 1b, or the like. The grades are:

Cadet, Year 1
Cadet, Year 2
Cadet, Year 3
Band one:
Journalist Grade 1
Journalist Grade 2
Journalist Grade 3
Journalist Grade 4
Band two:
Journalist Grade 5
Journalist Grade 6
Journalist Grade 7
Band three:
Journalist Grade 8
Journalist Grade 9
Journalist Grade 10
The majority of journalists above grade 10 are usually on a negotiated contract.

Appendix 3

Email Communication

Coyle, Kerry. 2005. subject line 'case query,' 13 June.
Coyle, Kerry. 2005. subject line 'case query,' 14 June.
Coyle, Kerry. 2006. subject line 'case update,' 24 April.
Thom, Helen. 2006. subject line 'sexual harassment policy,' 17 April.
'Susan.' 2004. subject line 'a few questions re interview,' 4 March.
'Stuart.' 2006. subject line 'further to our interview in 2004,' 16 January.
'Pat.' 2004. subject line 'thanks,' 5 February.
'Paul.' 2006. subject line 'our interview in December 2003,' 16 January.
Sophie Black. 2007. subject line 'story proposal,' 15 January.
Jane Worthington. 2007. subject line 'article idea,' 10 January.
MEAA source. 2007. subject line 'Aileen Keenan case,' 2 August.

References

Abhayaratna, Joanna, & Lattimore, Ralph. (2006). *Workforce participation rates: How does Australia compare?* *Staff working paper*, Productivity Commission, Canberra. Accessed 28 May 2007 from <http://www.pc.gov.au/research/swp/workforceparticipation/workforceparticipation.pdf.

Abu-Lughod, Lila. (1991). Writing against culture. In Richard Fox (Ed.), *Recapturing anthropology: Working in the present* (pp. 137–162). Sante Fe, NM: School of American Research, University of Washington Press.

Acker, Joan. (1990). Hierarchies, jobs, bodies: A theory of gendered organizations. *Gender and Society, 4*(2), 139–158.

Advertiser Newspapers Limited. (2003). EOWA (Equal Opportunity in the Workplace Agency) Report Online. Accessed 1 August 2006 from <http://www.eowa.gov.au> pp. 1–7.

Advertiser Newspapers Limited. (2006). EOWA report online. Accessed 9 July 2007 from <http://www.eowa.gov.au> pp. 1–10.

Albrow, Martin. (1990). *Globalisation, knowledge and society: Readings from international sociology.* London: Sage.

Albury, Kath. (2002). Amateurs, homies and DIY porn. In Kath Albury (Ed.), *Yes means yes: Getting explicit about heterosex* (pp. 105–126). Crows Nest, NSW: Allen and Unwin.

Aldridge, Meryl. (2001a). Lost expectations? Women journalists and the fall-out from the 'Toronto newspaper war.' *Media, Culture & Society, 23*(5), 607–624.

Aldridge, Meryl. (2001b). The paradigm contingent career? Women in regional newspaper journalism. *Sociological Research Online, 6*(3). Accessed 27 March 2003 from <http://www.socresonline.org.uk/6/3aldridge.html>.

Allen, Cameron, O'Donnell, Michael, & Peetz, David. (1999). More tasks, less secure, working harder: Three dimensions of labour utilisation. *Journal of Industrial Relations, 41*(4), 519–535.

Altmann, Carol. (2006). *After Port Arthur: Personal stories of courage and resilience ten years on from the tragedy that shocked a nation.* Sydney: Allen and Unwin.

AMP NATSEM. (2005). *Changing face of the Australian labour force 1985–2005,* AMP NATSEM Income and Wealth Report Issue 12 November 2005. Accessed 28 May 2007 from http://www.amp.com.au/group/3column/0,2449,CH27105%255FSI3,00.html.

Ardener, Shirley. (1974). Nudity, vulgarity and protest. *New Society, 27*(598), 704–705.

Ardener, Shirley. (1983). Arson, nudity and bombs among the Canadian Doukhobors: A question of identity. In Glynis M Breakwell (Ed.), *Threatened identities* (pp. 251–262). Chichester: Wiley.

Arthurs, Jane. (1994). Women and television. In Stuart Hood (Ed.), *Behind the screens* (pp. 82–101). London: Lawrence and Wishart.

Australian Bureau of Statistics (ABS). (1998, November). Career experience, catalogue no. 6254.0.

Bagdikian, Ben. (1983). *The media monopoly.* Boston, MA: Beacon Press.

Bagdikian, Ben. (2004). *The new media monopoly.* Boston, MA: Beacon Press.

Bacchi, Carol. (1998). Changing the sexual harassment agenda. In Moira Gatens & Alison Mackinnon (Eds.), *Gender and institutions: Welfare, work and citizenship* (pp. 75–89). Melbourne: Cambridge University Press.

Bacchi, Carol, & Jose, Jim. (1994). Dealing with sexual harassment: Persuade, discipline, or punish? *Australian Journal of Law and Society, 10,* 1–13.

Baehr, Helen, & Gray, Anne. (1996). *Turning it on: A reader in women and media.* New York: Arnold.

Bailey, Sue. (2001, August 2). Tassie shuns the whorehouse. *The Mercury,* p. 1.

Barcan, Ruth. (2000). Home on the rage: Nudity, celebrity, and ordinariness in the home girls/blokes pages. *Continuum: Journal of Media and Cultural Studies, 14*(2), 145–158.

Barcan, Ruth. (2002). Female exposure and the protesting woman. *Cultural Studies Review, 8*(2), 62–82.

Bartky, Sandra Lee. (1997). Foucault, femininity, and the modernisation of patriarchal power. In Katie Conboy, Nadia Medina and Sarah Stanbury (Eds.), *Writing on the body: Female embodiment and feminist theory* (pp. 129–154). New York: Columbia University Press.

Beasley, Maurine, & Gibbons, Shelia J. (1993). *Taking their place: A documentary history of women and journalism.* Washington, DC: The American University Press.

Beecher, Eric. (2005). The decline of the quality press. In Robert Manne (Ed.), *Do not disturb: Is the media failing Australia* (pp. 7–27). Melbourne: Black Inc.

Berger, John. (1990/1972). *Ways of seeing.* London: Penguin.

Binnie, Craig. (2004, August 30). Editor's building deals. *Herald Sun,* p. 26.

Binnie, Craig. (2005, March 15). Appeal on bias ruling. *Herald Sun,* p. 12.

Bordo, Susan. (1993). Reading the male body. *Michigan Quarterly Review, 32*(4), 696–737.

Bordo, Susan. (1999). *The male body: A new look at men in public and in private.* New York: Farrar, Straus and Giroux.

Bourdieu, Pierre. (1986). The forms of capital. In John Richardson (Ed.), *Handbook of theory and research for the sociology of education* (pp. 241–258). New York: Greenwood Press.

Boyd-Barrett, Oliver. (1977). Media imperialism: Towards an international framework for the analysis of media systems. In James Curran, Michael Gurevitch, & Janet Woollacott (Eds.), *Mass communication and society* (pp. 116–135). London: Arnold.

Boyd-Barrett, Oliver. (1998). Media imperialism reformulated. In Daya Kishan Thussu (Ed.), *Electronic empires: Global media and local resistance* (pp. 157–176). London: Arnold.

Breed, Warren. (1955). Social control in the newsroom: A functional analysis. *Social Forces, 33*(4), 326–335.

Breed, Warren. (2003/1955). Social control in the newsroom: A functional analysis. In Robert W. McChesney & Ben Scott (Ed.), *Our unfree press: 100 years of radical media criticism* (pp. 229–244). New York: The New Press.

Bridges, Lee. (1973). Race relations research: From colonization to neo-colonialism? Some random thoughts. *Race, 14*(3), 341–441.

Brittan, Arthur. (1989). *Masculinity and power*. Oxford: Blackwell.

Brown, William A., Deakin, Simon, Hudson, Maria, Pratten, Cliff, & Ryan, Paul. (1998). *The individualisation of employment contracts in Britain*. Employment Relations Research Series No 4. London: Department of Trade and Industry.

Brunner, Penelope, & Costello, Melinda. (2002). Where's the joke? The meaning behind sexual humor. Advancing Women in Leadership website. Online. Accessed 8 February 2005 from <http:/www.advancingwomen.com>.

Brunsdon, Charlotte. (1988). Feminism and soap opera. In Kath Davis, Julienne Dickey, & Teresa Stratford (Eds.), *Out of focus: Writing on women and the media* (pp. 147–150). London: The Women's Press.

Burrell, Gibson, & Hearn, Jeff. (1989). The sexuality of organization. In Jeff Hearn, Debra Sheppard, Peta Tancred-Sheriff, & Gibson Burrell (Eds.), *The sexuality of organisation* (pp. 1–28). London: Sage.

Butler, Judith. (1997). Performative acts and gender constitution: An essay in phenomenology and feminist theory. In Katie Conboy, Nadia Medina, & Sarah Stanbury (Eds.), *Writing on the body: Female embodiment and feminist theory* (pp. 401–417). New York: Columbia University Press.

Byerly, Carolyn, M. (1998). *Women, media and structure: Feminist research in an era of globalization*. Paper presented at the International Association for Media and Communication Research, Glasgow.

Byerly, Carolyn, M. (1999). News, feminism, and the dialectics of gender relations. In Marian Meyers (Ed.), *Mediated women: Representations in popular culture* (pp. 383–403). Cresskill, NJ: Hampton Press.

Byerly, Carolyn, M. (2004a). Feminist interventions in newsrooms. In Karen Ross & Carolyn Byerly (Eds.), *Women and media: International perspectives* (pp. 109–131). London: Blackwell.

Byerly, Carolyn, M. (2004b). Women and the concentration of media ownership. In Ramona R. Rush, Carol E. Oukrop, & Pamela J. Creedon (Eds.), *Seeking equity for women in journalism and mass communication: A 30-year update* (pp. 245–262). Mahwah, NJ: Erlbaum.

Byerly, Carolyn, M. (2005). After September 11: The formations of an oppositional discourse. *Feminist Media Studies, 5*(3), 281–296.

Byerly, Carolyn M., & Ross, Karen. (2006). *Women & media: A critical introduction*. Malden, MA, Oxford, and Carlton, Victoria: Blackwell.

Byerly, Carolyn M., & Warren, Catherine A. (1996). At the margins of centre: Organised protest in the newsroom. *Critical studies in mass communication, 12*(1), 1–19.

Byrnes, Holly, Grant, Sarah, & Barrett, Chris. (2006, December 2). Sydney confidential. *Daily Telegraph*, p. 27.

Califia, Pat. (1994). *Public sex: The culture of radical sex*. San Francisco: Cleis Press.

Carter, Cynthia, Branston, Gill, & Allan, Stuart (Eds.). (1998). *News, gender and power*. London and New York: Routledge.

Carter, Cynthia, & Steiner, Linda. (2004). Introduction to critical readings: Media and gender. In Cynthia Carter & Linda Steiner (Eds.), *Critical readings: Media and gender* (pp. 1–11). Berkshire: Open University Press.

Catalano, Christian. (2004, July 23). Andrew Jaspan new age editor-in-chief. *The Age*. Also Online. Accessed 5 August 2004 from <http://www.theage.com.au/articles /2004/07/22/1090464799544.html?from=moreStories>.

Catalano, Christian, & Porter, Jeni. (2005, November 19). Fairfax chief defends jobs cuts. *The Age*, p. B1.

Cheng, Cliff. (1996). Men and masculinities are not necessarily synonymous: Thoughts on organisational behaviour and occupational sociology. In Cliff Cheng (Ed.), *Masculinities in organisations* (pp. xi–xx). Thousand Oaks, CA: Sage.

Christmas, Linda. (1997). *Chaps of both sexes? Women decision-makers in newspapers: Do they make a difference?* London: BT Forum/Women in Journalism.

Clark, Kenneth. (1956). *The nude: A study in ideal form* (1st ed.). New York: Doubleday.

Cockburn, Cynthia. (1983). *Brothers*. London: Pluto Press.

Cockburn, Cynthia. (1986). *Machinery of dominance: Women, men and technical know-how*. London: Pluto Press.

Cockburn, Cynthia. (1991). *In the way of women: Men's resistance to sex equality in organizations*. London: Macmillan.

Colegate, Christina. (2004). "Does my bum look too big in this?": Getting a grip on our bodies. In *Just between you & me: The art of ethical relationships* (pp. 37–63). Sydney: Macmillan.

Coleridge, Nicolas. (1993). *Paper tycoons: The latest, greatest newspaper tycoons and how they won the world*. London: Heinemann.

Collinson, David L. (1992). *Managing the shopfloor: Subjectivity, masculinity and workplace culture*. Berlin: De Gruyter.

Collinson, David, & Hearn, Jeff. (1994). Naming men as men: Implications for work, organization and management. *Gender, Work and Organization, 1*(1), 2–22.

Collinson, David, & Hearn, Jeff. (1996). Breaking the silence: On men, masculinities and managements. In David Collinson & Jeff Hearn (Eds.), *Men as managers, managers as men: Critical perspectives on men, masculinities and managements* (pp. 1–24). London: Sage.

Compaine, Benjamin M., & Gomery, Douglas. (2000). *Who owns the media? Competition and concentration in the mass media industry*. Mahwah, NJ: Erlbaum.

Conboy, Katie, Medina, Nadia, & Stanbury, Sarah. (Eds.). (1997). Introduction. In *Writing on the body: Female embodiment and feminist theory* (pp. 1–12). New York: Columbia University Press.

Connell, Robert W. (1983). *Which way is up? Essays on sex, class, and culture*. London: Allen and Unwin.

Connell, Robert W. (1987). *Gender and power*. Sydney: Allen and Unwin.

Connell, Robert W. (1995). *Masculinities*. Berkeley: University of California Press.

Considine, Gillian, & Buchanan, John. (2000). *The hidden costs of understaffing: An analysis of contemporary nurses' working conditions in Victoria*. Sydney: Australian Centre of Industrial Relations Research and Training (ACIRRT).

Crawford, Mary. (2000). Only joking: Humor and sexuality. In Cheryl Travis & Jacquelyn White (Eds.), *Sexuality, society, and feminism* (pp. 213–236). Washington, DC: American Psychological Association.

Creed, Barbara. (2003). *Media matrix: Sexing the new reality*. Sydney: Allen and Unwin.

Creedon, Pamela. J. (1993). The challenge of re-visioning gender values. In Pamela J. Creedon (Ed.), *Women in mass communication* (2nd ed., pp. 3–23). Beverly Hills, CA: Sage.

Cunningham, Brent. (2003, July/August). Re-thinking objectivity. *Columbia Journalism Review*, pp. 24–32.

Dalton, Melville. (1959). *Men who manage: Fusions of feeling and theory in administration*. New York: Wiley.

Dannin, Ellen J. (1997). *Working free: The origin and impact of New Zealand's employment contracts act*. Auckland: Auckland University Press.

Davies Bros Pty Ltd. (1998). EOWA (Equal Opportunity in the Workplace Agency) Report Online. Accessed 1 August 2006 from <http://www.eowa.gov.au>.

Davies Bros Pty Ltd. (2003). EOWA Report Online. Accessed 1 August 2006 from <http://www.eowa.gov.au.> pp. 1–11.

Davies Bros Pty Ltd. (2004). EOWA Report. Online. Accessed 1 August 2006 from <http://www.eowa.gov.au> pp. 1–10.

Davies Bros Pty Ltd. (2006). EOWA Report Online. Accessed 9 July 2007 from <http://www.eowa.gov.au.> pp. 1–9.

Day, Mark. (2006, December 7). It takes more than a drunken outburst to get sacked. *The Australian*, Media section, p. 20.

Day, Mark, & Lehmann, John. (2005, October 27). Fairfax boss runs into job cuts fury. *The Australian*, Media section p. 15

de Beauvoir, Simone. (1978). *The second sex* (Howard Madison Parshley, Ed. & Trans.). New York: Knopf.

de Bruin, Marjan. (1999). Gender, media production and media output. *Media Development*, 2. Online. Accessed 4 April 2003 from http://www.wacc.org.uk/publications/md/md1999-2/bruin.html.

de Bruin, Marjan. (2000a). Looking beyond the "body count" in the Caribbean. *Media Development*, 3. Online. Accessed 5 May 2003 from <http://www.wacc.org.uk/publications/md/md2000-3/de_bruin.html>.

de Bruin, Marjan. (2000b). Gender, organisational and professional journalism. *Journalism*, 1(2), 217–238.

de Bruin, Marjan. (2004). Organizational, professional, and gender identities—Overlapping, coinciding and contradicting realities in Caribbean media practices. In Marjan de Bruin & Karen Ross (Eds.), *Gender and newsroom cultures: Identities at work* (pp. 1–16). Cresskill, NJ: Hampton Press.

de Bruin, Marjan, & Ross, Karen. (Eds.). (2004). *Gender and newsroom culture: Identities at work*. Cresskill, NJ: Hampton Press.

de Certeau, Michel. (1984). *The practice of everyday life*. Berkeley: University of California Press.

Delano, Anthony. (2003). Women journalists: What's the difference? *Journalism Studies*, 4(2), 273–286.

Djerf-Pierre, Monika, & Lofgren-Nilsson, Monica. (2001). *Sex-typing in the newsroom: Feminisation of Swedish television news production, 1958–2000*. Paper presented to the 15th Nordic Conference on Media and Communication Research, Reykjavik, Island.

Dodd, Andrew. (2000, August 10). Writer claims sexism at *Age*. *The Australian*, p. 5.

Dodson, Louise, Banham, Cynthia, & O'Mally, Nick. (2005, October 10). Your conditions are safe: Howard vow on changes. *The Sydney Morning Herald*, p. 1.

Dougary, Ginny. (1994). *The executive tart and other myths*. London: Virago.

Douglas, Jack D., & Rasmussen, Paul K. with Flanagan, Carol Abb. (1977). *The nude beach*. Beverly Hills, CA: Sage.

Dunlevy, Maurice. (2004a, August 4). Back in the stone age . . . Newspaper run by a "boys' club." *The Australian*, p. 7.

Dunlevy, Maurice. (2004b, August 6). $600 a week for phantom column. *The Australian*, p. 7.

Dunn, Anne. (2003). Ethics impossible? Advertising and the infomercial. In Catharine Lumby & Elspeth Probyn (Eds.), *Remote control: New media, new ethics* (pp. 133–151). Cambridge: Cambridge University Press.

Edgar, Patricia, & McPhee, Hilary. (1974). *Media she*. Melbourne: Heinemann.

Edmonds, Mike, Dennehy, Luke, & Danaher, Carla. (2004, October 8). Defence gets a mention. *Herald Sun* ("The Eye" column), p. 22.

Eisenstein, Zillah. (1997/1981). *The radical future of liberal feminism*. Boston, MA: Northeastern University Press.

Eveline, Joan. (1994). The politics of advantage. *Australian Feminist Studies*, 19, 129–154.

Eveline, Joan. (1998). Heavy, dirty and limp stories: Male advantage at work. In Moira Gatens & Alison Mackinnon (Eds.), *Gender and institutions: Welfare, work and citizenship* (pp. 90–106). Melbourne: Cambridge University Press.

Fanning, Ellen. (2004, August/September). Between the shock and a hard place. *The Walkley Magazine*, 28, p. 35.

Fairfax to slash 550 jobs to cut costs. (2008, August 26). Accessed 29 August 2008 from <http://www.news.com.au/business/story/0,27753,24242979-462,0.html>

Farley, Lin. (1978). *Sexual shakedown: Sexual harassment of women on the job*. New York: McGraw-Hill.

Fonow, Mary Margaret, & Cook, Judith A. (Eds.). (1991). *Beyond methodology: Feminist scholarship as lived research*. Bloomington: Indiana University Press.

Foucault, Michel. (1979). *The history of sexuality: Vol 1*. London: Penguin.

Frankenberg, Ruth. (1993). White on white: The interviewees and the method. In *White women, race matters: The social construction of whiteness* (pp. 23–42). Minneapolis: University of Minnesota Press.

Gallagher, Margaret. (1981). *Unequal opportunities: The case of women in the media*. Paris: UNESCO.

Gallagher, Margaret. (1987). *Women and media decision-making*. Paris: UNESCO.

Gallagher, Margaret. (1995). *An unfinished story: Gender patterns in media employment*. Paris: UNESCO.

Gallagher, Margaret. (2001). Reporting on gender in journalism: Why do so few women reach the top? In *Nieman Reports*. Online. Accessed 14 February 2003 from <http://www.nieman.harvard.edu/reports/01-4NRWinter/63-65.pdf>.

Gallagher, Margaret. (2002). *Women, media and democratic society: In pursuit of rights and freedoms*. Paper presented at United Nations Division for the Advancement of Women. Beirut, Lebanon.

Game, Ann, & Pringle, Rosemary. (1983). *Gender at work*. Sydney: Allen and Unwin.

Gamson, William A. (1984). *What's news: A game simulation of TV news*. New York: Free Press.

Garner, Helen. (1995). *The first stone: Some questions about sex and power*. Sydney: Pan Macmillan.

Garnham, Nicolas. (1990). *Capitalism and communication: Global culture and the economics of information*. London: Sage.

Gatens, Moira. (1998). Institutions, embodiment and sexual difference. In Moira Gatens & Alison Mackinnon (Eds.), *Gender and institutions: Welfare, work and citizenship* (pp. 1–18). Melbourne: Cambridge University Press.

Giddens, Anthony. (1990). *The consequences of modernity*. Cambridge: Polity.

Gill, Rosalind. (2003). From sexual objectification to sexual subjectification: The resexualisation of women's bodies in the media. *Feminist Media Studies, 3*(1), 100–106.

Gilligan, Carol. (1986). Remapping the moral domain: New images of the self in relationship. In Thomas Heller, Morton Sosna, & David Wellbery (Eds.), *Reconstructing individualism: Autonomy, individuality and the self in Western thought* (pp. 237–252). Stanford: Stanford University Press.

Gillwald, Alison. (1994). Women, democracy and media in South Africa. *Media Development, 2*, 27–32.

Gilson, Clive, & Wagar, Terry. (1996). Individual contracts and the impact of labour legislation: Trans-Tasman comparisons. *Australian Bulletin of Labour, 22*(4), 275–287.

Global Media Monitoring Report. (2005). Who makes the news? Accessed 7 February 2008 from http://www.whomakesthenews.org/who_makes_the_news/report_2005.

Gramsci, Antonio. (1971). *Selections from the prison notebooks*. London: Lawrence and Wishart.

Grosz, Elizabeth. (2001). Naked. In Terry Smith (Ed.), *Impossible presence: Surface and screen in the photogenic era* (pp. 209–222). Sydney: Power Publications.

Hall, Stuart, Critcher, Charles, Jefferson, Tony, Clarke, John, & Robert, Brian. (1978). *Policing the crisis*. London: Macmillan.

Hamner, Jalna, & Saunders, Sheila. (1984). *Well-founded fear: A community study of violence to women*. London: Hutchinson.

Haraway, Donna. (1988). Situated knowledges: The science question in feminism as a site of discourse on the privilege of partial perspective. *Feminist Studies, 14*(3). 575–599.

Harwood, Dick. (1997). *The media's relationship to fact fairness and gossip—Bias, cynicism, superficiality, and elitism*. Transcript of a forum at Columbia University Graduate

School of Journalism on December 4, 1997 in New York. Online. Accessed 18 August 2003 from <http://www.journalism.org/resources/education/ forums/ ccj/forum2/bias.asp>.

Haussegger, Virginia. (2005). *Wonder woman: The myth of "having it all."* Sydney: Allen and Unwin.

Hawkesworth, Mary E. (1989). Knowers, knowing, known: Feminist theory and claims of truth. *Signs: Journal of Women in Culture and Society, 14*, 533–554.

Hearn, Jeff, & Parkin, Wendy. (1987). *"Sex" at "work": The power and paradox of organisational sexuality.* Brighton: Wheatsheaf Books.

Heller, Zoe. (1999). Girl columns. In Stephen Glover (Ed.), *Penguin book of journalism: Secrets of the press* (pp. 10–17). London: Penguin.

Henningham, John. (1998). Australian journalists. In David H Weaver (Ed.), *The global journalist: News people around the world* (pp. 91–107). Cresskill, NJ: Hampton Press.

Hochschild, Arlie. (1983). *The managed heart: Commercialisation of human feeling.* Berkeley: University of California Press.

Hildebrand, Joe (2006, December 2). Joe Hildebrand column. *The Daily Telegraph*, p. 87.

Hill Collins, Patricia. (1986). Learning from the outsider within. *Social Problems, 33*(6), 14–29.

Hodge, Joanna. (1988). Subject, body and the exclusion of women from philosophy. In Morwenna Griffiths & Margaret Whitford (Eds.), *Feminist perspectives in philosophy* (pp. 152–168). Bloomington: Indiana University Press.

Huddy, Leonie. (1997). Feminists and feminism in the news. In Pippa Norris (Ed.), *Women, media, and politics* (pp. 183–204). New York and Oxford: Oxford University Press.

Human Rights and Equal Opportunity Commission (HREOC). (2002). *A bad business: Review of sexual harassment in employment complaints 2002.* Online. Accessed 28 July 2006 from <http://www.hreoc.gov.au/sex_discrimination/bad_business/docs/ factlegaldefinition.doc>.

HREOC. (2003). Executive summary. In *20 years on: The challenges continue: Sexual harassment in the Australian workforce.* Online. Accessed 28 July 2006 from <http://www.hreoc.gov.au/sex_discrimination/challenge_continues/data/exec_ summary.html>.

Jackall, Robert. (1988). *Moral mazes: The world of corporate managers.* New York: Oxford University Press.

Jackson, Sally. (2003a, February 27–March 5). Sisters bash heads against Perth paper's glass ceiling. *The Australian* (Media section), p. 3.

Jackson, Sally. (2003b, May 22). Equal work, but women journalists get less pay than their male counterparts. *The Australian* (features section), p. B3.

Jackson, Sally. (2004, March 11). Discrimination case lacking substance. *The Australian* (features section), p. 21.

Jeffreys, Elaine. (1991, Summer). What is 'difference' in feminist theory and practice? *Australian Feminist Studies, 14*, 1–13.

Jones, Kate. (2004a, August 4). Journo fights "old boys club." *Herald Sun*, p. 8.

Jones, Kate. (2004b, August 5). Editor asked to quit court. *Herald Sun*, p. 4.

Jones, Kate. (2004c, August 6). Age man called me a liar. *Herald Sun*, p. 6.

Jones, Kate. (2004d, August 7). Pay deals favoured men, hearing told. *Herald Sun*, p. 12.

Jones, Kate. (2004e, August 19). Male scribe's pay unfair, says editor. *Herald Sun*, edition 1, p. 13.

Jones, Kate. (2004f, August 19). Male scribe's pay "unfair." *Herald Sun*, edition 2, p. 13.

Jones, Kate. (2004g, August 20). Editor defends pay. *Herald Sun*, p. 11.

Jones, Kate. (2004h, August 21). Editor defends record. *Herald Sun*, p. 18.

Jones, Kate. (2004i, August 31). Age shows its cards. *Herald Sun*, p. 12.

Jones, Kate. (2004j, September 7). Age pay bonus was a "one-off." *Herald Sun*, p. 25.

Jones, Kate. (2004k, December 15). The age of workers' discontent. *Herald Sun*, p. 30.

Jones, Kate. (2004l, December 23). Ruling in sex case. *Herald Sun*, p. 13.

Joseph, Ammu. (2000). *Women in journalism: Making news.* New Delhi: Konark Publishers.

Joseph, Ammu. (2004). Working, watching and waiting: Women and issues of access, employment and decision-making in the media in India. In Karen Ross & Carolyn Byerly (Eds.), *Women and media: International perspectives* (pp. 132–156). London: Blackwell.

Kahn, William. (1989). Toward a sense of organizational humor: Implications for organizational diagnosis and change. *The Journal of Applied Behavioral Science*, 25, 45–63.

Kanter, Rosabeth Moss. (1975). Women and the structure of organizations: Explorations in theory and behavior. In Rosabeth Kanter & Marcia Millman (Eds.), *Another voice: Feminist perspectives on social life and social science* (pp. 34–74). New York: Doubleday.

Kanter, Rosabeth Moss. (1977a). Some effects of proportions on group life: Skewed sex ratios and responses to token women. *American Journal of Sociology*, 82(5), 965–990.

Kanter, Rosabeth Moss. (1977b). *Men and women of the corporation.* New York: Basic Books.

Kaszubska, Gosia. (2004, December 23). Fairfax's age-old boys club warned to pay up. *The Australian*, p. 4.

Kerfoot, Deborah, & Knights, David. (1993). Management, masculinity and manipulation: From paternalism to corporate strategy in financial services in Britain. *Journal of Management Studies*, 30, 659–677.

Kerfoot, Deborah, & Knights, David. (1996). "The best is yet to come?": The quest for embodiment in managerial work. In David Collinson & Jeff Hearn (Eds.), *Men as managers, managers as men* (pp. 78–98). London: Sage.

Kieran, Matthew. (1998). Objectivity, impartiality and good journalism. In *Media Ethics* (pp. 23–36). London: Routledge.

Kimmel, Michael S. (1994). Masculinities as homophobia: Fear, shame, and silence in the construction of gender identity. In Harry Brod & Michael Kaufman (Eds.), *Theorising masculinities* (pp. 119–141). Thousand Oaks, CA: Sage.

Kimmel, Michael S., & Messner, Michael A. (Eds.). (1989). *Men's lives.* New York: Macmillan.

Kramarae, Cheris (1992). Harassment and everyday life. In Lana F. Rakow (Ed.), *Women making meaning: New feminist directions in communication* (pp. 100–120). New York and London: Routledge & Kegan Paul.

Lafky, Sue A. (1991). Women journalists. In David Weaver & Cleveland Wilhoit (Eds.), *The American journalist: A portrait of US news people and their work* (pp. 160–181). Bloomington: Indiana University Press.

Language and pagination. (1996, April 21–June 2). *Insider*.

Leader Associated Newspapers Pty Ltd. (2004). EOWA (Equal Opportunity in the Workplace Agency) Report. Online. Accessed 12 April 2006 from <http://www.eowa.gov.au> pp. 1–6.

Lester, Libby. (2006). Journalism, reflexivity, and the natural state. *Australian Journal of Communication, 33*(2–3), 75–88.

Lester, Libby. (2007). *Giving ground: Media and environmental conflict in Australia*. Hobart: Quintus Press.

Lewis, Sue (2000). Masculinity and IT: Computing gender in the IT industry. *Quarterly Newsletter of the National Centre for Gender and Cultural Diversity, 1*(4) and Online. Accessed 5 November 2004 from <http://www.wisenet-australia.org/issue56/Masculinity%20and%20IT.htm>.

Lewis, Sue, McLean, Christopher, Copeland, Jane, & Lintern, Sue. (1998). Further explorations of masculinity and the culture of engineering. *Australian Journal of Engineering Education, 8*(1), 59–78.

Leys, Nick. (2004, December 23). Editor in the rough. *The Australian* ("Strewth" column), p. 9.

Limor, Yehiel, & Lavie, Aliza. (2002). The feminisation of the media: The case of Israel. Paper presented to the IAMCR (Gender and Communication section) conference, Barcelona.

Lovibond, Jane. (1998, October 9). A few stark realities. *The Mercury*, p. 5.

Lumby, Catharine. (1997). *Bad girls: The media, sex and feminism in the 90s*. St Leonards: Allen and Unwin.

Lumby, Catharine. (1999). *Gotcha: Life in a tabloid world*. Sydney: Allen and Unwin.

Lumby, Catharine. (2000). The dichotomy of pleasure and power is too simple. In an interview with Catharine Lumby, by Geert Lovink. Online. Accessed 25 May 2005 from <http://amsterdam.nettime.org/Lists-Archives/nettime-l-0009/msg00008.html>.

Lumby, Catharine. (2002). The future of journalism. In Stuart Cunningham & Graeme Turner (Eds.), *The media and communications in Australia* (pp. 320–329). Sydney: Allen and Unwin.

McCabe, Marita, & Hardman, Lisa. (2005). Attitudes and perceptions of workers to sexual harassment. *Journal of Social Psychology, 145*(6), 719–740.

McCallum, Ronald. (1996). The new millennium and the Higgins heritage. *Journal of Industrial Relations, 38*(2), 294–312.

McChesney, Robert W. (1999). *Rich media, poor democracy*. Urbana and Chicago: University of Illinois Press.

McChesney, Robert W. (2001). Global media, neoliberalism, and imperialism. *Monthly Review, 52*(10), 1–19. Online. Accessed 1 August 2005 from <http://www.monthlyreview.org/301rwm.htm>.

McChesney, Robert W., & Scott, Ben (Eds.). (2003). Introduction. In *Our unfree press: 100 years of radical media criticism* (pp. 1–30). New York: The New Press.

McIlwee, Judith, S., & Robinson, J. Gregg. (1992). *Women in engineering: Gender, power and workplace culture*. New York: State University of New York Press.

McKnight, David. (2003). "A world hungry for a new philosophy": Rupert Murdoch and the rise of neo-liberalism. *Journalism Studies, 4*(3), 347–358.

McLean, Christopher, Lewis, Sue, Copeland, Jane, Lintern, Sue, & O'Neill, Brian. (1997). Masculinity and the culture of engineering. *Australian Journal of Engineering Education, 7*(2), 143–156.

McLuhan, Marshall, & Fiore, Quentin. (1967). *The medium is the message: An inventory of effects*. New York: Bantam.

McRobbie, Angela. (1982). The politics of feminist research: Between talk, text and action. *Feminist Review, 12*, 46–57.

McRobbie, Angela. (1997). *More!* New sexualities in girls' and women's magazines. In Angela McRobbie (Ed.)., *Back to reality? Social experience and cultural studies* (pp. 190–205). Manchester: Manchester University Press.

McRobbie, Angela. (2000). The return to cultural production case study: Fashion journalism. In James Curran & Michael Gurevitch (Eds.), *Mass media and society* (3rd ed., pp. 255–267). London: Arnold.

McQuail, Denis. (2000). Global mass communication. In *McQuail's mass communication theory* (4th ed., pp. 216–240). London: Sage.

MacKinnon, Catharine A. (1979). *Sexual harassment of working women*. New Haven: Yale University Press.

MacLean, Sheena. (2006, February 23). Paper sales defy internet growth. *The Australia*, p. 17.

Mahtani, Minelle. (2005). Gendered news practices: Examining experiences of women journalists in different national contexts. In Stuart Allan (Ed.), *Journalism: Critical issues* (pp. 299–310). Berkshire: Open University Press.

Malone, Paul. (2003). Objective: Objectivity. *The Walkley Magazine, 22*, pp. 16–17.

Mangan, John (2004, November 16). The other end of the stick. *The Age*, A3 cover story, pp. 4–5.

Manne, Robert. (2005a, August 11). Is the media failing Australia? *The Media Report*. Online. Accessed 31 August 2005 from <http://www.abc.net.au/rn/talks/8.30/mediarpt/stories/s1435112.htm>.

Manne, Robert. (2005b). Introduction. In Robert Manne (Ed.), *Do not disturb: Is the media failing Australia?* (pp. 1–4). Melbourne: Black Inc.

Manne, Robert. (2005c). Murdoch and the war on Iraq. In Robert Manne (Ed.), *Do not disturb: Is the media failing Australia?* (pp. 75–98). Melbourne: Black Inc.

Marcus, Sharon. (1992). Fighting bodies, fighting words: A theory and politics of rape prevention. In Judith Butler & Joan Scott (Eds.), *Feminists theorise the political* (pp. 385–403). New York: Routledge.

Marjoribanks, Timothy. (2000). *News corporation, technology and the workplace: Global strategies, local change*. Cambridge: Cambridge University Press.

Martin, Patricia Yancey. (1996). Gendering and evaluating dynamics: Men, masculinities, and management. In David Collinson & Jeff Hearn (Eds.), *Men as managers,*

managers as men: Critical perspectives on men, masculinities and managements (pp. 186–209). London: Sage.

Martin, Roberta J., & Hine, Don W. (2004). Development and validation of the scale of uncivil workplace incivility questionnaire (UWBQ). In *Conference Proceedings for 2004 Annual Meeting of the Australian Psychological Association*. Sydney, NSW.

Mason, Gail. (2002). *The spectacle of violence: Homophobia, gender and knowledge*. London and New York: Routledge.

MEAA. (2004). Power at work. *Annual Report, 2003–2004*.

MEAA. (2006). Your rights at work. *Annual Report, 2005–2006*.

MEAA Foots Bill. (2004, March 18). *The Australian* (In Brief), p. 19

MEAA and IFJ (Media, Entertainment and Arts Alliance and International Federation of Journalists). (1996). *Women in the media in Asia: Participation and portrayal*. Sydney: Media, Entertainment and Arts Alliance.

Mead, Jenna. (Ed.). (1997). *BodyJamming: Sexual harassment, feminism and public life*. Sydney: Random House.

Meade, Amanda. (2005a, November 23). Nine offers redundancy packages in new push to slash costs. *The Australian*, p. 3.

Meade, Amanda. (2005b, November 24). The diary. *The Australian* (Media section), p. 18.

Meade, Amanda. (2007a, June 7). Cooper in fiery farewell. *The Australian* (Media section), p. 40.

Meade, Amanda. (2007b, July 26). And this one's for dad. *The Australian* (Media section), p. 36.

Melin-Higgins, Margareta. (1996). Female educators and male craftsmen?: The professional ideals among Swedish journalists. *Nordicom Review, 1*, 153–169.

Melin-Higgins, Margareta. (2004). Coping with journalism: Gendered newsroom culture. In Marjan de Bruin & Karen Ross (Eds.), *Gender and newsroom culture: Identities at work* (pp. 197–222). Cresskill NJ: Hampton Press.

Melin-Higgins, Margareta, & Djerf-Pierre, Monika. (1998). *Networking in newsrooms: Journalist and gender cultures*. Paper presented at the International Association for Media and Communication Research conference (IAMCR), Glasgow.

Messenger Press Pty Ltd. (2005). EOWA (Equal Opportunity in the Workplace Agency) Report Online. Accessed 1 August 2006 from <http://www.eowa.gov.au> pp. 1–10.

Meyers, Marian. (2000). Fracturing women. In Marian Meyers (Ed.), *Mediated women: Representations in popular culture* (pp. 3–19). Cresskill NJ: Hampton Press.

Miles, Margaret. (1991/1989). Nakedness, gender and religious meaning. In Margaret Miles (Ed.), *Carnal knowing: Female nakedness and religious meaning in the Christian west* (pp. 169–185). New York: Vintage.

Miller, Claire. (2001). Women are half the population, half the talent, half the experience. In *Equality and quality: A celebration of women in journalism*. Online. Accessed 14 September 2005 from <http://www.ifj.org/pdfs/eg.pdf>.

Mills, Kay. (1988). *A place in the news: From the women's pages to the front page*. New York: Dodd, Mead.

Milne, Glenn. (2006, December 3). What made me snap at the Walkleys. *The Sunday Telegraph*, p. 2.

Mitchell, Geraldine. (2006, December 2). Awards stoush blamed on drink, tablets. *Herald Sun*, p. 14.

Mitchell, Richard. (1997, August–September). Quantum leap to new era. *Insider*, vol. 2.

Morgan, David H. J. (1992). *Discovering men*. London and New York: Unwin Hyman/ Routledge.

Morgan, Jenny. (1995). Sexual harassment and the public/private dichotomy: Equality, morality and manners. In Margaret Thornton (Ed.), *Public and private: Feminist legal debates* (pp. 89–92). Melbourne: Oxford University Press.

Morehead, Alison, Steele, Mairi, Alexander, Michael, Stephen, Kerry, & Duffin, Linten. (1997). *Changes at work: The 1995 Australian workplace industrial relations survey*. Canberra: DEWSRB.

Mowlana, Hamid. (1997). *Global information and world communication* (2nd ed.). London: Sage.

Mulkay, Michael. (1988). *On humor: Its nature and its place in modern society*. London: Basil Blackwell.

Muller, Denis. (2005, August 31). Disconnected journalists and the public. *The Media Report*. Online. Accessed 1 February 2006 from <http://www.abc.net.au/rn/ talks/8.30/mediarpt/stories/s1444760.htm>.

Mulvey, Laura. (1975, Autumn). Visual pleasure and narrative cinema. *Screen*, 16(3).

Munro, Ian. (2004, December 23). Sex discrimination claim against age dismissed. *The Age*, p 4.

Murray, Lisa. (2005, July 20). Murdoch splashes $776m on the net. *The Sydney Morning Herald*, p. 25.

Nationwide News Ltd (NT Division). (2002). EOWA (Equal Opportunity in the Workplace Agency). Report. Online. Accessed 1 August 2006 from <http:// www.eowa.gov.au> pp. 1–12.

Nationwide News Ltd (NT Division). (2004). EOWA Report. Online. Accessed 1 August 2006 from <http://www.eowa.gov.au> pp. 1–4.

Nationwide News Ltd (NT Division). (2006). EOWA Report. Online. Accessed 18 July 2007 from <http://www.eowa.gov.au> pp. 1–9.

Negrin, Llewellyn. (2004). The female nude (part A): Representations of the ideal, lecture notes from Imaging the Body unit, University of Tasmania, pp. 1–13.

Nemy, Enid. (1975, August 19). Women begin to speak out against sexual harassment at work. *New York Times*, p. 38.

News Corporation. (2004). *Standards of business conduct*.

News Limited Corporation Affairs. (2005, November 16). News awards—winners announced. Media Release, p. 1–2.

Noble, Greg. (2005, October). Where has all the fieldwork gone? *Cultural Studies Associations of Australasia Newsletter*, pp. 13–15.

North, Louise C. (2004). Naked women, feminism and newsroom culture. *Australian Journal of Communication*, 31(2), 53–68.

North, Louise C. (2007). "Just a little bit of cheeky ribaldry"?: Newsroom discourses of sexually harassing behaviour. *Feminist Media Studies*, 7(1), 81–96.

Opoku-Mensah, Aida. (2004). Hanging in there: Women, gender, and newsroom cultures in Africa. In Marjan de Bruin & Karen Ross (Eds.), *Gender and newsroom cultures: Identities at work* (pp. 107–120). Cresskill NJ: Hampton Press.

Ouchi, William G. (1981). *Theory Z*. New York: Avon Books.

Outram, Dorinda. (1989). *The body in the French revolution*. New Haven: Yale University Press.

Oxenbridge, Sarah. (1999). The individualisation of employment relations in New Zealand: Trends and outcomes. In Stephen Deery & Richard Mitchell (Eds.), *Employment relations: Individualisation and union exclusion—An international study* (pp. 227–250). Sydney: Federation Press.

Paine, Michelle. (2002, August 31). A flesh offering from calendar girls. *The Mercury*, p. 5.

Paine, Michelle. (2003, March 23). Chilling out in name of disarmament. *The Mercury*, p. 3.

Parenti, Michael. (1986). *Inventing reality: The politics of the mass media*. New York: St. Martin's.

Pateman, Carole. (1988). *The sexual contract*. Cambridge: Polity.

Pearce, Sharyn. (1998). *Shameless scribblers: Australian women's journalism 1880–1995*. Rockhampton: Central Queensland University Press.

Peetz, David, & Murray, Georgina. (2005, Autumn). Individualisation and resistance at the coal face. *Just Labour*, 6–7, 56–71, and Online. Accessed 25 January 2006 from <http://www.justlabour.york.uca/volume67/pdfs/07%20Peetz%20Murray%20Press.pdf>.

Peters, Bettina. (2001). *Equality and quality: Setting standards for women in journalism*. International Federation of Journalists survey and report. Online. Accessed 5 March 2003 from <http://www.ifj.org/pdfs/ws.pdf>.

Peters, Tom, & Waterman, Bob. (1982). *In search of excellence*. New York: Warner Books.

Phillips, Anne. (1991). *Engendering democracy*. Cambridge: Polity Press.

Pierce, Jennifer L. (1995). *Gender trials: Emotional lives in contemporary law firms*. Berkeley: University of California Press.

Pieterse, Jan Nederveen. (1995). Globalisation as hybridisation. In Mike Featherstone, Scott Lash, & Roland Robertson (Eds.), *Global modernities* (pp. 45–68). London: Sage.

Pitt, Lisa. (2003). Masculinities@work: Gender inequality and the new media industries. *Feminist Media Studies*, 3(3), 378–382.

Plummer, Ken. (Ed.). (1992). *Modern homosexualities: Fragments of lesbian and gay experience*. London: Routledge.

Pocock, Barbara. (2003). *The work/life collision: What work is doing to Australians and what to do about it*. Annandale: The Federation Press.

Powell, Sian. (2006, December 1). Milne's main event. *The Australian* (Strewth column), p. 11.

Pringle, Rosemary. (1988). *Secretaries talk: Sexuality, power and work*. Sydney: Allen and Unwin.

Pringle, Rosemary. (1998). *Sex and medicine: Gender, power and authority in the medical profession*. Cambridge: Cambridge University Press.

Probert, Belinda, Ewer, Peter, & Whiting, Kim. (2000). Work versus life: Union strategies reconsidered. *Labour and Industry*, 11(1), 23–47.

Probyn, Elspeth, & Lumby, Catharine. (2003). Introduction: An ethics of engagement. In Catharine Lumby & Elspeth Probyn (Eds.), *Remote control: New media, new ethics* (pp. 1–10). Cambridge: Cambridge University Press.

Putnis, Peter, & Axford, Beverley. (2002). Communication and media studies in Australian universities. *Australian Journal of Communication*, 29(1), 1–20.

Queensland Newspapers Pty Ltd. (2001). EOWA (Equal Opportunity in the Workplace Agency) Report Online. Accessed 1 August, 2006 from <http://www.eowa.gov.au> pp. 1–10.

Queensland Newspapers Pty Ltd. (2003). EOWA Report Online. Accessed 1 August, 2006 from <http://www.eowa.gov.au> pp. 1–17.

Queensland Newspapers Pty Ltd. (2006). EOWA Report Online. Accessed 9 July, 2006 from <http://www.eowa.gov.au> pp. 1–16.

Quesada Tiongson, Mari Luz. (1999). The state of women and media in Asia: An overview. Online. Accessed 14 July, 2005 from <http:www.isiswomen.org/advocacy/media/1999/com00011.html>.

Quest Community Newspapers. (2005). EOWA (Equal Opportunity in the Workplace Agency) Report Online. Accessed 1 August 2006 from <http://www.eowa.gov.au> pp. 1–6.

Rantanen, Terhi. (2005). *The media and globalisation*. London: Sage.

Rapping. Elayne. (1994). *Media-tions: Forays into the culture and gender wars*. Boston: South End.

Read, Genevieve. (2001, September 21). Oldies put the fold back in centrefold. *The Mercury*, p. 1.

Reese, Steven D. (1990, December). The news paradigm and the ideology of objectivity: A socialist at the *Wall Street Journal*. *Critical Studies in Mass Communication*, 7(4), 390–409.

Reporter's Work Queried. (2004, August 18). *Herald Sun*, p. 22.

Richardson, Laurel. (1994). Writing: A method of inquiry. In Norman Denzin & Yvonna Lincoln (Eds.), *Handbook of qualitative research* (pp. 516–529). Thousand Oaks, CA: Sage.

Ricketson, Matthew, & Harrison, Dan. (2006, December 2). When press comes to shove. *The Age*, p. 3.

Ring, Laura. (1994). Sexual harassment and the production of gender. *A Journal of Feminist Cultural Studies*, 6(1), 129–166.

Robertson, Roland. (1990). Mapping the global condition: Globalisation as the central concept. *Theory, Culture & Society*, 7(2–3), 15–30.

Robinson, Paul. (2005, May 27). Business delighted, unions ready to fight. *The Age*, p. 3.

Roiphe, Katie (1993). *The morning after: Sex, fear and feminism*. London: Hamish Hamilton.

Roper, Michael, & Tosh, John. (Eds.). (1991). *Manful assertions, masculinities in Britain since 1800*. London: Routledge.

Rose, Gillian. (1999). Women and everyday spaces. In Janet Price & Margrit Shildrick (Eds.), *Feminist theory and the body: A reader* (pp. 359–370). Edinburgh: Edinburgh University Press.

Ross, Karen. (2001). Women at work: Journalism as en-gendered practice. *Journalism Studies*, 2(4), 531–544.

Ross, Karen. (2002). Selling women (down the river): Gendered relations and the political economy of broadcast news. In Eileen R. Meehan & Ellen Riordan (Eds.), *Sex & money: Feminism and political economy in the media* (pp. 112–129). Minneapolis: University of Minnesota Press.

Ross, Karen. (2004). Sex at work: Gender politics and newsroom culture. In Marjan de Bruin & Karen Ross (Eds.), *Gender and newsroom cultures: Identities at work*, (pp. 145–162). Cresskill, NJ: Hampton Press.

Ross, Karen, & Byerly, Carolyn. (Eds.). (2004). *Women and media: International perspectives*. London: Blackwell.

Rothfield, Phil, & Wilson, Rebecca. (2006, December 3). Bec and buzz column. *The Sunday Telegraph*, p. 57.

Rowe, William, & Schelling, Vivian. (1991). *Memory and modernity: Popular culture in Latin America*. London: Verso.

Rubin, Gayle. (1984). Thinking sex: Notes for a radical theory of the politics of sexuality. In Carole S. Vance (Ed.), *Pleasure and danger: Exploring female sexuality* (pp. 267–317). Boston: Routledge.

Sanders, Marlene. (1993). Television: The face of the network news is male. In Pamela Creedon (Ed.), *Women in mass communication* (2nd ed., pp. 167–171). London: Sage.

Savage, Desiree. (2003, Autumn). Our dirty secret. *The Walkley Magazine, 20*, p. 20.

Sex bias claim. (2005, February 24). *The Australian*, p. 17.

Schaffer, Kay. (1998). Scare words: "Feminism," postmodern consumer culture and the media. *Continuum: Journal of Media & Cultural Studies, 12*(3), 321–334.

Schudson, Michael. (1978). *Discovering the news*. New York: Basic Books.

Selznick, Philip. (1959). *The organisation weapon*. New York: Free Press of Glencoe.

Servaes, Jan, & Lie, Rico. (2000). Globalization: Consumption and identity: Towards researching nodal points. In Georgette Wang, Jan Servaes, & Anura Goonasekera (Eds.), *The new communication landscape: Demystifying media globalization* (pp. 307–332). London: Routledge

Shilling, Chris. (1991). Educating the body: Physical capital and the production of social inequalities. *Sociology, 25*(4), 653–672.

Shilling, Chris. (2004). Physical capital and situated action: A new direction for corporeal sociology. *British Journal of Sociology of Education, 25*(3), 473–487.

Shtargot, Sasha. (2004, August 7). Journalist not worthy of rise: Age. *The Age*, p. 11.

Simons, Margaret. (1999). *Fit to print: Inside the Canberra press gallery*. Sydney: UNSW Press.

Simons, Margaret. (2005). Inside the ABC. In Robert Manne (Ed.), *Do not disturb: Is the media failing Australia?* (pp. 121–149). Melbourne: Black Inc.

Simons, Margaret. (2007). *The content makers: Understanding the media in Australia*. Sydney: Penguin Books.

Singer, Jane. (2004). Strange bedfellows?: The diffusion of convergence in four news organisations. *Journalism Studies, 5*(1), 3–18.

Siochru, Sean, & Girard, Bruce. (2002). *Global media governance*. New York: Rowman and Littlefield.

Spender, Dale. (1995). *Nattering on the net: Women, power and cyberspace*. Melbourne: Spinifex Press.

Steiner, Linda. (1998). Newsroom accounts of power at work. In Cynthia Carter, Gill Branston, & Stuart Allan (Eds.), *News, gender and power* (pp. 145–159). London: Routledge.

Summers, Anne. (2003). *The end of equality: Work, babies and women's choices in 21st century Australia*. Milsons Point: Random House.

Summers, Anne. (1994/1975). *Damned whores and God's police: The colonisation of women in Australia*. Melbourne: Penguin Books.

Teleford, Laurie. (1996). Selves in bunkers: Organizational consequences of failing to verify alternative masculinities. In Cliff Cheng (Ed.), *Masculinities in organisations* (pp. 130–159). Thousand Oaks, CA: Sage.

Thompson, John B. (1995). *The media and modernity*. Cambridge: Polity.

Thompson, Paul, & McHugh, David. (1995). *Work organizations: A critical introduction*. Basingstoke: Macmillan.

Thornton, Margaret. (1994). The seductive allure of EEO. In Norma Grieve & Ailsa Burns (Eds.), *Australian women: Contemporary feminist thought* (pp. 215–224). Melbourne: Oxford University Press.

Thornton, Margaret. (1996). *Dissonance and distrust: Women in the legal profession*. Melbourne: Oxford University Press.

Thornton, Margaret. (2001). EEO in a neo-liberal climate. *Journal of Interdisciplinary Gender Studies*, 6(1), 77–104.

Tiddy, Josephine. (2001). *It's just not fair: Overcoming discrimination in Australia*. Sydney: ABC Books.

Top Gongs. (2007, February–March). *The Walkley Magazine*, 43, p. 7.

Trice, Harrison, M. (1993). *Occupational subcultures in the workplace*. Ithaca, NY: ILR Press.

Trice, Harrison M., & Beyer, Janice M. (1993). *The cultures of work organizations*. Englewood Cliffs, NJ: Prentice Hall.

Trioli, Virginia. (1996). *Generation F: Sex, power and the young feminist*. Melbourne: Minerva.

Uggen, Christopher, & Blackstone, Amy. (2004). Sexual harassment as a gendered expression of power. *American Sociological Review*, 69(1), 64–92.

Ullmann-Margalit, Edna. (1977). *The emergence of norms*. Oxford: Oxford University Press.

Union backs legal challenge to paper's perceived "Blokey" culture. (2004, August 26). *The Australian* (Media section), p. 43.

Valentine, Gill. (1992). Images of danger: Women's sources of information about the spatial distribution of male violence. *Area*, 24, 22–29.

van Zoonen, Liesbet (1989). Professional socialisation of feminist journalists in the Netherlands. *Women's Studies in Communication*, 12(2), 1–22.

van Zoonen, Liesbet (1994). *Feminist media studies*. London: Sage.

van Zoonen, Liesbet (1996). Feminist perspectives on the media. In James Curran & Michael Gurevitch (Eds.), *Mass media and society* (2nd ed., pp. 31–52). London: Arnold.

van Zoonen, Liesbet (1998a). A professional, unreliable, heroic marionette (m/f): Structure, agency and subjectivity in contemporary journalisms. *European Journal of Cultural Studies*, 1, 123–145.

van Zoonen, Liesbet (1998b). One of the girls?: The changing gender of journalism. In Cynthia Carter, Gill Branston, & Stuart Allan (Eds.), *News, gender and power* (pp. 33–46). London: Routledge.

Wajcman, Judy. (1991). *Feminism confronts technology.* Cambridge: Polity Press.

Walby, Sylvia. (1986). *Patriarchy at work.* Cambridge: Polity Press.

Walkerdine, Valerie. (2004). Neoliberalism, femininity and choice. In *Post Feminism and Sexual Citizenship* (seminar for the Economic and Social Research Council) Cardiff, Wales. Online. Accessed 1 August 2005 from <http://www.lse.ac.uk/collections/newFeminities/walkerdine.pdf>.

Walsh Childers, Kim, Chance, Jean, & Herzog, Kristin. (1996). Sexual harassment of women journalists. *Journalism and Mass Communication Quarterly, 73*(3), 559–581.

Waring, Peter. (1999). The rise of individualism in Australian industrial relations. *New Zealand Journal of Industrial Relations, 24*(3), 291–318.

Wark, McKenzie. (1999). *Celebrities, culture and cyberspace: The light on the hill in a postmodern world.* Sydney: Pluto Press Australia.

Warner, Michael. (1999). *The trouble with normal.* New York: Free Press.

Warren, Chris. (1995, August 31). Journalists and the new code of ethics. The Media Report. Online. Accessed 1 February 2006 from <http:www.abc.net.au/rn/talks/8.30/mediarpt/mstories/mr310802.htm>.

Weaver, Carolyn. (1992, September 23–27). A secret no more. *Washington Journalism Review,* pp. 23–27.

Weaver, David. H. (1997). Women as journalists. In Pippa Norris (Ed.), *Women, media and politics* (pp. 21–40). New York and Oxford: Oxford University Press.

Weaver, David. H. (1998). Journalists around the world: Commonalities and differences. In David H. Weaver (Ed.), *The global journalist: News people around the world* (pp. 455–480). Cresskill, NJ: Hampton Press.

Weeks, Jeffrey. (1977). *Coming out: Homosexual politics in Britain from the nineteenth century to the present.* London: Quartet.

Weiss, Gail. (1999). *Body images: Embodiment as intercorporeality.* New York: Routledge.

West Australian Newspapers Pty Ltd. (2002). EOWA (Equal Opportunity in the Workplace Agency) Report. Online. Accessed 1 August, 2006 from <http://www.eowa.gov.au> pp. 1–7.

West Australian Newspapers Pty Ltd. (2006). EOWA Report. Online. Accessed 9 July, 2006 from <http://www.eowa.gov.au> pp. 1–8.

Wharton, Amy, & Bird, Sharon. (1996). Stand by your man: Homosociality, work groups, and men's perception of difference. In Cliff Cheng (Ed.), *Masculinities in organizations* (pp. 97–114). Thousand Oaks, CA: Sage.

Whittock, Margaret. (2000). *Feminising the masculine?: Women in non-traditional employment.* Aldershot, Hampshire: Ashgate Publishing.

Witz, Anne, & Savage, Mike. (1992). The gender of organisations. In Mike Savage & Anne Witz (Eds.), *Gender and bureaucracy* (pp. 3–62). Oxford: Polity.

Wolff, Janet. (1990). *Feminine sentences: Essays on women and culture.* Berkeley: University of California Press.

Wolff, Janet. (1997). The global and the specific: Reconciling conflicting theories of culture. In Anthony D. King (Ed.), *Culture, globalisation and the world system* (pp. 161–173). Minneapolis: University of Minnesota Press.

Wood, Danielle. (2002, July 5). Calendar girls take next stage in the curtain call. *The Mercury,* p. 3.

Wooden, Mark. (2000). *The transformation of Australian industrial relations*. Sydney: Federation Press.

Woods, Guy. (2000). Australia 1975–2000-Part B: Labour force. Research Note 14 2000–01. Parliamentary Library. Online. Accessed 1 February 2006 from <http://www.aph.gov.au/Library/pubs/rn/2000-01/01RN14.htm>.

Wright, Rosemary. (1996). The occupational masculinity of computing. In Cliff Cheng (Ed.), *Masculinities in organisations* (pp. 77–96). Thousand Oaks, CA: Sage.

Wright, Susan. (1994). Culture in anthropology and organizational studies. In Susan Wright (Ed.), *Anthropology of organizations* (pp. 1–34). London and New York: Routledge.

Yallop, Richard. (2004a, August 7–8). Under the table at *The Age*. *The Weekend Australian*, p. 7.

Yallop, Richard. (2004b, August 19). Pay equity case told of clash over "column." *The Australian*, p. 3.

Yallop, Richard. (2004c, August 18). Catch-up on pay equity. *The Australian* (edition 2), p. 4.

Yallop, Richard. (2004d, August 18). Pay equity "passed over." *The Australian*, p. 4.

Yallop, Richard. (2004e, August 20). No mates' rates, says editor. *The Australian*, p. 6.

Yallop, Richard. (2004f, August 26). Discord on the home front reveals cracks in *The Age* façade. *The Australian* (Media section), pp. 41, 43.

Yallop, Richard. (2004g, September 9). Journo's gradings arbitrary, says judge. *The Australian* (Media section), p. 19.

Young, Iris Marion. (1988). Women recovering our clothes, perhaps. In Hugh J. Silverman & Donn Welton (Eds.), *Postmodernism and continental philosophy: Selected studies in phenomenology and existential philosophy* (pp. 144–152). Albany: State University of New York Press.

Yount, Kristen R. (1991). Ladies, flirts, and tomboys. *Journal of Contemporary Ethnography*, 19(4), 396–422.

Ziffer, Daniel. (2004a, August 4). *Age* a boys' club, claims journalist. *The Age*, p. 9.

Ziffer, Daniel. (2004b, August 5). Payment expected to end wage disparity, journalist tells discrimination case. *The Age*, p. 9.

Ziffer, Daniel. (2004c, August 6). "Mateship culture" at *Age*. *The Age*, p. 8.

Ziffer, Daniel. (2004d, August 19). Editor's high pay an anomaly: Manager. *The Age*, p. 8.

Ziffer, Daniel. (2004e, August 20). Editor not as good as predecessor, hearing told. *The Age*, p. 7.

Internet Resources

About APN news and media. Accessed 4 August 2006 from <http://www.apn.com.au/aboutus.asp>.

ACMA (Australian Comunications and Media Authority). Accessed 2 September 2005 from <http://www.acma.gov.au>.

AIRC (Australian Industrial Relations Commission): About the commission. Accessed 3 August 2005 from <http://www.airc.gov.au/research/about/about.html>.

APC (Australian Press Council): About the council. Accessed 4 August 2006 from <http://www.presscouncil.org.au/pcsite/apc.html>.

BBC News: Murdoch wins fight for Dow Jones. Accessed 1 August 2007 from www.news.bbc.co.uk/1/hi/business/6923474.stm.

Caslon Analytics—internet research, analysis, strategies, homepage. Accessed 4 August 2006 from <http://www.caslon.com.au>.

(EOWA) Equal Oppoirtunity in the Workplace Agency: Accessed 2 September 2005 from <http://www.eowa.gov.au>.

Fairfax New Zealand Publications. Accessed 29 July 2005 from <http://www.fairfaxnz.co.nz/publications/index.html>.

Harvard Magazine: Lady Godiva: The Naked Truth. Accessed 4 August 2006 from <http://www.harvard~magazine.com/on-line/o70377.htm>.

HREOC (Human Rights and Equal Opportunity Commission): Functions and powers. Accessed 3 August 2005 from <http://www.hreoc.gov.au/aboutthecommission/functions/index.html>.

HREOC: Who we are. Accessed 3 August 2005 from <http://www.hreoc.gov.au/info_sheet.html>.

HREOC: About the commission. Accessed 3 August 2005 from <http://www.hreoc.gov.au/aboutthecommission/index.html?

IFJ (International Federation of Journalists): IFJ condemns new Australian labour rules: A "charter for unscrupulous media employers." Accessed 29 July 2005 from <http://www.ifj.org/default.asp?Index=3263&Language=EN>.

Isis International. Our past. Accessed 26 October 2006 from <http://www.isiswomen.org>.

IWMF (International Women's Media Foundation) homepage. Accessed 4 August 2006 from <http://www.iwmf.org>.

MEAA (Media, Entertainment and Arts Alliance): Code of ethics. Accessed 20 September 2005 from <http://www.alliance.org.au/hot/ethicscode.htm>.

MEAA: What the industrial relations changes will mean for media workers. Accessed 29 July 2005 from <http://www.alliance.org.au/content/view/62/52/>.

Media Resource: Saturday newspaper readership plummets. Accessed 15 September 2005 from <http://www.bandt.com.au/news/38/0c02d238.asp>.

Media Resource, Ketupa. Accessed 3 August 2006 from <http://www.ketupa.net/murdoch.htm>.

Media Resource, Ketupa: Accessed 3 August 2006 from <http://www.ketupa.net/apn.htm>.

Naked For Peace homepage. Accessed 13 March 2004 from <http://www.sfheart.com/naked_for_peace.html>.

News Corporation Newspapers. Accessed 3 August 2006 from <http://www.newscorp.com/operations/newspapers.html>.

News Corporation Investor homepage. Accessed 1 September 2005 from <http://www.newscorp.com/investor>.

News Limited awards, 2007 winners. Accessed 30 September 2008 from <http://www.newsawards.com.au/07-winners.html>.

OEA (Office of Employment Advocate): What employers and employees are doing in their AWAs. Accessed 13 September 2005 from <http://www.oea.gov.au>.

OEA: Fairness test for workplace agreements. Accessed 2 August 2007 from http://www.oea.gov.au.

VCAT (Victorian Civil and Administrative Tribunal): About VCAT. Accessed 3 August 2005 from <http://www.vcat.vic.gov.au/CA256DBB0022825D/page/About+VCAT?OpenDocument&1=10-About+VCAT~&2=~&3=~>.

Author Index

Subject Index

LaVergne, TN USA
14 December 2010
208679LV00001B/89/P

9 781572 738737